CELLULOID SINGAPORE

Traditions in World Cinema

General Editors
Linda Badley (Middle Tennessee State University)
R. Barton Palmer (Clemson University)

Founding Editor
Steven Jay Schneider (New York University)

Titles in the series include:

Traditions in World Cinema
Linda Badley, R. Barton Palmer, and Steven Jay Schneider (eds)

Japanese Horror Cinema
Jay McRoy (ed.)

New Punk Cinema
Nicholas Rombes (ed.)

African Filmmaking
Roy Armes

Palestinian Cinema
Nurith Gertz and George Khleifi

Czech and Slovak Cinema
Peter Hames

The New Neapolitan Cinema
Alex Marlow-Mann

American Smart Cinema
Claire Perkins

The International Film Musical
Corey Creekmur and Linda Mokdad (eds)

Italian Neorealist Cinema
Torunn Haaland

Magic Realist Cinema in East Central Europe
Aga Skrodzka

Italian Post-Neorealist Cinema
Luca Barattoni

Spanish Horror Film
Antonio Lázaro-Reboll

Post-beur Cinema
Will Higbee

New Taiwanese Cinema in Focus
Flannery Wilson

International Noir
Homer B. Pettey and R. Barton Palmer (eds)

Films on Ice
Scott MacKenzie and Anna Westerståhl Stenport (eds)

Nordic Genre Film
Tommy Gustafsson and Pietari Kääpä (eds)

Contemporary Japanese Cinema Since Hana-Bi
Adam Bingham

Chinese Martial Arts Cinema (2nd edition)
Stephen Teo

Slow Cinema
Tiago de Luca and Nuno Barradas Jorge

Expressionism in Cinema
Olaf Brill and Gary D. Rhodes (eds)

French Language Road Cinema: Borders, Diasporas, Migration and 'New Europe'
Michael Gott

Transnational Film Remakes
Iain Robert Smith and Constantine Verevis

Coming-of-age Cinema in New Zealand
Alistair Fox

Celluloid Singapore
Edna Lim

edinburghuniversitypress.com/series/tiwc

CELLULOID SINGAPORE

Cinema, Performance and the National

Edna Lim

EDINBURGH
University Press

Edinburgh University Press is one of the leading university presses in the UK. We publish academic books and journals in our selected subject areas across the humanities and social sciences, combining cutting-edge scholarship with high editorial and production values to produce academic works of lasting importance. For more information visit our website: edinburghuniversitypress.com

© Edna Lim, 2018

Edinburgh University Press Ltd
The Tun – Holyrood Road
12 (2f) Jackson's Entry
Edinburgh EH8 8PJ

Typeset in 10/12.5 pt Sabon by
Servis Filmsetting Ltd, Stockport, Cheshire

A CIP record for this book is available from the British Library

ISBN 978 1 4744 0288 0 (hardback)
ISBN 978 1 4744 0289 7 (webready PDF)
ISBN 978 1 4744 3540 6 (epub)
ISBN 978 1 4744 5225 0 (paperback)

The right of Edna Lim to be identified as author of this work has been asserted in accordance with the Copyright, Designs and Patents Act 1988 and the Copyright and Related Rights Regulations 2003 (SI No. 2498).

CONTENTS

List of Figures — vi
Acknowledgements — viii
Traditions in World Cinema — x

1. Introduction — 1
2. Merdeka!: Merger, Separation and a Transnational Golden Age — 21
3. Influence, Hybridity and How the Past is a Foreign Country — 43
4. Nation-building, a Nun and a Bionic Boy — 69
5. Not so Foreign: the Case of *Saint Jack* — 92
6. One People, One Nation, One Singapore — 119
7. Revival Cinema: 'Other' Singaporeans in (An)other Singapore — 139
8. Singapore Cinema in Singapore — 165

Works Cited — 186
Index — 196

FIGURES

3.1	Court dance in *Hang Jebat*	53
3.2	Chombi and Kassim/Osman during 'Di Mana Kan Ku Cari Ganti'	54
3.3	Opening sequence in *Seniman Bujang Lapok*	58
3.4	First round of fashion show in *Labu dan Labi*	59
3.5	Second round of fashion show in *Labu dan Labi*	60
3.6	Tattered clothing in the kampong, versus formal wear in the city, in *Bujang Lapok*	61
3.7	Then and now: Robinson Road and Kampong Kling	63
4.1	Bell Church in *Bionic Boy*	84
4.2	Singapore tourist sites in *They Call Her . . . Cleopatra Wong*	86
5.1	Singapore as represented by the port, tavern and room upstairs in *Across to Singapore*	93
5.2	Li Ti and Leslie; Leslie dwarfed, humiliated and laughed at by prostitutes in the cell in Li Ti's room	95
5.3	Hotel, Macau cabaret, the mission, street, seedy bar and Rochor Canal in Singapore	97
5.4	Toh, the Little Person	107
5.5	Bugis Street in *Pretty Polly*	110
5.6	Jack greeting a diner at Bugis Street in *Saint Jack*	111
5.7	Bridgit and Lily's show	112
5.8	Shots in the opening 360-degree pan	113
5.9	The 'true garden city'	113
5.10	The final shot in *Saint Jack*	114

7.1	Opening sequence of *12 Storeys*	142
7.2	Meng and San San in the playground	145
7.3	Poh Huat's reality	150
7.4	Title shot in *Singapore Dreaming*	151
7.5	Ying's performance	156
7.6	Margaret performing *4'33'* in the void deck	158
7.7	National Day sequence and Melvyn at the station	162
8.1	Celebration dinner in *Meeting the Giant*	169
8.2	The hunched Yap Wah Pin and long shot of Hee Jin and his wife	172
8.3	The *pontianak* film in three ways: as the film we watch; viewed by diegetic audience; and on television	174
8.4	The little girl with the Pineapple statue captured via passing car	175
8.5	The Singapura	177
8.6	Singapore's sci-fi future	179

ACKNOWLEDGEMENTS

This book is, in many ways, the result of my encounters with Singapore films through watching, teaching and research. It has been in the making since I first launched a module called Singapore Film: Performance of Identity in the National University of Singapore's Theatre Studies Programme in 2004. Teaching such a module in Singapore to mostly Singaporeans is interesting because this is a topic that implicates everyone, myself included, and forces into consciousness our own relationship with and stake in this country and this national cinema. What constantly surprises me is the lack of familiarity with the cinema and films that form its corpus, especially those from the golden age and post-studio 70s. As someone who grew up in Singapore and in a Peranakan family that loves watching movies, the old Malay films of the golden age are part of my childhood, and watching them is like visiting old friends. Yet to many of my students, these films are like foreign films. The difference between what I see and what they see has informed much of my conception of this period. Through them, I have gained new perspectives on Singapore cinema that have shaped my research over the years, finally culminating in this book.

I am deeply grateful to Associate Professor Yong Li Lan for encouraging me to teach this module and setting me on this research path. This book would not be possible without your unfailing support. Thank you for being my fearless leader, mentor and friend.

I am also indebted to Associate Professor Timothy R. White, whose work on Hollywood and Asian cinemas is the foundation on which I built and developed my own ideas. I have relied much on your work on the golden age in this book, and I will always be grateful to you for laying those foundations and guiding this once-Literature student on her journey in film studies. Many thanks also to Ben Slater, whose lectures when he taught the Singapore film module with me, blog and brilliantly written *Kinda Hot* have provided crucial information and rich insights on the post-studio 70s and *Saint Jack*. My chapters on this period and this film rely greatly on your work and I am grateful to you for always being so kind and ready to help. Thanks also to Toh Hun Ping for allowing me to use his images of Robinson Road and Kampong Kling today in Figure 3.7. Images from *12 Storeys*, *Cinema* and *In the Room* in Figures 7.1, 7.2, 8.3, 8.5 and 8.6, as well as the cover of this book, are also reproduced with the kind permission of Zhao Wei Films.

I would also like to thank Drs Eleine Ng and Diego Fossati for their work on the Singapore Film research project so many years ago, Professor Rajeev Patke for his wisdom and advice, the Theatre Studies Programme, Department of English Language Literature and especially the Head of Department, Professor John Richardson, for supporting my work. Sincere thanks also to Edinburgh University Press for accepting this book, and particularly to Gillian Leslie and Richard Strachan for their generosity, kindness and assistance throughout this process. To my family and Tay Ping Hui, thank you for encouraging me, feeding me and always being there. To my friends, thank you for the laughs, adventures, deadline and your friendship. Finally, this book is dedicated to my beloved Grandmother – *terima kasih dan selamat jalan, Ma*.

TRADITIONS IN WORLD CINEMA

General editors: **Linda Badley and R. Barton Palmer**
Founding editor: **Steven Jay Schneider**

Traditions in World Cinema is a series of textbooks and monographs devoted to the analysis of currently popular and previously underexamined or undervalued film movements from around the globe. Also intended for general interest readers, the textbooks in this series offer undergraduate- and graduate-level film students accessible and comprehensive introductions to diverse traditions in world cinema. The monographs open up for advanced academic study more specialised groups of films, including those that require theoretically oriented approaches. Both textbooks and monographs provide thorough examinations of the industrial, cultural and socio-historical conditions of production and reception.

The flagship textbook for the series includes chapters by noted scholars on traditions of acknowledged importance (the French New Wave, German Expressionism), recent and emergent traditions (New Iranian, post-Cinema Novo), and those whose rightful claim to recognition has yet to be established (the Israeli persecution film, global found footage cinema). Other volumes concentrate on individual national, regional or global cinema traditions. As the introductory chapter to each volume makes clear, the films under discussion form a coherent group on the basis of substantive and relatively transparent, if not always obvious, commonalities. These commonalities may be formal, stylistic or thematic, and the groupings may, although they need not, be popularly identified as genres, cycles or movements (Japanese horror, Chinese martial arts cinema, Italian Neorealism). Indeed, in cases in which a group of films is not already commonly identified as a tradition, one purpose of the volume is to establish its claim to importance and make it visible (East Central European Magical Realist cinema, Palestinian cinema).

Textbooks and monographs include:

- An introduction that clarifies the rationale for the grouping of films under examination
- A concise history of the regional, national or transnational cinema in question
- A summary of previous published work on the tradition
- Contextual analysis of industrial, cultural and socio-historical conditions of production and reception
- Textual analysis of specific and notable films, with clear and judicious application of relevant film theoretical approaches
- Bibliograph(ies)/filmograph(ies)

Monographs may additionally include:

- Discussion of the dynamics of cross-cultural exchange in light of current research and thinking about cultural imperialism and globalisation, as well as issues of regional/national cinema or political/aesthetic movements (such as new waves, postmodernism or identity politics)
- Interview(s) with key filmmakers working within the tradition.

1. INTRODUCTION

Singapore is a small island measuring about 710 square kilometres at the southern tip of the Malaysian Peninsula. Yet its small size belies a complex historiography. Indeed, history itself became a subject of contention in the 1960s and '70s, when

> the political movement at that point in time, led by the People's Action Party (PAP) government, . . . declared that Singapore had no history, that the past was irrelevant, that Singapore's history started now. History had become unfashionable . . . It was even removed from the primary school syllabus in 1972, in favour of more 'practical' subjects that prepared students to be part of the workforce of the future.[1]

It was only in 1984 that a two-volume textbook titled *The Social and Economic History of Singapore* was issued to schools. The volumes, like C. M. Turnbull's seminal *A History of Modern Singapore*, trace the history of modern Singapore back to its founding by Sir Stamford Raffles, who established it as a trading post for the British Empire.[2] Turnbull's work became the basis of the state-sanctioned official historical narrative, the Singapore Story.[3] This narrative was publicly presented in an audio-visual show in 1997, called "The Singapore Story', and later made into a video screened at the then Singapore History Museum from 1997 to 2003.[4] This Singapore Story was also included in the National Education Programme launched by the Ministry of Education in 1997. The purpose of National Education is to develop national cohesion, the instinct for survival and confidence in the future, by fostering a sense of identity, pride and self-respect as Singaporeans; by knowing the Singapore story – how Singapore succeeded against the odds to become a nation; by understanding Singapore's unique challenges, constraints and vulnerabilities, which make us different from other countries; and by instilling the core values of our way of life, and the will to prevail, that ensures our continued success and well-being.[5]

According to Karl Hack and Jean-Louis Margoulin, the Story 'reached its apotheosis' in Lee Kuan Yew's books published thereafter: *The Singapore Story: Memoirs of Lee Kuan Yew*[6] and *From Third World to First: The Singapore Story.*[7]

So singular and entrenched was this Singapore Story that historians either subscribe to or work against it, creating a plurality of perspectives and 'a new wave of history about Singapore ... [that is] invaluable in telling us more about the variety of groups and possibilities ...'[8] Others, on the other hand, have taken a longer view, going back some seven hundred years to the island's place as a port settlement in the Straits of Melaka in the fourteenth century.[9] Here, 'the continuity between 14th and 21st centuries is not one of institutions or peoples, but rather of the need to reinvent in order to adapt to the rapidly shifting geostrategic and geo-commercial context around Singapore.'[10] As Karl Hack sees it, 'there is no single, unilinear "Singapore Story" for a historian to weave into a continuous whole'.[11] Singapore's story 'can be framed in multiple ways',[12] each reflecting the purpose of its telling.

To that end, *Celluloid Singapore* takes as its framing the *longue durée*, as it were, which establishes a transnational perspective that corresponds with the nature of cinematic practice in general and the transnational foundations of Singapore's cinema in particular. The island's multiple reinventions, from a transnational port polity with a cosmopolitan population to an independent, multicultural nation that is still externally oriented, also reflect the rather fractured history of film production in Singapore comprising three distinct periods: a golden age in the 1950s and 1960s, a post-studio era in the 1970s and revival in the 1990s. As such, the histories of 'the place that we now call Singapore'[13] and its film industry are layered trajectories of transformations that have enabled this cinema to be variously and correspondingly studied and considered – within broader modes of inquiry such as Malay, Chinese, transnational or postcolonial cinemas, for example, or on its own as Singapore cinema. These histories of reinventions and numerous approaches underscore this book's interest in Singapore and its cinema as multiple performances of multiple Singapores, and the volume traces the island's adjustments and transformations in relation to the three periods.

INTRODUCTION

THE LONGUE DURÉE

Derek Heng, in his study of the settlements of the island, identifies six key phases based on the turning points in its history:[14] 1) when it was known as Temasek (also spelt as Temasik) in the late thirteenth and fourteenth centuries and was the seat of exiled Srivijayan prince Parameswara, who ruled the island for a number of years before fleeing to Melaka and founding the sultanate there; 2) the decline of Temasek from the fifteenth to the early seventeenth centuries, when it was a Melaka Sultanate trading port and later nominally ruled by the Johor Sultanate; 3) Singapore as a trading factory under the East India Company, from Raffles' arrival in 1819 to the formation of the Straits Settlements (Singapore, Penang and Melaka) in 1826 and the Company's dissolution in 1858; 4) the period between 1867 and 1963, when Singapore was a Crown Colony of British government. During this time, the island was occupied by the Japanese between 1942 and 1945. The Straits Settlements was dissolved after the war and Singapore gained partial self-rule in 1953, when constitutional changes provided for an elected legislature and the appointment of a Chief Minister. Increasing anti-colonial sentiments in Singapore eventually led to full self-government in 1959, with the local People's Action Party winning forty-three of the fifty-one seats in the Legislative Assembly elections. The leader of the party, Lee Kuan Yew, became Singapore's first Prime Minister. The new government campaigned heavily for merger with neighbouring Malaya, viewing it as 'a historical necessity, if only for economic survival'.[15] Singapore and Malaya, together with Sabah and Sarawak, formed the Federation of Malaysia in 1963; 5) the short-lived period when Singapore was part of the Federation to its separation on 9 August 1965; and 6) from 1965, when Singapore became a sovereign and independent republic, whose government continues to be dominated by the People's Action Party today.

Heng's study of these phases shows a history of 'repeated adjustments to ... tap the trade between the Indian Ocean and South China Sea'.[16] All the phases were urban settlements 'devoid of a significant geographical hinterland', except for the British colonial phase. They 'functioned primarily as nodal points of exchange in international trade, and not as staple ports or as gateways to a significant geographical hinterland'.[17] With a small population base and absence of hinterland, the economies of these phases were externally oriented, capitalising on the island's location as a port city at the nexus of international trade in the region. With the exception of its time as part of Malaysia, the island has always served as a gateway to a larger economic entity.[18]

During the Temasek phase, the settlement was 'the only port-polity in the Southern Malay Peninsula region'.[19] It 'became the main gateway into the international and regional economic system for its immediate peripheral region'[20] by functioning as a transshipment and service centre for ships and traders, as well as establishing a niche export market through products such as lakawood incense, cotton and hornbill casques that were internationally in demand.[21] Temasek was thus 'at the apex of a pyramidal two-way exchange relationship, exerting a significant economic influence over the immediate region'.[22] As Heng notes, 'it was also during this phase that Singapore's economic sphere was at its largest, possibly extending into the Pulau Tujuh Islands near the Natunas and the northern islands in the Lingga Archipelago.'[23]

Although Temasek was a secondary port of the Melaka and Johor sultanates in the second phase, the external economy remained important and the island continued to export its products to Melaka, which was the key gateway in the region at this time. Archaeological discoveries of ceramics in Singapore also suggest that 'the settlement continued to maintain some trade with China and mainland Southeast Asia', albeit on a much smaller scale when compared to the Temasek phase.[24] Under the East India Company, Singapore once again became an entrepôt and transshipment port,[25] and served as an export gateway for the pepper industry and as 'the key Southeast Asian centre of trade in gambier'[26] in the 1830s. Although Singapore would cease making unique products for export in the fourth and fifth phases, the island has remained as a major transshipment hub between the larger regional markets up to the present.

External orientation also means the island's sphere of economic influence and activity depends on the political context of the region. The settlements were autonomous in only two of the six phases – during the Temasek phase 'when the settlement had its own raja'[27] and when it gained independence in 1965. The rest of the phases 'were characterised by the absence of political autonomy' as the island became part of larger political entities.[28] As such, external orientation also significantly impacted its social constitution:

> the absence of any significant domestic agrarian base, and the sparse populations of the settlement phases along the Melaka Straits region coast, necessitated an openness so as to attract the labour, goods and capital necessary for the success of the settlements' economic activities. Thus the population has been drawn from the neighbouring and further regions, facilitated by the transport links that converged at Singapore.[29]

Singapore was most cosmopolitan in the Temasek, East India Company and British colonial periods, when its

> population comprised migrants from the immediate area, the wider Melaka Straits region, and even from key states in Southeast Asia, the South China Sea and the Indian Ocean littoral. There was no 'local' population beyond a few *orang laut* or sea people and a very few long-

established Malays, with most of the indigenous population drawn from the coastal areas of the Melaka Straits region.[30]

As Anthony Reid posits, 'the mixed population of Chinese, Indians, Southeast Asians and Europeans in such cosmopolitan entrepôts [as Singapore] was not an accident of colonial displacement, but a necessity for the regional role in world trade.'[31] Indeed, the island, in all its settlement phases, can be defined as a 'transnational space', which Peter Jackson, Philip Crang and Claire Dwyer characterise as:

> *complex, multi-dimensional and multiply inhabited* [sic]. People from various backgrounds enter its spaces with a whole range of investments and from various positionalities. They may occupy its spaces momentarily ... or for a lifetime (as members of ethnically defined transnational communities). They may have residual affinities to the transnational identities of earlier migrant generations or emergent identities as a result of their own transnational experiences.[32]

Karl Hack and Jean-Louis Margolin argue that not only is Singapore at present 'most obviously a global city'[33] that owes 'its modern form to being part of the British world empire from 1819, but that its various rulers had already aspired to global status centuries before'.[34] They state that 'cities ... did not suddenly become global at some point in the late 20th century, but gradually over decades, if not centuries.'[35] For them:

> being a global city means that a city acts as a – and preferably the – major nodal point between a region and other parts of the world, attracting disproportionate amounts of foreign trade, personnel, international services and expertise coming to the area. Such cities – whether at the stage of aspiring to this status, or having achieved it – compete to place themselves at the centre of networks of trade, technology, tourism and services.[36]

In this sense, Singapore has always been a global city, serving as a nexus for international trade and services, with the corresponding flows of people, goods and services, since Temasek times. The emergence and early development of what would become a full-blown film industry in Singapore in the 1950s and '60s mirrors this historical positioning, similarly characterised by the transnational flow of capital, people, influences and connections as the island served as a hub and base of operations for a network of activities in the region. It is within this context of a global city that this book begins its examination of Singapore cinema.

Singapore Cinema: A Potted History of the Three Periods

The history of Singapore cinema is tied to the development of the island and comprises a series of disappearances and revivals in film production that have created three very distinct periods. According to C. M. Turnbull, 'the first movie, depicting Queen Victoria's funeral, was shown in the Town Hall in 1901.'[37] This screening has often been cited as the first recorded instance of film exhibition in Singapore. However, in the second edition of their book, *Latent Images: Film in Singapore*, Jan Uhde and Yvonne Uhde also cited 'an earlier screening'[38] noted by Thai film historian Anchalee Chaiworaporn that occurred on 3 August 1896. King Rama V of Thailand 'visited Singapore and was invited to see a short series of animated pictures at the Hurricane Palace in Singapore, afterwards saying "I could not remember the titles. They are a long roll of pictures put into a machine and the pictures were moving"'.[39] These were relatively private events, and films were not publicly screened till 1902 by 'an itinerant Parsi . . . named Basrai'.[40]

Based on these accounts, films had apparently arrived in Singapore soon after the Lumière brothers' first public screening of their films at the Salon Indien du Grand Café in Paris on 28 December 1895. However, film production did not begin until 1926, with a silent, Chinese-language documentary named *Xin Ke* (*The Immigrant,* Liu Pei Jing).[41] This is one of the first films to be made in Singapore with a known title. Although no prints remain and the details of the film are unclear, the existence of the film suggests that film production in the country occurred at about the same time as similar cinematic activity was emerging in other Asian countries such as Indonesia. The next known films to be made in Singapore are *Samarang*[42] (*Out to the Sea*, Ward Wing, 1933) and *Laila Majnun* (B. S. Rajans, 1934).[43] However, these early attempts at filmmaking came to a halt when the Japanese occupied Singapore in 1942. Film production would not be revived until the establishment of two major postwar studios, the Shaw Brothers' Malay Film Productions in 1947 and Cathay-Keris six years later. Together, these two studios dominated film production in Singapore in the 1950s and '60s, generating a prolific outpouring of primarily Malay-language films, while simultaneously developing a network of Chinese film production and distribution in Hong Kong. The 1950s and '60s is the first major period in the history of Singapore cinema and is generally regarded as the golden age of film production. Given the close ties between Singapore and Malaya at this time, the films produced catered to both markets (and Indonesia), and the industries in Singapore and Malaya collaborated and shared resources. It is, therefore, also no coincidence that the golden age experienced rapid decline after Singapore separated from Malaysia in 1965. It became more difficult and expensive to make films because the resources that were once shared now had to cross geopolitical lines. Key talents such as the influential P. Ramlee left Singapore for Studio Merdeka, a major studio in Kuala Lumpur, Malaysia. Malay Film Productions and Cathay-Keris eventually ceased production and closed in 1967 and 1972 respectively.

The decline in film production and closure of the two studios led to the second period in the 1970s, characterised by a small spate of independent productions. This period is often referred to as the post-studio era, and the films produced are markedly different from those of the golden age. Firstly, they are not Malay-language films but English and Mandarin ones. Secondly, whereas the earlier films tended to feature the rural landscapes of kampongs (or villages), these new films are much more urban and contemporary. They are also heavily influenced by popular spy and action films and television series such as James Bond and Bruce Lee films, and the *Six Million Dollar Man*. However, while some of the films were popular, output was limited and eventually ceased, resulting in a decade of silence in the 1980s. Interestingly, the decline in film production and ensuing silence coincided with intense state-driven efforts at nation-building and urban development after Singapore's independence.

Film production would not be revived until the 1990s, leading to the third major period that continues to the present. This period is perceived as a rebirth of Singapore cinema, emerging after the post-independence, formative years of nation-building in the 1970s and '80s when Singapore forged a distinct identity and differentiated itself from Malaysia. This revival cinema is a post-national one, and the films produced are different from those of the golden age and post-studio periods, just as the current constitution of the industry is also no longer recognisable as a legacy inherited from those times.

Each period therefore has unique characteristics and can be considered a different cinema. Indeed, they are often discussed as distinct eras, with little or no connection between them, creating a discursive fracturing in the understanding of Singapore cinema. As Gerald Sim notes, 'the historicist inclination' to distinguish the golden age and the revival 'is fostered by two obvious reasons: formal differences between the films themselves and the country's economic advance over the very period that production became dormant'.[44] Indeed, the films of the golden age are often discussed within a chronological, developmental trajectory of the industry.[45] Others have considered these films as reflections of a particular culture (as Malay films),[46] as part of the body of work of particular filmmakers[47] or studios[48] (as P. Ramlee films or Shaw Brothers films, for example) or to locate them within the context of that past – as colonial or postcolonial films,[49] for instance. While these studies are valuable, they also tend to contain these films in the past, designating them to either that time or a particular culture, and seeing them as films that were made in Singapore and not as Singapore films.[50] The post-studio period of the 1970s is often overlooked altogether in critical accounts of Singapore cinema. This is not a prolific period and the low production values of the films have often caused them to be perceived as B-movies. On the other hand, much of the critical work on Singapore cinema has focused on the films of the revival period. Apart from the usual accounting of these films within a historical trajectory, some have begun examining them alongside the national. Such considerations are only just emerging and are usually contained within larger discourses such as Chinese cinema[51] or the cinema of small nations,[52] for example.

Celluloid Singapore seeks to address the discursive fracturing and evolve the discussion into an examination of the nature of Singapore cinema as a national cinema, and how the films of each period fit within that rubric of understanding. It explores the films from these three periods to interrogate how they relate to each other and to the national. This book also challenges the easy identification of films from the revival as Singapore films because such recognition tends to pass as a rudimentary definition of Singapore films. The difficulty that arises is in applying this 'definition' to films of the earlier periods because they look like different kinds of films and depict a Singapore that is not as easily recognised today. So, if the films from the revival are clearly Singapore films, then how are those films from earlier periods also Singapore films?

What is a Singapore Film?

Discussions on Singapore cinema often raise the question: what is a Singapore film? Tackling the question raises further questions: why is this cinema called 'Singapore cinema' and not the much more grammatical 'Singaporean cinema'? Are the terms 'Singapore' and 'Singaporean' synonymous? If so, then do we understand 'Singapore' as also meaning 'Singaporean'? The application of such labels is obviously not so simple; what is 'Singapore' may not be 'Singaporean'.

The term 'Singaporean' denotes cultural specificity (as particular or distinctly Singaporean) as well as ownership (made by Singaporeans). However, it is rather limited because it does not account for those films that may be about Singapore but are not made by Singaporeans, like Peter Bogdanovich's *Saint Jack* (1979), a Hollywood production that has been regarded as a 'quintessential Singapore film'.[53] The term also fails to account for those films made by Singaporean individuals or companies that have nothing to do with Singapore. For example, *Infernal Affairs II* (Andrew Lau and Alan Mak, 2003) was co-produced by a Singapore production company, Raintree Pictures, but features a narrative about the triads in Hong Kong that has nothing much to do with Singapore at all. The term 'Singaporean' cinema is therefore an exclusive label that excludes the larger notion of an industry and the diversity of products such an industry may produce, as well as the potential for considering non-local productions as part of its cinema.

The term 'Singapore' cinema is a much broader label. It can refer to the entire local film industry and include products that are made by Singaporeans or Singaporean companies that have no culturally signifying qualities, as well as foreign films that re-present Singapore in some way, shape or form. However, denoting films as Singapore films then also qualifies them *as Singapore films*, which returns us to the opening question: What exactly are Singapore films? What do we mean when we say that a film is a Singapore film and another is not?

To classify and qualify films in this way highlights what they represent, and because the qualifier is the nation or country these films are then perceived, understood or claimed as representations of it; as products of a national cinema, if you will. According to Robert Stam, national cinema is premised on the notion that films are 'national and project national imaginaries; they are products of national industries, produced in national languages, portraying national situations and recycling national inter-texts (literatures, folklores, etc.).'[54] In theory, this definition seems rather obvious. However, in practice, applying such a definition is not so straightforward. When we qualify a film as a Singapore film, what exactly does it mean? Does the qualifier refer to the location, the filmmaker's or production company's origins, the extent to which a film represents a 'national imaginary', culture or people, or all of the above? How many of such criteria must a film fulfil before it can be considered a Singapore film?

Furthermore, Singapore is a migrant society and 'multiracialism is one of [its] founding myths'.[55] It has a heterogeneous population comprised of multiple races, ethnicities, languages, religions and cultures, raising the question of which represents the national? For example, the official, national language is Malay but Singapore's lingua franca is English and its population is dominated by Chinese. So, the national anthem, 'Majulah Singapura', is written in Malay but sung by a majority who do not readily understand its lyrics. In the context of cinema, to what extent can Malay films like those of the golden age be considered Singapore films when the majority of the population do not understand the language or perceive the culture presented as essentially foreign?

The problem of defining Singapore cinema and its films is the problem of identifying what we mean by 'Singapore', that is, the idea or identity of the nation rather than the geopolitical territory or material place of Singapore itself. According to Homi Bhabha, there is

> a particular ambivalence that haunts the idea of nation ... It is an ambivalence that emerges from a growing awareness that, despite the certainty with which historians speak of the 'origins' of nation as a sign of the 'modernity' of society, the cultural temporality of the nation inscribes a much more transitional social reality.[56]

This ambivalence pertains directly to the problem of defining what we mean by 'nation', especially after what Chris Berry describes as 'the deconstruction of the seeming naturalness of the idea of the nation'.[57] Central to this deconstruction is Benedict Anderson's theorising of the nation as 'an imagined political community' comprised of the collective imagination of a community who will 'never know most of their fellow-members, yet in the minds of each lives the image of their communion'.[58] His definition of nation as constituted through actions that circulate or produce an image or idea of community emphasises the constructedness and performativity of nationhood and the experience of belonging. Such a conception creates what Bhabha calls 'the impossible unity of the nation'.[59] As Ann Anagnost notes, not only is the nation 'an "impossible unity" that must be narrated into being in both time and space', but 'the very impossibility of the nation as a unified subject means that this narrating activity is never final'.[60] Therefore, the nation is not only constituted by narratives or 'narrated into being',[61] but a process of *being constituted*.[62]

This process is about national identity formation and identification, and is essentially a performative one where doing is being. This is Judith Butler's view of performative, and her work on the performativity of identity explains how nations can be construed as a process of being constituted. To extrapolate, nation, like gender, 'ought not to be construed as a stable identity or locus of agency from which various acts follow; rather [it] is an identity tenuously constituted in time, instituted in an exterior space through a stylized repetition of acts.'[63] These acts are performative gestures that perform rather than actually reflect a stable identity. As such, identity, whether gender or national, is 'real only to the extent that it is performed'.[64] If this is so, then the question of what 'Singapore' is needs to be reframed to how Singapore is constituted or performed into being, and by whom or what. This also opens the possibility that there may be more than one process at work, resulting in multiple performances, each producing a 'Singapore'. Since there is no singular meaning ascribed to the term 'Singapore', what then is the value of defining a film as a Singapore film or not? This book suggests that of greater value is not the question of what a Singapore film is, but *how* a film can be considered a Singapore film.

Given the now taken for granted view that nations are unstable, dynamic and constituted, it would be naïve to conceive of national cinema as merely reflecting and expressing 'a pre-existing national identity, consciousness, or culture'.[65] Writing about Indian cinema, Sumita Chakravarty, citing Eric Hobsbawm, states that 'the film medium may be said to approximate ... the tension contained within nationalism itself, namely the cultural singularity evoked by the concept (the "nation" as collectively linked by ties of common history, place of origin and language) and the reality of nations ... in the contemporary world as inevitably diverse and plural.'[66] Susan Hayward goes a step further by positing what she calls 'the paradox of national cinema'.[67] For her, 'national cinema ... will always – in its forming – go against the underlying principles of nationalism and be at cross-purposes with the originating idea of the *nation* as a unified identity.'[68] So the value of a national cinema lies in its continued ability to 'problematise a nation – by exposing its masquerade of unity'.[69]

Adding to the complexity of the situation is the debunking of Anderson's view that the nation is also 'imagined as both inherently limited and sovereign' and geopolitically determined as nations have 'finite, if elastic boundaries, beyond which lie other nations'.[70] Such a conception limits the idea of the nation to geopolitical boundaries. As Andrew Higson argues, this delimiting is problematic because 'borders are always leaky and there is a considerable degree of movement across them (even in the most authoritarian states).'[71] Anderson's imagined communities overlooks not only the diasporic community and 'the cultural difference and diversity that invariably marks both the inhabitants of a particular nation-state and the members of more geographically dispersed "national" communities'.[72] It also fails to account for the ways that media practices cross borders. Hollywood, of course, is the prime example here since its mode of film production, distribution and exhibition is much more international than specifically national. A typical example is the recent remake of *Ben Hur* (2016), which is an American film that features a narrative set in Jerusalem during the Roman Empire but was principally shot in Italy, directed by the Kazakh Timur Bekmambetov and starred two Brits (Jack Huston and Tony Kebbell) in leading roles alongside a generally international cast that also includes Americans like Sofia Black-D'Elia and Morgan Freeman as well as Israeli, Danish and Brazilian actors Ayelet Zurer, Pilou Asbae and Rodrigo Santoro respectively. It was released in fifty-five countries in 2016 alone, not to mention subsequent international distribution of the film in various formats such as DVD.[73]

Asian cinematic practice has also become increasingly transnational. One of the earliest examples of this trend is *Crouching Tiger, Hidden Dragon*, which is listed as a Taiwan/Hong Kong/USA/China film, but entered the Oscars as the Taiwanese entry. It was produced by eight companies, including Columbia, Sony Pictures (USA, and also Japanese!), EDKO Film from Hong Kong and the mainland Chinese China Film Co-Production Corp. It features an international crew comprising Taiwanese director Ang Lee, Hong Kong action choreographer Yuen Wo-ping and cinematographer Peter Pau, all of whom are now based in the US. Original music is composed by Tan Dun, who is from China, and features musical performances by world-renowned cellist Yo-Yo Ma, who was born in Paris but is also now based in the US. Matching its international crew is an international cast that includes Hong Kong's Chow Yun-fat, Malaysia's Michelle Yeoh, China's Zhang Ziyi and Taiwan's Chang Chen. Furthermore, according to James Schamus:

> The film was shot in almost every corner of China, including the Gobi Desert and the Taklamakan Plateau, north of Tibet, near the Kurdistan border. We were based for a time in Urumchi where all the street signs are in Chinese and Arabic, all [the] way down south to the Bamboo Forest at Anji. [Then] North to Cheng De where the famous summer palace is ... The studio work was done in Beijing, we recorded the music in Shanghai, and we did the post-production looping in Hong Kong. So it is really bringing together every conceivable image you could have of China.[74]

The composite, international nature of film practices such as those in the examples above raise questions about the place of the national in the global transactions and interactions that exist within and across cinemas. Where is the national in the context of international production and global circulation, as well as the reception and consumption of films by heterogeneous audiences? The rubric of national cinema seems an inadequate framework for discussion, and Chris Berry notes that 'the 1990s saw something of a shift away not only from the "national cinema" model but from issues of the national in general, and a corresponding growth of interest in all that might be marked as "transnational"'.[75] As I previously noted,[76] this resulted very quickly in what Mette Hjort terms 'the "transnational turn" in film studies',[77] particularly in work on Asian cinema, where transnationalism was welcomed as a critical framework capable of advancing the field beyond area studies. In view of such developments, it may seem almost outmoded now to raise the spectre of national cinema. However, within a few years, transnationalism is already in danger of burning out. According to Hjort:

> there is anecdotal evidence to suggest that a number of film scholars are tiring of the endless incantation of 'transnational' and are beginning to ask themselves whether the very cinematic phenomena currently being described in 2009 as transnational would not, just some ten years previously, have been discussed in terms of a new allegedly outdated national cinemas paradigm.[78]

As Berry warns, 'to turn away from the national in the current era is to confuse deconstruction with destruction ... [I]f the idea of the territorial nation state as a transcendent and exclusive ideal form is no longer tenable, that does not mean either that the form or issues of the national disappear altogether.'[79] Reinforcing this idea, Elizabeth Ezra and Terry Rowden state that 'the transnational at once transcends the national and pre-supposes it'.[80] Such conceptions of transnationalism call for 'a renewed focus on national cinema as a simultaneous point of access and departure' that views the national within the context of the global and requires the interaction between cinema and nation to be reframed.[81] As Berry argues, '[w]ithin this framework, the national is no longer confined to the form of the territorial nation-state but multiple, proliferating, contested and overlapping.'[82]

This framing of the national cultivates an understanding of cinemas as participating in a global network while also functioning within the remits of their particular cultural, social and political movements and transformations. The discursive mode of national cinema is reconfigured from an expressive model reflecting the fixed and stable characteristics of a nation to a new analytical framework of cinema and the national that can extend 'beyond specific national cinema projects' and include 'the idea of a national cinema industry'.[83] As Berry concludes, 'only an approach that sees cinema and the national as a multidimensional problematic can move beyond the national cinemas approach without losing sight of the national altogether and in the process, capture the complexity of the national in the transnational era.'[84] The transnational era obviously refers to contemporary exchanges and flows between nations and industries. However, it could also refer to current thinking about transnationalism as an 'intermediate and open term' receptive to the 'modalities of geopolitical forms, social relations and especially the variant *scale* [sic] on which relations in film history have occurred that give this key term its dynamic force, and its utility as a frame for hypotheses'.[85] It is a conceptual tool that can be applied to contemporary cinematic practices and those of prior periods as well.

Thus, both transnationalism and the national are recuperated as potentially constitutive rather than mutually exclusive conceptions that can be considered alongside each other within a broader perspective of cinema as 'inter-national'.[86] Whereas the term 'international' is 'predicated on political systems in a latent relationship of parity',[87] the hyphen emphasises 'the inter-relation and inter-action of connections'[88] and influences that occur as a result of cinema's mobility and the relationship between cinemas. As such, a national cinema can also be transnational, and transnational flows and practices can impact or inform a cinema's relationship with the national. Given Singapore's history and positioning as a transnational space, this conception of the transnational and national is crucial not only to this book but also to considerations of this nation. It is particularly pertinent to discussions on the golden age when the industry was transnational and the inter-action of influences from other cinemas and performance forms is apparent in the hybridity of the films and conventions of that period.

Dudley Andrew notes that 'quite distinct strains of national and regional styles and genres surely tell several histories . . . , each harbouring its particular idea of cinema.'[89] It is this 'distinct strain' in Singapore films that this book aims to uncover and, in the process, discover how these constitute a 'particular idea of [Singapore] cinema' as a national cinema. *Celluloid Singapore* takes up the challenge of finding the national in Singapore cinema. At stake is not the question of *what* this national cinema is, but *how* it is national.

Celluloid Singapore

As the title of this book suggests, the focus is not only on Singapore cinema but on the ways that Singapore is (re)presented or performed on screen. References to Singapore on screen can be traced back to the 1920s, in such Hollywood films as *Across to Singapore* (1928), *Singapore Woman* (1941) and *Singapore* (1947). These films were not actually shot in Singapore. Instead, 'Singapore' was created in a Hollywood studio with rickshaws, wooden huts, parrots, sarongs and assorted Asian extras. In *Singapore*, for example, Singapore is presented as an exotic tropical isle that does not resemble Singapore in the 1940s, much less the present. For a local audience especially, these foreign depictions tend to be perceived as inaccurate, as feeding into Orientalist discourses that imagine the other as exotic, rural or native. It is easy, therefore, to see these Singapores as foreign or perspectives from the outside. On the other hand, locally made films are expected to mirror some kind of social, political or cultural essence or reality that exists in the nation, as national allegories in Jameson's terms.[90] This requires audiences to identify what they see as Singapore and the films as Singapore films. Such desire to find the national in films sees local representations as more 'realistic', creating a dichotomy between local and foreign productions, between inside and outside perspectives, where the 'reality' of the former is pitted against the inaccuracy of the latter. However, whether a film is realistic or not is not the point. This is because while the medium of film is capable of capturing material reality, what we actually see in a film is not 'realistic'.

Certainly, film's ontological relationship with reality has been the subject of much preoccupation in film theory, resulting in the realist position that film records reality and the formalist view that film renders reality. In trying to reconcile this divide, Irving Singer states that while 'reality may be revealed through photographic images, . . . the use of these images shows the extent to which reality has been transformed'.[91] Pierre Sorlin argues that 'although they refer directly to the world, pictures are inserted in representations which compel us to pay more attention to some aspect of their referent. Films borrow their material from reality and offer us a reshaped reality, an interpretation of it.'[92] As such, Dudley Andrew notes:

> cinema perception is a mode of 'seeing as' wherein we see an array of light and shadow as a particular object and we see several hundred fragments of a full film as a particular world. Far from being a rare occurrence in perception, or a particularly devious one, cinema here joins myriad

other instances of 'seeing as', instances in which we notice an oscillation between what our senses deliver to us and how we identify this.[93]

For Nataša Ďurovičová, the medium, 'built ... on the paired desires to bring the distant closer and to make the proximate strange enough to be worth seeing',[94] is 'indebted at once to photographic capture of space and to movement, mobility, displacement'.[95] As such, watching a film involves what she calls a 'double vision'[96] that requires the spectator 'to see his or herself as an Other even while seeing the other as a variant of one's self.'[97]

This is similar to Richard Bauman's conception of the 'consciousness of doubleness' in performance as explained by Marvin Carlson:

> all performance involves a consciousness of doubleness, according to which the actual execution of an action is placed in mental comparison with a potential, an ideal, or a remembered model of that action. Normally this comparison is made by an observer of the action – the theatre public, the school teacher, the scientist – but the double consciousness, not the external observation, is what is most central [. . .] Performance is always performance *for* someone, some audience that recognizes and validates it as performance even when, as is occasionally the case, that audience is the self.[98]

The introduction of consciousness differentiates 'performing' from 'doing' and enables normative actions that may otherwise be opaque, perfunctory or mundane (that is, doing) to be regarded as performance. This is a mode of 'seeing as' that can be applied to film, where consciousness can occur on the part of the person or thing performing, such as the various, deliberate processes of filmmaking or a film's verisimilitude, or on the part of the people watching who are conscious of the constructedness of what is being performed.[99] So, to see a film as performance is to see it as 'an action carried out for someone, an action involved in the peculiar doubling that comes with consciousness and with the elusive other that performance is not but which it constantly struggles in vain to embody'.[100]

In the context of this book, films that are made or set in or about Singapore are approached as cinematic performances of Singapore that consciously reference or (re)present it. They each produce a Singapore and call upon audiences to regard their Singapore *as Singapore*, regardless of whether they are locally produced or not. So, 'the elusive other' that these performances 'struggle to embody' is Singapore, and the doubling that occurs is between (the idea of) the nation and the performance of it in these films. Together, these films add to and negotiate with the multiple ways that Singapore can and has been performed on film and elsewhere.

The title, *Celluloid Singapore*, therefore implies that the Singapore we collectively see on screen is not only a transformed version of material reality, or different from the Singapore that is performed or understood elsewhere. Celluloid Singapore is essentially already (an)other Singapore. Here, the parentheses emphasise a simultaneous understanding of these cinematic performances as variations of different Singapores (another) that also address, contest or subvert other performances of the nation (an other).

This book addresses the 'consciousness of doubleness' between cinema and nation according to the rather neat division of film production in Singapore into three distinct periods. These three periods also constitute the three main sections of this book: 1) Malay cinema and the golden age; 2) B-movies and the post-studio 1970s; and 3) counter-performance and the revival. Each section has two chapters that collectively take on the discursive fracturing identified above as they consider the ways in which the films from each period depict a different Singapore and require a different 'mode of seeing [them] as' Singapore films. The results, however, are unique but also coherent ways in which this cinema engages with the national.

The first section examines the Malay cinema of the golden age as a pre-national cinema in the sense that it is pre-independence. Although Singapore was not yet an independent nation, it was by then already a discrete political unit that existed as part of the British Straits Settlements, then a Crown Colony, before achieving partial self-rule in 1953 and full self-government in 1959. The first chapter examines the golden age as a transnational cinema that mimics Singapore's positioning as a transnational space. Borrowing Sheldon Lu's argument on Chinese cinema, this chapter argues that film production in Singapore arose as 'an event of transnational capital from its beginning'.[101] To that end, it considers the development, practices and migrant constitution of the film industry vis-à-vis the sociopolitical circumstances of this burgeoning nation, including Singapore's complex relationship with Malaysia, and places Singapore cinema within the larger transnational network of film production and distribution in the region, Hong Kong and China.

The next chapter focuses on the films of the period and discusses two ways that these films could be considered Singapore films. First, when viewed within the context of its time, the golden age is a cinema of hybrid films that is essentially culturally heterogeneous and consistent with the transnational nature of the industry and Singapore. The hybridity of the films is apparent in the narrative, musical style and language, which reveal a diversity of influences ranging from other cinematic conventions, such as those from Indian and Hollywood cinemas, and more culturally specific performance practices like *bangsawan* theatre. Second, when viewed from the vantage point of contemporary Singapore, these films have become somewhat foreign since many of the conventions and spaces are no longer practised or visible. In short, they are problematically perceived as old films, reinforcing their distance and difference from the films of the revival especially. This part of the chapter challenges the tendency to relegate golden age films to the past and argues that watching these films now creates a 'consciousness of doubling' between the Singapore in the films and the one materially present today. What we see is (an)other Singapore being performed at each viewing, and it is precisely because of this that the films from the golden age can be considered Singapore films.

The next section sees the post-studio period of the 1970s as an important turning point that marks the transition from the pre-national cinema of the golden age to the post-national one today. The first chapter explores the sociopolitical context of post-independent Singapore, such as the state's efforts at nation-building, the global focus of its policies and the arrival of television, which resulted in a changing audience and the development of a different cinema that was also internationally oriented. Like the country within which it operates, this is a cinema in transition and the films perform a Singapore that is either absent or foreign. The next chapter develops on the topic of foreignness in Singapore films and discusses the ways that Singapore has been depicted in films made outside the country, especially by Hollywood. It addresses the tendency to polarise local- and foreign-made films as inside/outside perspectives and argues that they all perform a Singapore that is equally foreign regardless of where they were made. The chapter also problematises the tendency to limit the study of national cinema to locally-made films by making the case for how a Hollywood production like *Saint Jack* (Peter Bogdanovich, 1979) can be considered a Singapore film.

Singapore's revival cinema is a post-national one, emerging after Singapore had already transitioned from *Third to First World*, as heralded by the title of the late Mr Lee Kuan Yew's memoirs. Central to the section on the revival is the performance of national identity, primarily the difference between the state's version of the nation and the other Singapores produced by this cinema. My prior work on the revival[102] offers a framework for analysis that the chapters here develop and expand on. The first chapter explores a series of acts and gestures that constitute the state's performance of a successful Singapore as a unified, homogeneous national identity, including the Singapore Story, policies, speeches and the ubiquitous annual National Day Parade. The second chapter argues that films of the revival engage the national through a relational force of counter-performative strategies present in the narrative, film style, language, the use of space and the prevalence of the 'other' Singaporean.[103] Together, these films not only produce different Singapores. They perform (an) other Singapore.

By way of conclusion, the last chapter discusses current developments in Singapore cinema through recent films like *Ilo Ilo* (Anthony Chen, 2013), *Meeting the Giant* (Tay Ping Hui, 2014) and *To Singapore with Love* (Tan

Pin Pin, 2014). It also examines the *7 Letters* anthology of films (2015) and Eric Khoo's *In the Room* (2015) as tributes against the context of Singapore's fiftieth birthday celebrations. Analysis of these films shows that although the industry has grown, the existence of other Singaporeans in (an)other Singapore continues to persist. The chapter also develops and expands on my prior argument on Singapore cinema's position as (an)other cinema in Singapore.

The three periods studied here are essentially three distinct cinemas that collectively comprise Singapore cinema. However, despite the ways in which these cinemas may be different, they create a trajectory of cinematic performance that is much more coherent and similar than the distinct fracturing of their history seems to suggest. Together, they constitute a national cinema through different performances of the nation, requiring different modes of seeing celluloid Singapore as Singapore.

Notes

1. P. J. Thum, 'Constance Mary Turnbull', 11.
2. C. M.Turnbull, *History*, xii.
3. Thum, 12.
4. Karl Hack, 'Framing', 6.
5. Ministry of Education, 'Launch of National Education'.
6. Kuan Yew Lee, *The Singapore Story*.
7. Kuan Yew Lee, *From Third World to First*.
8. Karl Hack and Jean-Louis Margolin, 'Global City', 7.
9. See, for example, Derek Heng, 'Longue Durée'; Chong Guan Kwa, Tai Yong Tan and Derek Heng, *700 Year History*.
10. Hack, 22.
11. Margolin, 4.
12. Hack, 26.
13. Ibid.
14. Heng, 58–9.
15. Michael Hill and Lian Kwen Fee, *Politics*, 50.
16. Heng, 58.
17. Ibid., 61.
18. Ibid., 69.
19. Ibid., 62.
20. Ibid., 64.
21. Ibid., 62.
22. Ibid., 64.
23. Ibid., 64–5.
24. Ibid., 62.
25. Ibid., 63.
26. Ibid., 62.
27. Ibid., 59.
28. Ibid.
29. Ibid., 66.
30. Ibid.
31. Anthony Reid, 'Cosmopolis and Nation', 37.
32. Peter Jackson, Philip Crang and Claire Dwyer, 'Introduction'.

33. Margolin, 28.
34. Ibid., 29.
35. Ibid.
36. Ibid.
37. C. M. Turnbull, 126.
38. Jan Uhde and Yvonne Ng Uhde, *Latent Images*, 2nd edn, 14.
39. Anchalee Chaiworaporn, cited in ibid.
40. Ibid.
41. Raphael Millet, *Singapore Cinema*, 18.
42. Uhde and Uhde, 19.
43. Ibid., 16.
44. Gerald Sim, 'Historicizing Singapore Cinema', 362.
45. See, for example, Jan Uhde and Yvonne Ng Uhde, *Latent Images*.
46. See, for example, Syed Muhd Khairudin Aljunied, 'Films as Social History'.
47. See, for example, Timothy Barnard, 'The Ambivalence'.
48. See, for example, Kay Tong Lim, *Cathay*.
49. See, for example, Rohani Hashim and David Hanan, *Malay Comedy*.
50. Edna Lim, 'Singapore Cinema', 20.
51. Song Hwee Lim, '*15*', 9–16.
52. Tan See Kam and Jeremy Fernando, 'Singapore', 127–43.
53. Philip Cheah, quoted in Ben Slater, *Kinda Hot*, second cover.
54. Robert Stam, *Film Theory*, 289.
55. Michael Hill and Lian Kwen Fee, *Politics*, 4.
56. Homi Bhabha, 'Narrating the Nation', 1.
57. Chris Berry, 'From National Cinema', 153.
58. Benedict Anderson, *Imagined Communities*, 6.
59. Bhabha, 1.
60. Ann Anagnost, *National Past-Times*, 2.
61. Ibid.
62. Edna Lim, 'Counterperformance', 188.
63. Judith Butler, *Gender Trouble*, 179.
64. Judith Butler, 'Performative Acts', 278.
65. Andrew Higson, *Waving the Flag*, 5.
66. Sumita S. Chakravarty, 'Fragmenting', 223.
67. Susan Hayward, 'Framing', 95.
68. Ibid.
69. Ibid., 101.
70. Anderson, 6.
71. Andrew Higson, 'Limiting Imagination', 67.
72. Ibid., 66.
73. IMDb, '*Ben Hur*'.
74. Linda Sunshine, *Crouching Tiger*, 46.
75. Berry, 150.
76. Edna Lim and Lilian Chee, 'Asian Cinemas', 2.
77. Mette Hjort, 'On the Plurality', 13.
78. Ibid., 12.
79. Berry, 154.
80. Elizabeth Ezra and Terry Rowden, 'General Introduction', 4.
81. Lim and Chee, 4.
82. Berry, 149.
83. Chris Berry and Mary Farquhar, *China on Screen*, 9.
84. Berry, 156.

85. Nataša Ďurovičová, 'Preface', x.
86. Lim and Chee, 3.
87. Ďurovičová, x.
88. Lim and Chee, 3.
89. Dudley Andrew, 'Time Zones', 62.
90. Fredric Jameson, 'Third World Literature'.
91. Irving Singer, *Reality Transformed*, 7.
92. Pierre Sorlin, 'That Most Irritating', 265.
93. Dudley Andrew, *Concepts*, 38.
94. Nataša Ďurovičová, 'Vector', 90.
95. Ibid., 92.
96. Ibid., 91.
97. Ibid.
98. Marvin Carlson, *Performance*, 5.
99. Lim and Chee, 5.
100. Carlson, 5.
101. Sheldon Hsiao-Peng Lu, 'Historical Introduction', 4.
102. Edna Lim, 'Coming'; Lim, 'Counterperformance'; Lim, 'Singapore Cinema'.
103. Lim, 'Coming'.

2. *MERDEKA!*: MERGER, SEPARATION AND A TRANSNATIONAL GOLDEN AGE

Early Cinema: Transnational from the Beginning

Film production did not begin in earnest in Singapore until the 1930s, with *Samarang (Out to the Sea,* Ward Wing, 1933) and *Laila Majnun* (B. S. Rajans, 1934). Although there are records of an earlier film, *Xin Ke (The Immigrant,* Liu Pei Jing, 1926), 'there is no evidence that [the production company or the film] left any permanent filmmaking legacy in the city'.[1] On the other hand, *Samarang* and *Laila Majnun* were advertised as bona fide Malayan films even though they were both produced by foreigners.

Samarang was directed by an American, Ward Wing of World Wide Pictures, written by American scriptwriter and actress Lori Bara, and produced by United Artists. It premiered in 1933 in the United States before opening in Singapore in 1934. Described as 'a simple story of love amid smiling brown pearl-fishers, having as its background a forbidding jungle', Jan Uhde and Yvonne Uhde believe that *Samarang* was 'likely inspired by'[2] Robert Flaherty and Friedrich Murnau's *Tabu: A Story of the South Sea.* The film was shot in Singapore and 'featured a multiracial cast that may be described as typically Singaporean'.[3] Some of these actors were already famous local *bangsawan* (a type of Malay opera) performers. *Samarang* was publicised as 'Malaya's First Sensational Thriller – filmed entirely in Singapore with local artists' when it was released in Singapore.[4]

Laila Majnun (also spelt *Leila Majnun*) was directed by B. S. Rajans, a film-maker from India who would eventually become 'the founding director of

Singapore cinema', and produced by Motilal Chemical, a Bombay company that supplied projector lamp carbons to Malayan cinemas.[5] As Raphael Millet notes, the 'story itself is not really Malay as it was mainly inspired by Arabic folklore, specifically *One Thousand and One Nights*, and also partly Shakespeare's *Romeo and Juliet*.'[6] *Laila Majnun* was also likely influenced by *Leila Majnu* (1931), a very popular, 'all talking, singing, dancing' Hindustani film, and 'introduced an Indian-influenced filmmaking style that was to dominate local Malay productions for years to come'.[7] The film also featured a local cast of popular *bangsawan* performers as well as Arabian and Egyptian dancers. It was released one day after *Samarang* and marketed as 'The First Spectacular Colossal Malay Talkie ... entirely produced in Singapore'.[8]

According to Uhde and Uhde, 'the simultaneous appearances of *Samarang* and *Laila Majnun* indicate that local film production was already taking root.'[9] By the mid-1930s, two companies that would dominate the golden age of Singapore cinema were also established. The first is Shaw Brothers Pte Ltd, whose story begins with a company called Tian Yi Film Co. in Shanghai.[10] It made silent films and was established in 1924 by Runje Shaw, the eldest of Shaw Yuh Hsuen's five sons. The others are Runde, Runme, Run Run and Runfun. Runme, who oversaw the company's film distribution business, eventually left for Singapore to expand the family fortune in the region. In 1927 his brother, Run Run, joined him and they formed the Hai Seng Company, which would later become Shaw Brothers Pte Ltd. Hai Seng's initial business was distributing films made by Tian Yi and other companies in China. However, the brothers soon decided to venture into film exhibition and opened their first cinema in Singapore in 1927. By the end of the 1930s, the Shaw Brothers had 139 cinemas in Malaya, Singapore, Thailand and Indochina. The Shaws eventually added film production to their business in Singapore and Hong Kong, and became a major player in both countries, creating not only an international film empire but also a fully vertically integrated one similar to the major Hollywood studios like MGM or Paramount.

In Hong Kong, Run Run and Runme, together with their siblings in China, set up the Nan Hua Film Company in 1936 and the Nanyang Film Company in 1937. The latter company was active until the early 1950s and produced about ninety feature films, of which seventy were made between 1937 and 1941.[11] Indeed, the use of the term 'Nanyang' in its name clearly reflects the company's focus. Literally translated, 'Nanyang' means the South Seas, and was used to refer to those areas in Southeast Asia to which migrants from China settled. According to Wang Gung Wu, 'for the people of south China, the Nanyang was both a land of wealth and opportunity as well as a romantic place filled with wild or charming and easy-going people.'[12]

As they were already producing Chinese films in both Shanghai and Hong Kong, the brothers focused on the Malay audience in Singapore by importing films from Indonesia and making their own locally. They established their own production studios at 8 Jalan Ampas in Singapore in 1937 and made a total of eight Malay films from 1938 to 1941. However, these Malay films were actually made by Chinese filmmakers who worked with the brothers in Hong Kong. As Millet notes, these films 'were very much inspired by their previous works in Hong Kong'.[13] They were based on Chinese stories, not Malay ones, creating a confusing mix that neither appealed to the target audience of Malays nor the Chinese. They were not box-office successes, 'as "the Malay patrons seemed to reject" stories and themes adapted from Chinese films, which they could not relate to'.[14]

Ten years after the Shaws first set foot on the island, another Singapore family, the Lokes, entered the film business. Loke Wan Tho, who would become a major player in later years, was only two when his father, yet another successful businessman, died. His mother took over the business as Loke's trustee and, together with a relative called Khoo Teik Ee and an Englishman named Max Baker, established Associated Theatres Ltd to venture into the film exhibition business. The company was based in Singapore and Kuala Lumpur and would later become Cathay Organisation in 1959, the second of the two companies that would dominate the industry in the golden age.

However, just as these two companies were flourishing, the Japanese occupied the island in 1942. Singapore was renamed Syonan and filmmaking activities came to a halt except for a handful of Japanese propaganda films produced by Nippon Eiga Sya Production between 1942 and 1943. Although it was still possible to watch Western films at the beginning of the Occupation, those from Allied nations were eventually banned. Film exhibition came under the control of the Eiga Haikyusha, 'one of the Japanese occupation monopolies also known as kaishas'.[15] Uhde and Uhde, citing Chin Kee Onn, note that '[m]any of the films available in Singapore and Malaya were Japanese, but . . . the local population evidently patronized and enjoyed them although they were aware that these films were meant to be propaganda.'[16] Film production would not be revived until after the war, leading to the development of the golden age.

I have relied much on the detailed and thorough accounts of these film activities in Singapore in these early years by Uhde and Uhde, Raphael Millet and Timothy White in my own brief re-telling above. It is an abbreviated history of early Singapore cinema because the objective is not to rehash prior research, but rather to highlight the international character of all these activities. The emergence and early development of what would become a full-blown film industry in Singapore in the 1950s and '60s mirrors Singapore's own historical positioning as a transnational space, similarly characterised by the flow of capital, people, influences and connections as the island served as a hub and base of operations for a network of activities in the region. Film, at its appearance and establishment in Singapore, was an international enterprise, or in

Sheldon Lu's terms, 'an event of transnational capital from its beginning'.[17] It remained so throughout the golden age of the 1950s and '60s, as well as the post-studio era of the 1970s.

POSTWAR SINGAPORE AND MALAYA: SEPARATE BUT LINKED

The Japanese Occupation between 1942 and 1945 was a critical point in Singapore's history, as the occupier's brutal treatment of the locals gave rise to nationalistic sentiments and political action that would eventually lead to independence. This was especially so among the Chinese, whom the Japanese suspected were supporters of the British or Kuomingtang in China. They became prime targets early on. To purge anti-Japanese elements, the occupiers launched Operation Clean Up or *sook ching* three days after the British surrendered. All Chinese males between eighteen and fifty years of age had to report to registration centres. Those identified as anti-Japanese were taken out to sea to be sent overboard or shot.[18] This massacre lasted for three weeks, and hundreds more were killed in 'a mopping-up operation' that followed.[19] According to Turnbull, 'it is impossible to say how many Chinese died in [these] massacres ... The Japanese later admitted to killing 5000 but the figure was probably closer to 25,000, and many Chinese put the total much higher.'[20]

Throughout the Occupation, 'contempt was mixed with dread: the everyday fear of beatings and face slappings, the constant haunting terror of arrest, prison, torture and death.'[21] It was 'a time of rumour, fear and secrecy, suspicion and informing, when it was unsafe to voice any opinions at all'.[22] When the Japanese finally surrendered in 1945, Singapore once again returned to the British. However, the British returned to 'a different Singapore, and a changed Southeast Asia ... The old unquestioning trust in British protection had been forever shattered'.[23] Life after Occupation was marked by severe food shortages, exorbitant prices for basic necessities, and crime. The harbour was choked and the railway, docks and most of the godowns had been damaged or destroyed. The city was 'dilapidated – the roads full of portholes – while water, electricity, gas and telephone services were run down. Overcrowding, poverty and disease were chronic'.[24]

In addition, the Chinese were exceedingly unhappy with the war crimes commission's punishment of *sook ching* perpetrators; only a Japanese major-general and colonel were condemned to death, while five others were sentenced to life imprisonment. Turnbull states that 'the Chinese community were incensed at the leniency of a verdict so disproportionate to the enormity of the crime.'[25] According to the Discovery Channel's companion book to its documentary on *The History of Singapore* (2005), 'many began to argue that the spilling of so much Chinese blood on Singapore soil justified a moral claim to govern the island that had not existed before.'[26] The book also cites Lee

Kuan Yew, who said that 'it was the catastrophic consequences of the war that changed mindsets, that my generation decided, "No, this doesn't make sense. We should be able to run this as well as the British did, if not better".'[27]

Meanwhile, Britain, beleaguered and almost bankrupt by the war, dissolved the Straits Settlements and proposed the formation of a Malayan Union that involved convincing the Malay sultans to give up their sovereignty and grant citizenship rights to immigrants. The plan excluded Singapore, which would remain a separate Crown Colony with a British governor, while 'currency, higher education, immigration, income tax, civil aviation, posts, and telegraphs were to be administered on a pan-Malayan basis.'[28] The Malayan Union was enforced in 1946 with Kuala Lumpur as its capital, despite vocal opposition in both Singapore and Malaya. Minority parties in Singapore called for its inclusion based variously on their ideas of a Malayan Malaya, Singapore's centrality in Malayan commerce, politics and culture, or objection to the separation of Malays between the island and the peninsula. The exclusion of Singapore stoked nationalistic sentiments that were already emerging as a result of the Japanese Occupation. According to Michael Hill and Lian Kwen Fee,

> contrary to a view proposed by some accounts of nation building in Singapore, the birth of nationhood began, not in 1959 when the colony was given self-government, nor in 1965 when it separated from Malaysia and became independent, but in the aftermath of the Second World War and the Malayan Union proposal of 1946.[29]

On the other hand, the United Malays National Organisation (UMNO) in Malaya incited widespread nationalistic sentiments among the Malay community by arguing that the sultans being forced to surrender their sovereignty and the granting of equal citizenship to immigrants was not fair to the Malays.[30]

The differing reactions to the Malayan Union in both Singapore and Malaya reflected their contrasting visions of Malaya. In Singapore, the majority Chinese population had shifted from a sojourning outlook to 'a more settled and Malaya-orientated'[31] one, with ties to families and businesses in the peninsula. As Hack notes, 'many developed a Malayan Chinese identity.'[32] The number of locally born Chinese had also increased from 38 per cent in 1931 to 60 per cent in 1947, and 72 per cent by 1953. The Indian population too rose quickly between 1947 and 1957, two-thirds of which came from the Federation. Although the Indians had stronger ties to their homeland than the Chinese, increasing numbers were also settling in Singapore and regarding it as their home.[33] According to Hack, 'the "Malayan" trend amongst the Chinese and many English-educated was beyond politics, and reflected across almost all non-Malay political groups.'[34] This Malayan outlook was a syncretic one 'in which the Malay would provide the language but would not necessarily dominate politically or culturally'.[35] On the other hand, the peninsula was predominantly Malay and experienced the rise of Malay nationalism 'through a combination of Islamic reform, growth of a Malay print community, a feeling that Malay interests and primacy had to be fought for against Chinese economic preponderance, and a growing sense of a pan-Malayan Malay identity'.[36] Its cause was to protect the rights of a *bangsa Melayu* (Malay state or community), whose core identity was Malay, while other races were considered 'non-indigenous and outside the core-identity of the region'.[37]

Accepting that 'communal differences were too deep to create an immediate self-governing state with racial equality',[38] the British restructured the Malayan Union to safeguard Malay rights, restore sovereignty to the sultans and strictly limit citizenship requirements while retaining a centralised government. Based on this, a new Federation was formed in 1948 that continued to exclude Singapore because the Malay leaders felt that the Chinese would otherwise outnumber the Malays. According to Hack, the different names that the Federation was referred to 'reflected schizophrenia over its identity':

> To anyone whose lingua franca was English, it was the Federation of Malaya, a body 'in-waiting' for cross-communal politics and ultimate reunification with Singapore. For Malay-speakers it was the *Persekutuan Tanah Melayu* [sic] or 'Federation of Malay Lands,' with sovereignty residing in the Malay sultans (charged with protecting Malay interests), and a flag which included a crescent as the symbol of Islam.[39]

Despite this difference in political views, the island had, in reality and for a long time, been closely tied to the peninsula in more ways than one. Roads, railways, postal services, airlines and tertiary education were pan-Malayan as Singapore and Malaya shared a causeway (built in 1923), a railway service, an airline (Malayan Airways, which was established in 1947) and a university (Raffles College, which was established in 1928, became the University of Malaya in 1949). They also shared sporting events such as football and rugby, as their Malaya Cup included Singapore in their leagues. As such, Hack notes that by the 1950s the use of the term 'Malaya' was not limited to the peninsula but had also in effect 'come . . . to be accepted as a term which included Singapore'.[40]

Postwar Cinema and Golden Age: a Malay Cinema in a Transnational Industry

It was within this context of separation, commonality and rising nationalistic sentiments that the film industry in Singapore revived after the Occupation, and developed into a cinema that was essentially shared by both the island

and the Federation until Studio Merdeka opened in Kuala Lumpur in 1960. Cathay and Shaw began reopening their cinemas almost as soon as the war was over and released many pre-war Chinese titles that had been hidden in Thailand. Eventually 'the high demand for films prompted a number of companies to venture into home production.'[41] The first postwar film to be made in Singapore is *Seruan Merdeka* (*The Call for Freedom* aka *The Call for Independence*) by B. S. Rajans in 1946.[42] It was a Malay-language film produced by Malayan Arts Production, an independent company owned by an Indian businessman. Although it was not commercially successful – because the main cinemas owned by Shaw and Cathay refused to screen films that were not their own – Millet counts this film as 'the real starting point for what would turn out to be a 25-year golden age of film for Singapore'.[43] He does not explain his statement but a possible reason could be that this is a Malay film made by a prominent director who would eventually be known as 'the founding father of Singapore cinema'.[44] The other films produced were largely Chinese-language films made by independent companies. They included *The Light of Malaya* (Liu Man, 1946) by the New China Film Company and several others by Zhong Hua Film, like Cai Weijun's *The Blood and Tears of the Overseas Chinese* (*Hua qiao xue lei*, aka *Blood and Tears of the Chinese Immigrants*, 1946) and Yin Hailing's *Lost Souls Abroad* (aka *Souls of Overseas Expeditions*, 1946) and *Honour and Sin* (*Nanyang xiao jie*, aka *Miss Nanyang*, 1947). Shaw also made a number of Mandarin films about the Japanese Occupation. Three were directed by Wu Cun, a mainland Chinese: *Song of Singapore* (*Xin jia po zi ge*, 1946), *Second Home* (*Di er gu xiang*, aka *My Second Homeland*, 1947) and *Unbearable Days* (*Du ri ru nian*, aka *A Day is like a Year*, 1947).[45] However, although the existence of these films suggests that a revival of film production was rather diverse, they also did not lead to further Chinese-language productions.

On the other hand, Shaw also released a number of Malay-language films that were produced before the Occupation. The success of these films led Shaw to reopen its studios and establish a new production company named Malay Film Productions (MFP) at Jalan Ampas in 1947 'to produce films, and cater to the local Malay audience, not only in Singapore but also in Malaya, which was then the fastest expanding market in the region, albeit a predominantly Malay one'.[46] This time, Shaw Brothers hired Indian talent such as B. S. Rajans. MFP, together with its exhibition arm Malayan Theatres Ltd, enabled Shaw to once again model itself on the vertically integrated major Hollywood studios, controlling all aspects of the film business, including its own stable of contracted stars and talent. Through this set-up, Shaw had, in effect, 'kicked off the Studio Era in Singapore'.[47]

Competition in the film industry soon emerged, as a number of independent film companies entered the market. One of these was Nusantara Film. The name Nusantara means 'Malay archipelago' and Millet posits this suggests its 'intention to reach across borders and cover the whole Malay archipelago'.[48] Little is known about this company except that it produced six or seven films over a period of less than three years. Nonetheless, its contribution to the industry is interesting in terms of the diversity of actors and directors it introduced,[49] especially when compared to Shaw. Instead of Indian talent, Nusantara hired Indonesian and Malayan directors and actors with varying experience, including A. R. Tompel, a Malayan who cut his teeth in the business as Rajan's assistant director at MFP. Its first two films, *Pelangi* (Naz Achnas, 1950) and *Sesal Tak Sudah* (A. R. Tompel, 1950), featured new faces, different from those contracted to MFP. Its later films also cast actors who were 'more established in the Singapore scene'.[50] One of its films, *Seniyati*, was 'interestingly codirected by A. R. Tompel and Chow Wing Kok, thus bringing together both Malay and Chinese references and influences'.[51] However, Nusantara lacked the kind of muscle that a studio like Shaw's MFP obviously had in terms of financing and access; Shaw had its own cinemas, Nusantara did not. So Nusantara depended heavily on independent exhibitors, which were slowly dying out as Shaw and Associated Theatres (Cathay) gradually bought them. Nusantara was eventually squeezed out and closed in 1954.

Another independent player of note is Abraham Ho Ah Loke who, like Shaw and Cathay, first ventured into the film business through exhibition in the 1920s. By 1934 he had already owned and sold to Shaw a string of cinemas in Northern Malaya before beginning to acquire a new chain in Kuala Lumpur, Ipoh and Penang a few years later. As Millet notes, 'by the beginning of World War II, he was a major force in the exhibition business, and was duly known as North Malaysia's movie tycoon.'[52] He fled to Thailand during the war and returned to Malaya in 1945. In 1948, Ho collaborated with Cathay's Loke Wan Tho to form a new film exhibition company called Associated, International and Loke Theatres. In 1951, he started two studios. The first was Keris Film Studio and the second was Rimau Film Productions, a joint venture with an Indian film distributor for Cathay[53] that would later be renamed Keris Film Productions. Under this label, Ho would produce some of the most interesting films of the 1950s, including *Buloh Perindu* (aka *Magic Flute*, 1953), which was made in collaboration with Loke Wan Tho and believed to be the first colour Malay-language film.[54] The partnership between Ho and Loke deepened and eventually led to the formation of the Cathay-Keris studio in 1953.

Initially Cathay's mainstay was the exhibition business, but it did not screen Malay films because Shaw, which distributed these films, did not distribute them to Cathay's theatres. So Cathay made a deal with a UK-based company to distribute its films in Malaya, Hong Kong and Thailand. Loke started to recognise the potential of the Malayan film market and began delving into film production with Ho before they finally formed Cathay-Keris together. As Cathay was already a serious player in the exhibition business, Cathay-Keris became the first real threat to the Shaw empire which, prior to this, enjoyed a virtual monopoly.

By the time Cathay-Keris was established, Shaw's MFP had already made a total of thirty-seven films between 1947 and 1952. With the entry of Cathay-Keris, production increased. In the 1950s, MFP averaged about ten films a year, while Cathay-Keris averaged about five. By the early 1960s, their combined output of Malay films was about eighteen a year. The industry high was in 1958, with twenty Malay films (eleven by MFP and nine by Cathay-Keris). By the time it closed in 1967, MFP had produced about 160 movies, 'making it the most prolific production unit ever in the history of Singapore.'[55] This 'creative and fertile period spanning the 1950s and early 1960s has come to be regarded as the golden age of Malay cinema in Singapore'.[56] The period would be best remembered for its stars such as Saloma, Zaiton, Latifah Omar, Ahmad Daud, Jins Shamsudin and, of course, P. Ramlee, the figure most associated with, and who in some ways is, the face of the golden age.

Although audiences flocked to the cinemas to watch their favourite stars, most of whom were Malay, the business of making, distributing and exhibiting films was transnational in practice. These films were financed by, and made in studios owned by, Chinese businessmen who also distributed and exhibited them. The cinematographers, editors and technical specialists were also Chinese. The directors were mostly Indian; some were born in Singapore while others were discovered in India and brought to the country because there was a lack of experienced local talent. Shaw was the first to practise this, choosing 'the first of these directors based on their talent but also, more pragmatically, their familiarity with Malay culture and language'.[57] A number of them would eventually leave Shaw's MFP to join Cathay-Keris. They included L. Krishnan who, with thirty films, is known as 'Singapore's most prolific director';[58] B. N. Rao, whose films were some of the most successful of the period, including the very popular *pontianak* (female vampire) series that has now become a cult classic; and B. S. Rajans, the first Indian director Shaw hired and who 'holds a very special place in Singapore film history'.[59] Although he died in 1955, just as film production was ramping up, Rajans was one of the most prolific filmmakers of the period, with a total of twenty-eight films. Among these are landmark works that paved the way for subsequent filmmakers and the industry, such as the first Malay talkie – *Leila Majnun* (1933), Singapore's first postwar film – *Seruan Merdeka* (1946), the first Singapore studio film – *Cinta* (*Love*, 1948) and *Buloh Perindu* (*Magic Flute*, 1953), the first film produced by Cathay-Keris.[60] B. N. Rao and L. Krishnan also respectively created the *pontianak* and *orang minyak* (oily man), creatures that would become iconic characters of the Malay horror genre in this decade. These Indian directors did not merely make

Malay films. They significantly influenced them. They were responsible for a number of major breakthroughs in the industry, including the use of colour and making film adaptations of local novels, as well as the practice of using outdoor locations. These Indian directors also influenced not only the stories and themes but also the acting style and use of music and dance in Malay films, which would become conventional in Malay cinema. They gave the Malay films 'an unmistakable Indian-Malay flavour rich in song and dance, which became very popular with Malay viewers and also quite a few Singaporean Chinese'.[61] It was in fact the popularity of their films that made the business of Malay films viable. They not only paved the way for, but also laid the foundations of, this golden age of Malay cinema.

To add to its stable of Indian talent, Shaw also created a Filipino connection when it hired award-winning filmmakers like Eddy Infante, T. C. Santos, Ramon Estella, Lamberto Avellana and Rolf Bayer. Collectively, they made a total of sixteen films in Singapore during this period. Of these, eleven were helmed by Ramon Estella, including a number of *pontianak* and other horror films for both MFP and Cathay-Keris. Although most of the Filipino directors, with the exception of Ramon Estella, did not remain in Singapore for long, they brought with them their Hollywood influences. According to Millet, 'many of them were very Hollywood-oriented, and some were even trained by Americans. Their screenplays tended to be remakes of Hollywood films and their movies were replete with Western themes.'[62]

Even though the Indian directors remained in Singapore much longer than their Filipino counterparts, many would also eventually leave between 1959 and 1963, leaving the stage clear for Malay talents to fill their shoes. In fact, before 1959, only the singers, dancers and actors were Malay. The exceptions were A. R. Tompel,[63] Naz Achnas, Jaafar Winyo and Haji Mahadi, who began directing their own films between 1950 and 1954, followed by P. Ramlee, S. Roomai Noor and Jamil Sulong between 1955 and 1959. Of these, the multitalented P. Ramlee was the most versatile and prolific. He was the chief talent at MFP, where he not only directed and acted in films, but also wrote scripts, composed music and sang the songs. In total, he sang about 360 songs, acted in forty films and directed sixteen during his time in Singapore,[64] making him the most successful director as well as actor, writer, songwriter and singer of the period.

The influx of Malay talent into the industry after 1959 coincided with the individual paths Malaya and Singapore were taking to independence as they negotiated their complicated relationship and differing visions of a Malay Malaya and a Malayan one. In 1957, the Federation of Malaya was granted independence within the British Commonwealth, though it had been dealing with the communist insurgency led by the military arm of the Malayan Communist Party since 1948.[65] Armed conflict escalated to such an extent that a state of emergency was declared in the Federation, which would last for the next twelve years. Emergency was declared in Singapore in June 1948 and led to the vigorous clamping down of anything that was deemed to be politically subversive. Many arrests were made, several organisations were declared illegal, and the Malayan Communist Party itself was banned.[66]

In the meantime, Singapore attained partial internal self-rule in 1955, with locally elected members holding twenty-five seats in the Legislative Assembly. From the Assembly, a Chief Minister and Council of Ministers would be chosen to serve as head of state and cabinet respectively, while the British would continue to have veto power as well as control over internal security and foreign affairs. In 1958, the UK parliament passed the State of Singapore Act, and a new constitution granted the local government near-total internal self-rule with control of all domestic affairs, including internal security, while the British continued to oversee foreign affairs and external defence, with the proviso for a further review in June 1963. A new Legislative Assembly was elected in 1959 and the People's Action Party (PAP) swept to power with forty-three of the fifty-one seats. The party's leader, a young Cambridge-educated lawyer, Lee Kuan Yew, became Singapore's first Prime Minister.

In Singapore, the ideal all along, on the part of the British and the various local governments, was merger with the Federation. The Legislative Assembly, in a statement to the newly independent Federation of Malaya, said, 'We of Singapore look forward to that day when our strength will be added to your strength and our separation will be ended.'[67] Putting it more bluntly, in his address to the crowd at City Hall on taking office in 1959, Lee Kuan Yew said that 'it is but a step towards merger with the Federation of Malaya and *Merdeka* [independence].'[68] This desire for merger was founded on the corresponding idea of a syncretised Malayan Malaya. The PAP ideal, as outlined by Hack, was one in which

> there could be a 'Socialist Society,' where 'All men are equal, and no privilege should accompany the accident of birth, race, rank, religion or sex'. Rewards should correspond to 'work and ability', which together defined a person's 'worth' to society, though Malay was accepted as the national language for good.[69]

Thus began the campaign for merger with the Federation.

However, the Federation, led by the United Malays National Organisation, had a very different view – Malay culture already presented 'a pre-existent basis for national culture' and 'should continue to define "Malayan" or "Malaysian" culture'.[70] Indeed, Malay nationalism, which had been brewing since the end of the Second World War, gained tremendous momentum in the 1950s. Malay intellectuals engaged in critical debates over the development of Malay society. As Timothy Barnard notes, in addition to the presence of a film industry, Singapore was enticing to Malays attracted to many other forms of media, as the port city was the technological centre of the Malay Peninsula. The post-war newspaper industry was one of the leading intellectual engines for the Malay community, and was based in Singapore.[71]

One of the most influential groups was the ASAS 50 (Angkatan Sasterawan 50: Generation of the Writers of the 1950s), the first literary association in postwar Malaya, and the questioning of the basic assumptions that underpin Malay identity resulted in the flourishing of art in Singapore and Kuala Lumpur. Another influential group was the Singapore Malay Journalist Association, which demanded that 'Malay films should be directed by Malays'[72] and a greater push towards ownership of the arts and representation. The political and social awakening of Malay society paved the way for more Malays to enter the film industry in Singapore. The industry, too, made more of an effort to put Malays at the helm. A number of actors such as Salleh Ghani, Omar Rojik, M. Amin, Mat Sentul and Noordin Ahmad started directing their own films from 1960 onwards. An exception to this trend of actors-turned-directors is Hussein Haniff, who began as a film editor at Cathay-Keris and rose to become one of the studio's key talents.

The year 1959 seems to have been a turning point in this golden age cinema, since it augured the arrival of more Malay directors. Timothy Barnard identifies two films that year by Jamil Sulong that mark this point: *Batu Belah Batu Bertangkup* (*Stone Splits, Stone Closes*) and *Raja Laksamana Bintan* (*The Admiral of Bintan*). They are based on Malay tales and, therefore, reflect local taste and 'sentiments of *merdeka*'.[73] As such, Barnard concludes that 1959 'began a period in which films drew their inspiration from local legends, histories and tales. No longer would they be direct translations of Indian films; a local perspective would now reign.'[74] Assuming that 'local' refers to local Malay culture, it would seem that, based on content alone, the films made before 1959 when Indian directors dominated the industry are somehow less authentic as Malay films than those made by Malay filmmakers. Amir Muhammad also notes that 'a particularly obnoxious essay in the film journal of UiTM Shah Alam (a university open only to ethnic Malays) even claimed that Malay cinema really only "began" when Malays became directors.' This, he declares, 'is bollocks'.[75]

On the one hand, under the helm of Malay directors more films mined stories from historical narratives such as the *Sejarah Melayu* or the *Hikayat Hang Tuah*. These are important texts in Malay culture, occupying the same status as *The Iliad* and *The Odyssey* to Europeans and the *Mahabharata* and *Ramayana* to Indians,[76] and became the basis of films like *Hang Jebat* (Hussein Haniff, 1961). Malay folktales were also a rich resource for films such as

Bawang Merah Bawang Puteh (S. Roomai Noor, 1959) and *Batu Belah Batu Bertangkup*.[77] This is consistent with the rise of Malay nationalism and the questioning of Malay identity at this time. These two films are particularly significant as both Noor and Sulong were journalists in the 1940s and became active members of the intellectual movement advocating greater Malay identity in Malay films.

On the other hand, these sources of stories were not the exclusive purview of Malay directors, since Indian directors also used them. This is evident in films like *Hang Tuah* (1956), which was made by Indian director Pani Majumdar and drawn from the *Hikayat Hang Tuah*. The figure of the *pontianak* popularised in films made by the Indian B. N. Rao and the Filipino Ramon Estella is also drawn from Malay lore. Furthermore, in his survey of 120 Malay films, Amir Muhammad notes a number of films made by Indian directors with Islamic settings, concerns and references, including *Nasib* (B. S. Rajans, 1949), *Iman* (K. R. S. Sastry, 1954) and *Noor Islam* (K. M. Basker, 1960). Some films by Malay directors, like Jamil Sulong's own *Raja Bersiong* (1968) and Hussein Haniff's *Dang Anom* (1962), had pre-Islamic settings. Others contradict, make fun of or critique aspects of Islamic teachings and values, such as *Nasib Si Labu Labi* (P. Ramlee, 1963) and *Seniman Bujang Lapok* (P. Ramlee, 1961).[78]

So, content alone is an insufficient qualifier of authenticity, if authenticity can be measured at all. What is deemed authentic is subjective and subject to questions of perspective and address – authentic to whom? To a large extent, the content, culture, race or ethnicities of stars and language visibly identify the films as Malay films. Indeed, the milieu depicted in most of these films is not only Malay but also mostly racially homogeneous. Other races are usually left out or relegated to minor or cameo roles. This is true even in *Aloha* (B. S. Rajans, 1950), which depicts a Hawaii populated solely by Malays. However, all or a combination of these attributes characterise the Malay films of this period, regardless of the race or ethnicity of the filmmakers. Indeed, these elements could very well have been deemed to constitute authentic performances of Malay identity by the directors themselves. So, from their perspective, they are, in effect, making Malay films.

Moreover, by 1959 the transnational roots of the industry had already been firmly established. Many of the Indian filmmakers had local assistants who learnt the craft through working with them. This spawned 'the rise of home-based professional infrastructure'.[79] As such, the influx of Malay talent in the industry was not a break with but a continuation of established practices. Indeed, as Muhammad argues,

> the earliest Malay directors actually built upon what the earlier Indian directors did; there is no obvious point of rupture. How can anyone watch

Penarik Beca (directed by a Malay in 1955) and not notice the obvious thematic and stylistic continuation from a film like *Miskin* (directed by an ethnic Indian in 1952)?[80]

William van der Heide also notes that 'it is an interesting paradox that *Penarik Beca* [P. Ramlee, 1956], the first film by a major Malay filmmaker, has more Indian attributes than *Hujan Panas*, which was made by an Indian director.'[81] In his study of Malaysian cinema, van der Heide also details the similarities and links with Indian cinema in six film examples from the period.[82] Two of these were directed by Indians, namely *Hujan Panas* (B. N. Rao, 1953) and *Hang Tuah*, and he notes how they negotiated with local culture and Malay history, as well as the influence of *bangsawan* and *wayang kulit*, to be discussed in the next chapter. Both Muhammad's and van der Heide's studies show that there are overlaps between the films made by Indian and Malay directors.

The Malay films produced in Singapore also had a transnational market, as they catered to domestic audiences as well as those in the Federation and Indonesia. As Uhde and Uhde claim, 'about 80 per cent of the box-office takings of Singapore's Malay films came from what is now Malaysia.'[83] Their classifying of these films as 'Singapore's Malay films' is interesting because while this period is known as the golden age of Malay cinema, it could also be deemed as the golden age of film production in Singapore. This dual characterisation of this period as the golden age of both Malay cinema and film production in Singapore is important because they occur simultaneously but are not synonymous. The characterisation mimics the unique condition of separation and commonality between the peninsula and Singapore at this time, and underscores the contesting claims that both Malaysia and Singapore would make to the films of this period after separation in 1965.

As a cinema of Malay films, it spans both Singapore and Malaya. What was perceived as local content was culled from a Malay culture common in both countries. Many of its talents came from Malaya and Singapore, and the films they made were distributed to and popular in both markets. So, based on the general acceptance of the term 'Malaya' as referring to both the peninsula and Singapore even though they were politically separate entities, this Malay cinema is as pan-Malayan as the airline, railway and sporting leagues mentioned above. In fact, one could even go so far as to say that this is a Malayan cinema.

However, it is also possible to see this period as the golden age of film production in Singapore, since that was where the films were made. Hence Uhde and Uhde's reference to them as 'Singapore's Malay films'. Millet also notes that 'even though the Malay film industry from the 1940s and mid-1960s was a shared entity, claimed by both Singapore and Malaya . . . Malay film would more often than not be a Singapore affair (at least until the Malaysian Merdeka

Studio opened its doors in Kuala Lumpur in 1960).'[84] This is because, prior to the establishment of Studio Merdeka, the studios in Singapore were the main source of Malay films in the region. As such, this is, in effect, a Malay cinema that developed out of the film industry in Singapore. The proliferation of these locally produced films in the 1950s and '60s also marks a high point in the history and development of Singapore cinema that remains unmatched today. Furthermore, the transnational roots of filmic activity in the early years of this industry had continued and flourished after the Japanese Occupation, creating a multiracial and multicultural industry that significantly impacted and influenced the films it produced. So, while this period was indeed the golden age of Malay cinema, it was also an age that arose out of and in tandem with the golden age of the film industry in Singapore, whose practices very much mirrored the transnational space within which it was housed. This is further reinforced by the expansion of film production and distribution as Singapore companies ventured beyond the immediate region of Southeast Asia to Hong Kong and became part of Hong Kong's cinematic golden age during the same period.

Chinese Cinema: Singapore in a Larger Transnational Network

While the studios focused on producing Malay films, Chinese films were largely made in China and Hong Kong and imported to Singapore. Shaw had already established this practice before the war and would continue to do so in the 1950s and '60s in Hong Kong, alongside Cathay and other Chinese companies based in Singapore. As such, although Singapore did not produce more than a handful of Chinese films during this golden age of film production, these Singapore-based companies, with their filmmaking activities in Hong Kong, placed Singapore within a transnational network that spanned beyond the immediate region of Southeast Asia.

Even though Shaw was already producing films in Hong Kong through its Nanyang Film Company, it was Cathay that really pushed up the scale of Chinese film production there when it set up its own studio, Motion Picture & General Investment Co. Ltd (MP&GI) in 1956, three years after the establishment of Cathay-Keris in Singapore. The growth of Cathay's two studios was simultaneous. While Cathay-Keris contributed significantly to the proliferation of Malay films in Singapore, MP&GI did the same for Hong Kong's postwar cinema. Between its years of operation from 1956 to 1970, MP&GI made approximately 250 films, and distributed them in Hong Kong, Taiwan and Southeast Asia. Its films, such as *Mambo Girl* (1957), were not only big box-office hits and launched the careers of some of Hong Kong cinema's most beloved and enduring stars like Lin Dai and Ge Lan, but they also received critical acclaim at film festivals. For example, *Golden Lotus* (1957) and *Our*

Sister Hedy (1958) won the Best Actress and Best Picture Awards at the Fourth and Fifth Asian Film Festivals respectively.

Around the same time, Kong Ngee, another pre-war film distributor and exhibitor of Chinese films in Singapore, also entered the film production business in Hong Kong. It initially commissioned films from Hong Kong filmmakers before opening the Kong Ngee Film Production Company in 1955 to produce its own films there, while its head office remained in Singapore. Like Shaw and Cathay, Kong Ngee's production arm in Hong Kong also served its distribution network in Southeast Asia. It made approximately eighty Cantonese films between the mid-1950s and mid-1970s, making the studio one of the Big Four producers of Cantonese cinema in Hong Kong.[85] Its films also featured popular stars of the period like Patrick Tse Yin, Patsy Kar Ling, Nam Hong and Kong Suet. According to Millet, 'even though most of Kong Ngee's movies were Cantonese, and deeply rooted in Cantonese culture, a number of them were either totally or partially shot in Singapore, particularly for some exterior scenes.'[86] These included *The Whispering Palms* (aka *Ye Lin Ye* or *Ye Lum Yu*), *Blood Valley* (aka *Xue Ran Xiang Xi Gu*, *Blood Stains in the Valley of Love* or *Bloodshed in the Valley of Love*) and *China Wife* (aka *Tang Shan A Shao* or *She Married an Overseas Chinese*), which were all made in 1957 and are collectively known as the Nanyang Trilogy (or *Nanyang San Bo*).

Eng Wah, another Singapore-based company that established its distribution and exhibition business on the island after the war, also made a foray into film production in Hong Kong in the late 1950s. Its Eng Wah Film Production Company specialised in Hokkien films before eventually also making Cantonese films in the 1960s. Some of its film titles, such as *Peranakan Nonya* (1958), *Love of Malaya* (aka *Ma Lai Ya Zhi Lian*, 1959) and *Miss Singapore* (*Xin Jia Po Xiao Jie*, 1959), reflect the company's Southeast Asian origins.[87]

Meanwhile, Shaw, which was the first to make films in Hong Kong, had renamed its Nanyang Film Company as Shaw Father and Sons Film Company in 1950 and was not faring as well. Unable to compete with either Cathay's MP&GI, Kong Ngee or the other Hong Kong film studios, Shaw ceased film production in 1957, while continuing to distribute and exhibit foreign-language films. In 1958, Run Run Shaw left Singapore for Hong Kong and established Shaw Brothers, a company that still exists today. Mimicking the practices of MP&GI and Kong Ngee, the new company made a number of Cantonese films that were also partially shot in Singapore. These included its own Nanyang Trilogy comprising *The Merdeka Bridge* (aka *Du Li Qian Zhi Lian*, or *Chinta di Jabatan Merdeka*), *Bride from Another Town* (aka *Guo Bu Xin Niang*) and *When Durians Bloom* (aka *Liu Lian Piao Xiang*, or *The Fragrance of Durians*). These films were shot back-to-back in 1959 and featured the same cast of well-known actors such as Patricia Lam Fung, Cheung Ying Choy and Lung Kong. In 1961, Shaw Brothers opened a new studio and competed head-to-head with Cathay's MP&GI, which had a five-year head start. By 1964, Shaw Brothers dominated the Hong Kong market and Asian film festivals. It specialised in and popularised the martial arts genre with such landmark films as Chang Cheh's *One Armed Swordsman* (aka *Du Bi Duo*, 1967) and King Hu's *Come Drink with Me* (1966). According to Millet, the Shaw Brothers also 'found inspiration . . . in their Malay catalogue when ideas were badly needed'[88] in films like the *Oily Maniac* (aka *You Gui Zi*, 1976), which directly referenced the popular and strange oily man in its Malay horror films. Shaw's domination in Hong Kong also meant that the films it made there would also come to dominate the cinemas in Asia through its distribution and exhibition network.

As such, although Chinese film production was primarily located in Hong Kong, these companies, with their strong ties to Singapore and their distribution and exhibition muscle extending across Southeast Asia, created film businesses and practices that were transnationally organised and operated. Singapore was an integral part of this network, serving as an avenue for distribution and exhibition, a target market because its population was predominantly Chinese, or as an extended resource for stories and locations for the Hong Kong studios. So, even though the 1950s and '60s was the golden age of film production and Malay films in Singapore, the film activities that sprung from, and included, Singapore were much more far-reaching and international. However, the Chinese films produced by the ventures in Hong Kong complemented as well as competed with the Malay films made in Singapore for a share of the box office. Indeed, as we shall see later, the success of its Chinese films would eventually be one of the factors that led Shaw to scale down its production of Malay films in Singapore before relocating to Kuala Lumpur altogether.

Merger and Separation

As Hong Kong cinema was flourishing, Ho Ah Loke left Cathay-Keris and established Merdeka Film Productions Ltd (also known as Studio Merdeka) in Kuala Lumpur in 1960. By July 1961, the PAP government in Singapore and its UMNO equivalent in Malaya had begun negotiations on a merger. The terms were published in the 'Command 33' Singapore White Paper on 15 November: Singapore would continue to control education and labour on the island but only have fifteen seats in the Federal government, which was not proportionate representation relative to its population. Its citizens would become Malaysian nationals, not full citizens. As such, they would only have voting rights in Singapore and not in Malaya. Vociferous arguments on the merits of the terms ensued, reflecting differing visions of what a merger should be, particularly from the Barisan Socialis (a party formed by expelled members of the 'progressive' wing of the PAP). Some in the Assembly also called the terms a 'sell-out'.[89] A referendum with various options for merger was called in September 1962. Seventy-one per cent voted for the PAP-brokered deal and Singapore became part of the Federation of Malaysia in 1963.

This marriage, however, was not a happy one. More detailed accounts of the union have been provided elsewhere and this chapter will not go over them except to note that, among other things, political manoeuvring on both sides, unhappiness over the execution of the terms of merger, dealing with Indonesia's *Konfrontasi*[90] and the race riots that erupted in Singapore in July and September 1963 reflected and strained the already tenuous relationship between the PAP and UMNO. At the heart of what Hack describes as 'a political "civil war"'[91] is not the clash of tactics or personalities between the two leading parties but the differing and ultimately incompatible visions of 'Malaysian' and 'Malayan' held by both sides. Hack notes that 'the PAP and the UMNO images of decolonisation, and of the "Malayan" (in its political, cultural and economic guises) were rooted in radically different trajectories, one Malay-centered and the other Malayan-centered.'[92] While

> the PAP viewed Singapore as a services, planning and advanced industrial centre for Malaya, and as its New York ... [UMNO] viewed Singapore as a quarantine area in which a Chinese and communist threat could be contained, ... [and] as a 'price' to be paid for including 'Malays' in the Borneo territories in [the] Federation of Malay lands.[93]

In July 1965, both parties began discussions for a looser arrangement and, by 9 August, 1965, Singapore was officially separated from Malaysia and became an independent nation.

The political situation and Singapore's separation in 1965 'cannot be underestimated as it tore apart a cultural unity which had existed for generations.'[94] Separation resulted in the corresponding segregation of the film industry, with one in Singapore and another in Kuala Lumpur, and the division of resources between the two. It became more difficult to share resources, because doing so now involved crossing political and economic boundaries. Although, Millet states, 'the years between 1961 and 1966 were the most prolific and successful for the entire group of Malay directors,'[95] Uhde and Uhde also note the effects of other changes on the industry at this time. Apart from the arrival of television and dwindling box-office receipts, the *Konfrontasi* had also severely impeded the export of Malay films to Indonesia, and the high cost of production due to strikes, rising wages and the adoption of new technologies such as widescreen and colour were also rapidly surpassing the limited box-office revenue derived from the markets in Singapore and the Federation.[96] Cathay-Keris was losing money and struggled to recover from the untimely deaths of its visionary leader, Loke, in 1964 and its key talent, Hussein Haniff, in 1966. Shaw, with Run Run focusing on its business in Hong Kong and the larger market for Chinese films, began relocating its Malay film production to Kuala Lumpur by first moving major talents like P. Ramlee to Studio Merdeka as early as 1964 before eventually buying up the studio in 1966 and closing MFP in Singapore in 1967. Cathay-Keris hung on but, unable to compete with the Malay films produced by the rapidly developing Indonesian film industry, it eventually folded in 1972.

The closure of these studios ended a golden age of film production and Malay cinema in Singapore that had lasted for about a decade. Separation also eventually led to the reconstitution of the film industry as Singapore and Malaysian cinemas with distinct interests and different trajectories of development. However, while this may be so, the films that were made during this golden age remain to this day a legacy shared by the cinemas of both Malaysia and Singapore, and the same films are included in the historical accounts of both.

Sharing has not been easy and both parties have contentiously claimed the films. For example, in 1999, the 12th Singapore International Film Festival, together with the Singapore Film Commission and Shaw Organization, screened eight of P. Ramlee's films under the banner: 'Tribute to P. Ramlee: Celebrating Singapore's Pioneer Film-maker.'[97] This event also included an exhibition of his work at Shaw's cinemas. Singapore's Minister of Information and the Arts stated at the opening ceremony that 'there would be no P. Ramlee without Singapore'.[98] This was cited in the Malaysian newspaper *Harian Metro*, and sparked a debate on the ownership of P. Ramlee's work. The paper argued that his work belonged to Malaysia, not Singapore. In response, the Malaysian Information Minister also said that Ramlee was a Malaysian citizen and its 'asset', and 'other countries have no right over the works of the Malay movie legend.'[99] Although it was later clarified that the Singapore minister's statement was not a real claim on Ramlee's body of work but a quote from Ramlee's friend and colleague, Yunor Ef, this incident ignited a controversy that reflects the difficulty in sharing his body of work. The Malaysian claim is centred on Ramlee's nationality (he is Malaysian) and the fact that his films are Malay films. The Singaporean claim is that Malay Films Productions made these films and he worked for them as a paid employee.

These disparate claims apply not only to P. Ramlee's work, but also to the Malay films produced by the industry that thrived in Singapore. Part of the problem is that these films pre-date or were made during the independence, merger and separation of both countries, and claims from both sides continue to reflect and restage their opposing views of Malayan identity – a Malayan Malaya versus a Malay one. The other part of the problem is that while this period was the golden age of Malay cinema, it was also the golden age of film production in Singapore as discussed above. These are Malay films produced by an industry that is transnational in practice, a characteristic consistent with Singapore's own positioning as a transnational space. So, while the films depict Malay culture and identity during this time, they also equally reflect the transnational nature of the cinema that produced them. This is evident in the hybridity of the films themselves as a result of the multiple influences that have come to bear on this cinema and its filmmakers. It is, therefore, the international character of this cinema and the films it produced that enables the golden age to be read and understood as Singapore cinema.

NOTES

1. Jan Uhde and Yvonne Ng Uhde, *Latent*, 2nd edn, 19.
2. Ibid.
3. Ibid., 20.
4. Ibid.
5. Ibid., 16.
6. Millet, 21.
7. Uhde, 17.
8. Ibid., 16.
9. Ibid., 20.
10. Tian Yi Film Co. is also known as Unique Film Company and Unique Film Productions: Millet, 17.
11. Ibid., 24.
12. Wang Gung Wu, 'South China', 75.
13. Millet, 24.
14. Uhde, 22.
15. Ibid., 24.
16. Ibid., 25.
17. Lu, 4.
18. C. M. Turnbull, 198.
19. Ibid.
20. Ibid.
21. Ibid., 211.
22. Ibid.
23. Ibid., 223.
24. Ibid., 229.
25. Ibid., 231.
26. Discovery Communications, *History*, 106.
27. Ibid.
28. C. M. Turnbull, 233.
29. Hill and Fee, 3.
30. C. M. Turnbull, 234.
31. Karl Hack, 'Malayan Trajectory', 252.
32. Ibid., 253.
33. C. M. Turnbull, 237–8.
34. Hack, 'Malayan Trajectory', 254.
35. Ibid., 263.
36. Ibid., 252.
37. Ibid., 263.

38. C. M. Turnbull, 235.
39. Hack, 'Malayan Trajectory', 257.
40. Ibid., 262.
41. Uhde, 25.
42. Millet, 28.
43. Ibid., 29.
44. Ibid., 40.
45. Uhde, 26–7.
46. Millet, 29.
47. Ibid.
48. Ibid., 31.
49. Ibid.
50. Ibid.
51. Ibid.
52. Ibid., 32.
53. Sources contradict as to Rimau's actual partners. While Uhde and Uhde state that it is Gian Singh, an Indian distributor for Cathay, Millet claims that it is a joint venture between Cathay and an Indian partner, Hardial Singh. Uhde, 26; Millet, 32.
54. According to Uhde and Uhde, 'some maintain that Ho's earlier and less-known *Perwira lautan teduh* [sic] (Warrior of the Calm Seas, 1952), directed by Jaafar Wiryo, holds this distinction': Uhde, 29.
55. Millet, 29.
56. Uhde, 30.
57. Millet, 39.
58. Ibid., 41.
59. Ibid.
60. Ibid.
61. Uhde, 28.
62. Millet, 46.
63. Tompel began directing his own films at Nusantara as early as 1950.
64. Millet, 48.
65. The Malayan Communist Party had acquired an aura of prestige and heroism due to the extensive resistance activities of its military arm, the Malayan People's Anti-Japanese Army, during the Japanese Occupation. Its army was disbanded in 1946 and the party began working through several front organisations such as trade and labour unions. Although it initially gained strong mass support, many Singaporean workers were disillusioned by the end of 1947. By 1948, the party had lost its stronghold in Singapore and revived its military arm in the Federation: C. M. Turnbull, 237.
66. Political repression during the Emergency eased in 1953. Singapore released a number of its political detainees, some of whom fled the island. The Malayan Communist Party capitalised on the easing of tensions and began infiltrating Chinese middle schools and labour unions.
67. C. M. Turnbull, 268.
68. Hack, 'Malayan Trajectory', 265.
69. Ibid.
70. Ibid., 266.
71. Timothy P. Barnard, 'Decolonization', 70.
72. Uhde, 44.
73. He defines *merdeka* as meaning more than independence but a break from colonialism in the mindset of the people: Barnard, 66–7.

74. Ibid.
75. Amir Muhammad, *120 Malay Movies*, 27.
76. Barnard, 79.
77. William van der Heide, *Malaysian Cinema*, 72.
78. Muhammad.
79. Uhde, 28.
80. Muhammad, 27.
81. Heide, 70.
82. Muhammad, 27.
83. Uhde, 325, footnote 61.
84. Millet, 30.
85. The others were Union, Overseas Chinese Films and Sun Luen.
86. Millet, 58.
87. Ibid., 59.
88. Ibid., 61.
89. Hack, 'Malayan Trajectory', 273.
90. *Konfrontasi* (or Confrontation) was Indonesia's protest against the formation of the Federation of Malaysia. It involved 'armed incursions, bomb attacks and other subversive acts aimed at destabilising the states that were to be included in the Federation, namely, Singapore, Malaya, Sarawak, Brunei and North Borneo (now known as Sabah).': 'History Sg: Indonesia Announces Konfrontasi.'
91. Hack, 'Malayan Trajectory', 282.
92. Ibid., 280.
93. Ibid., 283.
94. Uhde, 47.
95. Millet, 62.
96. Uhde, 47.
97. Millet, 38.
98. Elisabeth Gwee, 'Come See'.
99. 'No Claim Made on P. Ramlee's Works'; 'P. Ramlee's Works Belong to Us, Says Kl.'

3. INFLUENCE, HYBRIDITY AND HOW THE PAST IS A FOREIGN COUNTRY

The hybridity of golden age Malay films points to influences that were more wide-ranging than the nationalities of the talents that made them. As writers like Millet have pointed out, these are 'less direct and internalised, but nonetheless undeniable and observable'.[1] They include Indian and Hollywood cinemas, Arabic films, particularly Egyptian ones,[2] as well as Japanese cinema, which many of the filmmakers were exposed to during the Occupation. For instance, Timothy White details the influence of Yasugiro Ozu in the low camera height in *Bujang Lapok*, (P. Ramlee, 1957), Kenji Mizuguchi in the crane shots in *Ibu Mertua Ku* (P. Ramlee, 1962) and the references to Akira Kurosawa's *Rashomon* in the cinematography of *Sergeant Hassan* (Lamberto V. Avellana, 1958).[3] William van der Heide also traces the commonalities between the work of these Japanese filmmakers and *Hang Jebat*.[4] However, both writers note that these types of shots are not sustained in the films. The influence is stylistic in nature, reflecting the formal hybridity of these Malay films. These films were not as culturally specific as the term 'golden age of Malay cinema' might suggest. As Millet puts it, 'while Malay on the face of it, Singapore cinema was in fact characterized by a great internal cultural heterogeneity.'[5] This is not surprising, since this period was also the golden age of film production in Singapore and the industry was a transnational one.

Writing on the Malay films of this period often notes the influence of *bangsawan* and *wayang kulit* (shadow puppetry). However, although Millet describes them as 'two pre- or proto-cinematic forms directly originating from the Malay world',[6] they were, in fact, originally hybridised forms of performance. *Bangsawan* is a musical, theatrical form often characterised as Malay opera. It started in Penang in the late 1800s and became popular in Malaya and Singapore in the 1920s and '30s. It is an offshoot[7] or adaptation of Parsi Theatre (*wayang parsi* in Malay), a popular form of entertainment for the Indians in the British army. From Parsi Theatre, *bangsawan* derived its proscenium staging, the practice of entry fees[8] as well as the use of music and dance performances between acts (known as extra turns).[9] Literally meaning aristocracy or nobility, *bangsawan* centres almost exclusively on royalty, with an eclectic narrative style that is similar to Parsi Theatre, mixing Arab-Persian romances, Indian epics, European plays, particularly Shakespeare's, and Victorian melodramas, and, later, Malay and Chinese stories. It featured:

> a combination of song, dance, and melodramatic narrative; charging entrance fees; and freely borrowing elements of both the traditional (stories, martial art styles, and role types) and the then modern (stories, perspective scenery, new lighting techniques, touring groups, multiple ethnicities/mestizo performers in the company, and Western musical instruments or dance styles as well as local Malay, Indian, and Chinese instruments and movement styles).[10]

Bangsawan is not only a hybridised form of performance. It is built on the foundational influence of another hybridised form, *wayang kulit*. *Bangsawan*'s *wayang* roots are apparent in their shared narrative focus on royalty and similar plot structures, where scenes begin in the court or palace before moving outdoors to more natural environments and then back to the court or palace. Like *wayang kulit*, *bangsawan* also featured stock characters such as clearly defined heroes and villains. However, *wayang kulit* is also a performance form that has Indian roots. Its stories are generally culled from Indian epics, particularly the *Mahabharata* and the *Ramayana*, although these would also become localised. Citing Tan Sooi Boon's extensive study on *bangsawan*, van der Heide notes that 'the Wayang [sic] represents an "uneasy" amalgam of Malay animism, Hindu-derived narratives and hero figures, and Islamic prayers.'[11]

However, unlike Parsi Theatre, *bangsawan* was performed in Malay and not Hindustani. This made it more popular since Malay was a common language across the races in Singapore and also made the performance form more easily identified or claimed as Malay. The songs, stories and music also became more and more Malay from the 1920s. Yet *bangsawan* also had multiethnic performers and audiences. According to Mohd Effindi Samsuddin and Rahmah Bujang, 'actors were generally ethnically appropriate to the roles they played, and the stories presented could be Western (perhaps portrayed by Eurasians), Indian or Middle Eastern (by Indians), Chinese, or Malay.'[12] As such, they conclude that, by the 1930s, *bangsawan* was 'a cross-cultural form that treated heroism from many cultures other than Malay'.[13] It was a very popular form of entertainment across races, and its cross-cultural qualities made it a true reflection of the cosmopolitan society of colonial Malaya, which saw the intermingling of Chinese, Malays and Indians. In its heyday in the 1920s and '30s, *bangsawan* was the main source of entertainment and its performers were popular stars and trendsetters. As such, it is not surprising that early filmmakers would see *bangsawan* theatre as a resource for talent and stories. This is evident in the first locally produced Malay film, *Laila Majnun*, which featured a main cast of *bangsawan* performers. Its story of the star-crossed lovers, Laila and Majnun, was also popularised in *bangsawan* performances with the same title. This overlap of stories between *bangsawan* and Malay films is not uncommon, as both mined the same resource.

The influence of *bangsawan* and *wayang kulit* on the films of the golden age denotes the hybridised roots of this cinema. Furthermore, the ways in which both forms have been localised reflect how this Malay cinema also borrowed from and adapted a variety of sources, conventions and styles.

Narrative

Narratively, the influence of *bangsawan* is most evident in period films such as L. Krishnan's *Raden Mas* (1959). It is based on a Malay legend about a princess called Raden Mas, the daughter of the Pangeran (brother of a Javanese sultan) and a court dancer, Mas Ayu. The sultan objects to the marriage and the discord results in the burning of the Pangeran's palace. Mas Ayu dies in the fire and the Pangeran flees with his baby daughter to Temasek, where she grows up, is ill-treated by her stepmother and dies trying to shield her father from an attack. This story is a well-known one and has been popularised in *bangsawan* performances. The film follows the legendary tale and has a standard cast of stock *bangsawan* characters that populate the royal court. They include the *raja/datuk* (king/nobleman), *permaisuri/datin* (queen/nobleman's wife), *mentri-mentri* (ministers), *dayang* (female palace attendants) and *hulubalang* (warriors). Its main characters, the Pangeran Agung and Raden Mas, are also the equivalents of *bangsawan*'s *orang muda* (young man/hero) and *seri panggung* (female lead).[14] To clearly define heroic characters, *bangsawan*'s young heroes and female leads are usually good-looking, have refined manners and are able to sing or are skilled in martial arts. Similarly, in the film, the Pangeran and Raden Mas are played by two very popular stars of the period, namely matinee idol M. Amin, and Latifah Omar, who was Miss Singapore Universe in 1953. The Pangeran is very skilled in the Malay martial art of *Silat*, while Raden Mas has a beautiful singing voice.

In a *bangsawan* performance, 'there is always a palace garden scene, a court scene, a fighting scene between the hero and villain, a romantic scene between the hero and the heroine, and an adventure scene wherein the hero is, for example, traveling on a mission.'[15] Similarly, the film begins in the sultan's court, where the Pangeran is formally given his title and meets Mas Ayu. He declares his love for her in the garden. A jealous minister burns the Pangeran's home and kills Mas Ayu. The Pangeran fights with and defeats the minister. He also takes his daughter and flees. His adventure includes an encounter with some Chinese seamen who give them food and passage to Kerimun. There, he and his daughter live a simple life as ordinary folk. This is only the first half of the film but it already fulfils the standard narrative elements of *bangsawan* theatre. In terms of performance, the film's extended fight sequences and equally long song-and-dance numbers also follow *bangsawan*'s emphasis on 'expansive movement skills'[16] in dance and martial arts.

William van der Heide's study also details the influence of Hindi cinema on narrative style in a number of ways, such as the use of the tableau, darsan (seeing the divine image in a man), and the modelling of the male protagonist on the Majnun lover or the Devdas figure. The Majnun lover is the Arabic equivalent of Shakespeare's Romeo in the popular story of Laila and Majnun, a pairing that recurs in Indian and Malay films, and from which this archetype is derived. He is a passive, unhappy character, half of a pair of star-crossed lovers who is inconsolable at the loss of his love. The Devdas figure is based on the Majnun lover and popularised in Hindi films in the 1950s. Equally passive, this character type signifies 'romantic obsession and failure, having an almost morbid obsession with loss, the beloved, the mother, childhood and home'.[17] P. Ramlee's characters especially seem to be modelled on the Majnun/Devdas types.

The influence of Hindi cinema is also apparent in the tendency towards 'loosely structured, digressive narratives'[18] and dependence on chance and coincidence to motivate action. Unlike Hollywood narratives, which are anchored in realism, verisimilitude, the Aristotelian emphasis on mimesis, unities of time and place, and coherent narrative development based on cause and effect, Hindi cinema, particularly Bollywood, is founded on the ancient Sanskrit Natyasastra dramatic theory. This theory of drama is concerned with moving the spectator through a succession of moods conveyed by highly stylised devices like acting style, song and dance. This produces a different kind of narrative, characterised by loose causality, overblown melodramatic dialogue and exaggerated stylised acting. Slippage between registers does not have to be marked, and continuities of space and time are not as important or clearly articulated. Psychological characterisation is not as important as clearly defined characters that are either virtuous or evil, creating an obvious dichotomy to serve 'a conclusion of "moral ordering" rather than narrative conclusion'.[19] Likewise, the characters in these Malay films tend to be obviously good and bad. The good ones are virtuous and hard-working, if somewhat naïve, while the bad ones are just plain evil, lazy, greedy and cunning. These are not psychologically-based characters but archetypes whose actions are accordingly motivated. The perceived digressions and dependence on chance and coincidences in these Malay films also relate to the narratives' focus on expressing moral tales and conclusions based on themes or issues.

A prime example of how the films embody these influences is *Penarik Beca*. The digressive nature of the narrative is signalled in the first few scenes. Images of a clock tower and vehicles on the roads are followed by a tracking shot of a newspaper boy running through the streets. The shot ends as the boy passes Marzuki and rests as the latter hails a trishaw ridden by Amran. This opening sequence is more than a minute long and has no real relevance to the narrative, which effectively begins when the camera rests on Marzuki. Amran delivers Marzuki to his big house but the latter refuses to pay the full fare, reflecting Marzuki's character as a rich but mean-spirited bully. Deprived of his earnings, Amran can only afford to buy one packet of rice, but is given another by the kind-hearted proprietor. Returning home to his dilapidated shack, Amran generously gives an old beggar outside his door a packet of food and the other to his ailing mother. When she asks why there was only one portion, he lies that he had already eaten. These scenes have a loose causality and do not add to narrative action, but rather serve to clearly define Marzuki and Amran as bad and good characters respectively, while also using them to draw the obvious lines between the mean rich and the virtuous poor.

Seeing through his lie, Amran's mother gives him half her meal. As he eats, a clash of thunder and flash of lightning announce the arrival of a storm. The dark lighting, strong gusts of wind and rain leaking through the roof together create a scene that seems drawn from horror conventions, while Amran and his mother look about helplessly. As he closes a window, a tracking shot shows the rain flooding his food before fading to black. This sequence in the shack is nearly four minutes long and fosters a sympathetic view of Amran's plight and poverty, serving the film's thematic concerns rather than causality in the Hollywood style. The use of lightning and thunder is also borrowed from Indian cinema and used to signal the fatefulness of particular events or actions, invoke a higher order, heavenly justice, or as a cinematic equivalent of pathetic fallacy. Similarly, in this film, these effects heighten the moment and emphasise the (melo)drama. This scene is reminiscent of a similar one in *Miskin* (K. M. Basker, 1952), in which rain leaks through the roof of yet another dilapidated hut inhabited by poor characters, underscoring 'the obvious thematic and stylistic continuation'[20] between the two films mentioned by Muhammad.

The narrative is also motivated by a series of coincidences that van der Heide describes as 'used without "camouflage" or self-consciousness; as in the Wayang [sic] and in [Hindi] films like *Awara*, coincidence is the true motor of the narrative'.[21] For example, Marzuki's daughter, Azizah, goes to the movies and is harassed by a group of men led by Ghazali. Amran happens to be there and saves her but is beaten up in the process. Grateful to him, and aware of his extreme poverty, she hires Amran to ferry her to and from her sewing and cooking class every day. Later, a car knocks down Marzuki and the driver is none other than Ghazali. Marzuki forgives Ghazali and entrusts him with the care of his family while he recovers in hospital. Ghazali plots to marry Azizah and tells Marzuki exaggerated tales of her relationship with Amran. Just then, Azizah arrives in Amran's trishaw, whereupon the enraged Marzuki fires him. The next day, Azizah visits Amran and is coincidentally spotted by one of Ghazali's friends. Marzuki and Ghazali promptly arrive, even though the film does not show that the sighting was reported. Marzuki flies into another rage, beats Azizah, threatens Amran and insults his mother. Marzuki agrees to let Ghazali marry Azizah to save her from Amran. The maid overhears and warns Azizah, who flees to Amran's home. Ghazali inexplicably appears and a fight ensues. Ghazali flings a knife at Amran but wounds his mother instead. He goes to Marzuki's house to demand money. Just then, Amran appears and vanquishes Ghazali in an extended fight. These chance encounters conveniently enable the characters to meet and set up dramatic actions in which characters behave according to type. Marzuki is a rich but prejudiced bully and easily duped. Amran is poor, upright and powerless, while Ghazali is just greedy and unscrupulous. These coincidences propel dramatic action and forward the thematic concerns of the film, leading to a moral end where Marzuki finally comes to his senses, repents and accepts Amran.

The influence of Hollywood cinema is also apparent in films like *Bawang Puteh, Bawang Merah*. The film's title comprises the names of the two half-sisters in the film, who are daughters of each of Ali's two wives, Kundur and Labu respectively. Kundur is the central villain and she is introduced as the jealous wife by the *bangsawan*-style song that begins the film, matched with an image of her quarrelling with Ali. Later, after Ali dies, she bullies and beats Merah, and causes Labu to drown in the well. Labu turns into a fish and is caught by the mean Kundur, who cooks and feeds the fish to Merah. Merah buries the fish bones in a clearing and it grows into a big tree with a swing. As she swings and sings, her melodious voice attracts the attention of a passing Prince. His ministers secretly follow her home to discover her identity. Kundur tells them that the girl they saw is her daughter, Puteh, and they all go to the tree so she can prove her identity. Unfortunately, Puteh cannot sing and the swing refuses to move. Kundur then admits that she has another daughter and Merah is brought forward. Merah proves that she is the girl on the swing and marries the Prince. However, the evil Kundur is not done. With the help of another bomoh, or shaman, she entrances Merah and instructs her to tie an axe above the bedroom door so that it will fall on the Prince when he enters the room. The Prince is badly injured and Merah is tied to a stake to be burnt. However, natural forces including thunder, lightning and an earthquake disrupt the proceedings and a woman who coincidentally saw Kundur suspiciously hanging around outside the Prince's room that night comes forward and reveals Kundur as the true culprit. The Prince sentences her to be tied and burnt but Merah intervenes and he acquiesces. Kundur begs Merah's forgiveness and promises to turn over a new leaf. Merah and the Prince live happily ever after. This story is based on Malay folklore, and although the film follows a version of the tale rather closely, it is also clearly influenced by Disney's *Snow White* and *Cinderella*. Kundur plays out both the bad character archetype who is just plain mean, as well as that of Disney's evil stepmother in her ill-treatment of Merah. Like Cinderella and Snow White, Merah also speaks to animals such as a goat, rabbit and cat, although the only creature that talks to her is a parrot. She tells them her woes and finds comfort in their company. In fact, the ants even help her find her mother's fish bones. The Prince's attraction to her singing also recalls similar scenes in the Disney films. Indeed, the film even opens like a fairy tale, albeit in its own terms, with the *bangsawan*-style song that tells the story of Ali and his wives.

In addition to Indian and Hollywood cinema, White also notes the influence of the Japanese genres of the *shomin-geki* (comedies about the lower-middle class) and *nansensu-mono* ('nonsense comedy') on the narrative style of these Malay films, particularly the latter in P. Ramlee's comedies. These nonsense comedy films

> are slightly racy comedies, often featuring a group of about three young men seeking to meet women and make money with a minimum amount of effort. They include many sight gags, jokes built around mistaken identity, mothers-in-law, and girlfriends with angry fathers, and usually conclude in ways that are implausible, at best.[22]

The combined influence of *nansensu-mono* and Hindi cinema is apparent in *Labu dan Labi* (P. Ramlee, 1962), which takes the tendency towards loosely structured or digressive narratives to the extreme. The title characters are servants employed by a rich man named Haji Bakhil ('bakhil' means stingy). They are both secretly in love with his daughter, Manusah. However, much of the film is not really about either one getting the girl, or forwarding a linear narrative. Instead it consists of a series of episodic, digressive sequences spawned from the collective imagination of Labu and Labi as they try to fall asleep. In the first sequence, they imagine that they are a magistrate and a doctor respectively, meeting at a nightclub where a relative of Bakhil, who looks exactly like him, is a waiter. In this hilarious sequence they conduct their conversation with each other in exaggerated English or British-accented Malay. The sequence comprises a fashion show, a musical sequence performed by the singer-actress Saloma playing herself and, later, a scene in which both servants end up fighting to win her affection. Manusah does not even appear and the sequence has nothing to do with their desire for her. Instead, it serves the thematic concerns of the film, such as the characters' desire for a better life through their imagining of the conversations and lifestyle that a magistrate or doctor would have, and class differences as they invert the real divisions between themselves and their employer. The rest of the film proceeds in much the same way: they repeatedly try to sleep but end up imagining outrageous scenarios that end in a fight and then are berated by Bakhil for making too much noise. Each gets more and more ridiculous except the last, which is also the only one in which Manusah actually appears. In the second scenario, Labu is 'a Malayan Tarzan' and Labi is 'an educated tiger', while the third is a spoof of the Western, in which Labu is the brother of Jesse James and Labi is the brother of Nat King Cole. In the last sequence, Labu discovers a treasure trove, becomes a rich man and schemes to marry Manusah through the use of black magic. Again, the sequence ends in a fight, and they are once more interrupted by reality. Labu and Labi decide that they have to go to sleep and the film ends.

The Musical Form

Bangsawan's greatest influence on the films of the period is perhaps in the use of songs and dance. In *bangsawan*, extra turns or interludes featuring a song, dance or comic skit in front of the curtains are required to facilitate scene changes backstage. These 'did not necessarily have anything to do with the plot and could just be a hit song or fashionable new dance'.[23] Film does not need extra turns for the same purpose. Instead, musical sequences are often used to delay action or to relieve tension after a dramatic build-up. It can also be similarly unmotivated by the narrative. As Timothy White observes:

> the musical number in Malay films often appears in films and at moments that seem, to the Western viewer, quite inappropriate. It is not unusual for a perfectly serious Malay drama to include songs, and often comic songs, at the most serious and dramatic moments.[24]

Citing the example of the 'The Satay Man' song in the horror film *Anak Pontianak* (Ramon Estella, 1958), which is performed by the comical character of the satay man and a group of children, White argues that 'this number serves absolutely no purpose in terms of narrative cause and effect. Instead, it serves as a break for the audience, a moment at which tension is released, after which tension is once more increased.'[25] While White attributes this musical sequence to the influence of *bangsawan* theatre, he also concludes that such sequences 'have become part of what audiences, and filmmakers, expected to experience during a dramatic performance'.[26]

However, the musical form in these films borrows not only from *bangsawan* but Indian and Hollywood cinemas as well. While the influence of Indian cinema could be attributed to the Indian filmmakers themselves, Hollywood's comes from simple exposure. As White notes,

> after World War 2, Hollywood used the backlog of films that had not been seen in occupied countries, including Malaya, to flood these countries with these films. This had the effect not only of stunting the growth of native film industries, but also of saturating filmmakers (and future filmmakers) in these countries with the classical Hollywood style.[27]

In the Hollywood model, musicals are a specific genre with its own codes and conventions that distinguish it from other genres like the Western or science fiction. There are also two distinct types of Hollywood musical. The backstage musical is the earliest form. Its characters are singers and/or dancers, providing clear, realistic motivation for singing and dancing. For example, the narratives could be about the staging of a show and the musical sequences could be rehearsals or actual performances within the films, such as in *The Broadway Melody* (Harry Beaumont, 1929). However, although the music is diegetic, the songs themselves need not relate to the narrative and can function as pure performance numbers. The backstage musical later evolved into the integrated musical where the opposite happens. Characters have no reason to be singing or dancing in integrated musicals. The music is non-diegetic but the songs reflect the narrative by revealing a character's thoughts or emotions, such as in *Meet Me in St Louis* (Vincente Minnelli, 1944). These sequences are seen as spontaneous actions that erupt from the moment and require greater suspension of disbelief on the part of the audience. These two forms of Hollywood musicals are almost mutually exclusive and rarely overlap; the films are either one type of musical or another. Although some later backstage musicals like *Shall We Dance?* (Mark Sandrich, 1937) can contain sequences such as 'Let's Call the Whole Thing Off' that seem to relate more closely to the narrative than those of earlier films, the songs are still not as tightly or clearly woven as those in integrated musicals would be. In short, the backstage and integrated musical forms are quite distinct and the films either conform to, or are more clearly aligned with, one type or the other.

In Malay films, musical sequences could be as realistically motivated as a Hollywood backstage number, in which characters who sing or dance are performers in the films themselves. They could be nightclub singers or musicians in contemporary films such as the characters of Hassan and Kassim Selamat in *Anaku Sazali* (Phani Majumbar, 1956) and *Ibu Mertua Ku* (P. Ramlee,

1962), or *dayangs* (court maidens) in historical ones like Mas Ayu in *Raden Mas*. Alternatively, these sequences could also be unrealistically motivated, like those in P. Ramlee's *Bujang Lapok* series of films, in which the characters are not performers but 'ordinary folk'. As such, there is no reason for them to sing or dance, but the songs are integrated into the narrative. The songs could externalise a character's thoughts or be about an event that has occurred or may not happen, such as a love song or a dream sequence.

Although this seems consistent with the Hollywood model, there are two key differences that can be attributed to the specific influence of Bollywood cinema. Firstly, musical sequences are 'included, and in fact often required'[28] in almost all films, regardless of genre. As such, it is not at all surprising, but instead rather common, to find musical sequences in Malay historical epics, comedies, melodramas and horror films, making the musical form conventional to, and a mode of articulation in, the films of the period as a whole. Secondly, these musical sequences can vary, overlap and have multiple functions in a single film. For example, in *Hang Jebat* the first musical sequence is a formal performance in the palace that is very much like Hollywood's backstage musicals. Court dancers perform for an audience of courtiers and the sultan, and the cinematography is also reminiscent of Busby Berkeley's complex choreography (see Figure 3.1). However, later on, the love song that the character Dang Baru sings expresses her love and longing for Hang Jebat and is akin to Hollywood's integrated musical style. This is further reinforced when the music overlaps with their conversation when they discuss their feelings for each other. Interestingly, Hang Jebat, who is a renowned warrior, never sings or dances. This is consistent with his character, and the realism that underpins the backstage musical style.

When the character performing the number is also a singer or musician, more variations and overlaps between the degree of realistic motivation and narrative integration can occur. For example, in *Ibu Mertua Ku*, Kassim Selamat is a popular saxophonist and singer, and the film opens with a live radio performance of one of his songs, 'Jangan Tingalkan Daku' ('Don't Leave Me'). His performance is consistent with his character and therefore realistically motivated by the narrative, like a backstage musical would be. This sequence intercuts between Kassim performing in the studio and Sabariah, a big fan and daughter of a wealthy widow, swooning in bed as she listens to the song on the radio, making the music diegetic in both scenes and reinforcing the realistic motivation of the musical moment. This sequence can be perceived as a pure performance piece, like that in a backstage musical. However, the love song contextualises Sabariah's infatuation with Kassim and motivates her to call the station to speak with him and set a date to meet. It also explains the expediency of their falling in love, causing her to break her engagement with an eye specialist, Dr Ismadi. Her mother opposes the relationship and

Figure 3.1 Court dance in *Hang Jebat*

disowns Sabariah. The couple move to Penang, where they quickly descend into poverty. Pregnant and unable to cope, Sabariah returns to Singapore. Not knowing that her mother had told Kassim that she had died and kept her letters to him, Sabariah divorces her husband and marries Dr Ismadi. As such, the song also predicts the end of Kassim and Sabariah's relationship when she actually does leave him.

Meanwhile, Kassim goes blind with grief and is taken in by a kind woman whose daughter, Chombi, is mourning the recent death of her husband. Chombi hears Kassim, now calling himself Osman, singing the song 'Di Mana Kan Ku Cari Ganti' ('Where Can I Find a Replacement?') in the next room and comes out of her grief-stricken state. This song is realistically motivated since it is sung by a character who is also a performer. It is also simply performed, sung only by Kassim/Osman with no musical accompaniment, since he has given away his prized saxophone. However, the song itself also expresses both Kassim's and Chombi's feelings of loss, and presages their eventually taking the place of the other's lost love. This is reinforced by superimposing images of Chombi and her husband in the background in a close-up of her. Similarly, a shot of Kassim/Osman singing in the foreground also shows him and Sabariah in the window in the background (see Figure 3.2). These shots

Figure 3.2 Chombi and Kassim/Osman during 'Di Mana Kan Ku Cari Ganti'

make it explicitly clear that the song reflects Chombi's loss (and the object of her grief), and how this is mirrored against Kassim's own.

Osman's real identity is revealed when he plays a borrowed saxophone. This musical number is the most unrealistic in the film, since he performs with non-diegetic percussion and string accompaniment. Yet the long sequence emphasises Kassim's talent and is enjoyed as pure performance, adding to the variation in the types of musical sequences in the film. Kassim, as Osman, later performs 'Jeritan Batinku' ('Cry of My Soul') in a concert in Singapore. Sabariah and Dr Ismadi, who are in the audience, immediately recognise him. This last musical sequence is consistent with the overlaps and variations between backstage and integrated musical styles throughout the film. It is realistically motivated as a concert performance, with Kassim/Osman singing on stage to an audience in the auditorium, but the song speaks of his anguish, which disturbs Sabariah so much that she leaves during the performance, and also motivates her into asking Dr Ismadi to help Kassim restore his eyesight in the next scene.

In addition, like Bollywood cinema, the Malay films also practise the use of playback singers. Stars such as Normadiah or Saloma, who were also well-known singers, were frequently credited as playback singers in films such as *Bujang Lapok*, and *Anaku Sazali* (Phani Majumdar, 1956). Perhaps the most famous playback singer of all is P. Ramlee, who was first hired as such by B. S. Rajans but later sang his own songs when he became an actor.[29] Indeed, much of the pleasure of watching these films lies in hearing these songs performed by popular singers. The musical sequences are deliberate pauses in the flow of each film, with still shots that enable the audience to enjoy the performances without distraction.

Therefore, while the influences on Malay cinema's narrative and musical form can be traced back to *bangsawan*, Hollywood, Indian and Japanese cinemas' use of music does not strictly conform to one musical style or the other. Instead the films have amalgamated and adapted these various styles to create unique, hybrid applications of international influences that reflect the transnational roots and practices of this cinema.

Language

The international quality of these films is also apparent in the language. Generally, the films use a less formal, more colloquial variety of Malay known as Bazaar Malay. Described as a Malay-lexified pidgin, it is a hybrid of Malay and the languages and dialects spoken by various communities, and variations exist depending on the range of languages that came into contact with Malay. For example, Bazaar Malay in Singapore is influenced by Hokkien and Teochew Chinese. Bazaar Malay pre-dates colonial times and, as its name suggests, emerged as a language of trade. It was the lingua franca for inter-ethnic communication for centuries across Southeast Asia, including Singapore.[30] It was not only the common language of communication across ethnic groups but also 'within the same ethnic group, speaking mutually unintelligible linguistic codes, e.g. [sic] among Indian groups speaking different languages'.[31]

Exceptions to the use of Bazaar Malay were period films like *Hang Jebat* and *Raden Mas*, which tended towards a more formal Malay. This is consistent with the courtly style of language in *bangsawan* performances, which features rhythmic dialogue comprised of metaphors, similes and rhymed verses.[32] However, the dialogue in *Raden Mas*, for example, is also peppered with references to the story's Javanese provenance. The characters use Javanese terms of address such as *kangmas* or *dimas*, where 'kang' refers to an older or close friend, 'di' refers to a younger man or boy and 'mas' means gold. Furthermore, as many of the actors came from all over the region,

> it was common for these actors to play their roles in their own dialects, or at least use their own regional accents ... The end result was that the language used in some films was not necessarily representative of the character being portrayed, but rather of the actor playing the part.[33]

This was apparently not an issue with anyone making or watching the films. Consequently, the language in these films is international, whether Bazaar Malay or a more formal variety, or spoken in a local or regional dialect or accent, and clearly reflects the transnational character of the industry, its audience and Singapore. So, even though these were Malay films, and they were not subtitled, the films were able to transcend an exclusively Malay audience and appeal to a larger speech community that included different races and ethnic groups.

INILAH SINGAPURA?[34]

It is perhaps in the setting of these films that the 'consciousness of doubling' most visibly occurs between Malay cinema and Singapore. Whereas period and horror films like *Hang Jebat* and *Sumpah Orang Minyak* (P. Ramlee, 1956) tend to be located in rural settings, more contemporary films show us glimpses of Singapore during the time. These films capture local landmarks and street scenes in their opening sequences or in establishing shots that clearly locate the films in Singapore. For example, the opening sequence of *Madu Tiga* (*Rivals Three*, P. Ramlee, 1964) begins with a long shot of the front of Shaw Building before cutting to a back view and car park to establish the arrival of one of its characters. Cathay-Keris films tend to open with the image of Cathay cinema in lieu of a studio logo. This is a practice that is consistent in a number of films from this studio. Although these are usually daytime images, *Serangan Orang Minyak* (*The Oily Man Strikes Again*, L. Krishnan, 1958) opens with a long shot of Cathay cinema and hotel at night instead. This is an exception that is consistent with the horror genre of the film. This opening image is followed by a pre-credit sequence that shows the ghostly release of a man from prison before a close-up identifies the space as the Pearl's Hill Prison in Singapore. While these shots economically establish the specific setting of the opening scene, such sequences can also be extended to include a variety of locations. For example, in *Seniman Bujang Lapok* the opening sequence begins with a low-angle shot of the statue of Sir Stamford Raffles before panning to a street view of Empress Place and cutting to Connaught Drive with a view of City Hall. From there, the camera follows a lorry advertising MFP's upcoming film *Panji Semerang* (to be shown at Rex and Sky theatres) as it journeys past Capitol theatre on Stamford Road (showing *The Great Imposter*) and Lido theatre on Orchard Road (showing *Cimarron*) before finally travelling through a village (see Figure 3.3). The emphasis on cinemas and film advertising serves its narrative of three bachelors trying to be movie stars. However, the images also unmistakably locate the film in Singapore.

Such images of Singapore locations in these and other Malay films are not surprising, since they were filmed locally. However, they also establish a clear cultural context that frames the narrative as urban and occurring within a Singapore milieu, which is modern and cosmopolitan. According to Hack, 'many Singapore-based urbanites and even kampong (village) dwellers of the island might see themselves as urban Malayans. Singapore was increasingly a space to experiment with being modern, urban and Malayan.'[35] Barnard also identifies Singapore as the 'technological centre of the Malay Peninsula'.[36] Indeed, in its quest for merger, Singapore positioned itself 'as the most modern, and most economically and financially developed part of that new country [the Federation of Malaysia]; and . . . as the advanced manufacturing centre for a Malayan economic hinterland.'[37] As such, although the films depict a Malay perspective of Singapore, this perspective is also modern and cosmopolitan, where traditions coexist with Western influences. This is apparent in aspects of mise-en-scène like the nightclubs that characters either work in or frequent, and the cars they drive, as well as their costumes, which range from the more traditional sarongs and *kebayas* to Western-style suits and dresses.

The natural mingling of such styles is most apparent during the 'international' fashion show in *Labu dan Labi*. The emcee Aziz Satar (playing himself) characterises the show as international and this is reflected in the multiracial models and outfits. They range from the Chinese Jolly Kwan wearing 'Rainbow' (a *cheongsam*-style dress) and the Caucasian Linda Lumb in 'An Evening in Paris' (a Western-style dress) to the Indian Miss Nirmala in 'Party' (a modern saree) and the Malay Sarimah in a tight-fitting, *kebaya*-style outfit called 'Sukma Rindu' (see Figure 3.4).

The next round features more conventional versions of these outfits corresponding with the models' race. This time the outfits no longer have fancy names but are more simply and literally identified as 'Cheongsam', 'Summer' (dress) and 'Saree' respectively. However, Kwan's Cheongsam is styled with

Figure 3.3 Opening sequence in *Seniman Bujang Lapok*

long gloves, giving the look a more modern sensibility similar to Linda Lumb's summer dress and short gloves that follow (see Figure 3.5).

The only exception is Sarimah, who appears in a *kebaya* named 'Bintang Hati' (star of the heart), which pairs a tight-fitting sarong with a Western-

Figure 3.4 First round of fashion show in *Labu dan Labi*

influenced cowl-neck blouse. Although this outfit is supposed to be the more conventional iteration of the *kebaya* as compared to 'Sukma Rindu', it is also the least traditional of all the outfits in this round. The models' walk, posture and poses on the runway, as well as the accompanying music, equate these multiple races and styles, casting them as simultaneously particular and international. The patrons of the club are also from a variety of races and dressed in a number of different styles. The men are in suits and the women are either in Western-style dresses or *kebayas*. Despite the appearance of multiple races, the perspective of the scene and the film as a whole is decidedly Malay, like the rest of the films of this cinema. Yet, like Sarimah's 'Hati Bintang', the contemporary films perform the culture with a modern international sensibility that reflects the cosmopolitan setting of Singapore.

On the other hand, other films depict a more complex negotiation between modernity and tradition. A prime example is *Bujang Lapok*, which I discussed in an earlier work.[38] The film questions the place of tradition in modernity by showing a clear contrast between 'the formal, transactional, functional nature of the city and the idyll and community spirit (*gotong royong*) associated with the kampong'.[39] This is effectively conveyed in the first few scenes. Ramlee, Sudin and Ajiz are three friends who share a room in the kampong and work in

Figure 3.5 Second round of fashion show in *Labu dan Labi*

the city as a perfume salesman, an office worker and a lorry driver respectively. The film opens with Ramlee attempting to sell perfume to Sudin's boss. Ramlee and Sudin do not acknowledge each other in the office, and it is only later when they meet with Ajiz at his lorry outside the office that we realise these three men are friends. In contrast, the kampong's spirit of community is immediately established after the three friends leave the city and head home. They happily share the cost of a chicken, which a neighbour cleans for them. They make their meal with a stove borrowed from their landlady and eat it together. The frequency of three-shots of the friends in these scenes underscores their unity and camaraderie, which are reinforced in an extended comic sequence following their return to the kampong. The three men deliberately strip the layers of their 'formal' work attire to reveal tattered underwear beneath. As they make fun of each other, the scene draws attention to the difference between the city and kampong through their clothes (see Figure 3.6).

The use of costume to highlight the formality of the city is further reinforced each time Ramlee dresses in a formal suit for his dates in the city. There, the women he meets repeatedly cheat him. As White notes, 'in each [date], the urban coffee shop is a site in which Ramlee, seeking a romantic relationship, is cheated of both companionship and money.'[40] In contrast to the women in the

HOW THE PAST IS A FOREIGN COUNTRY

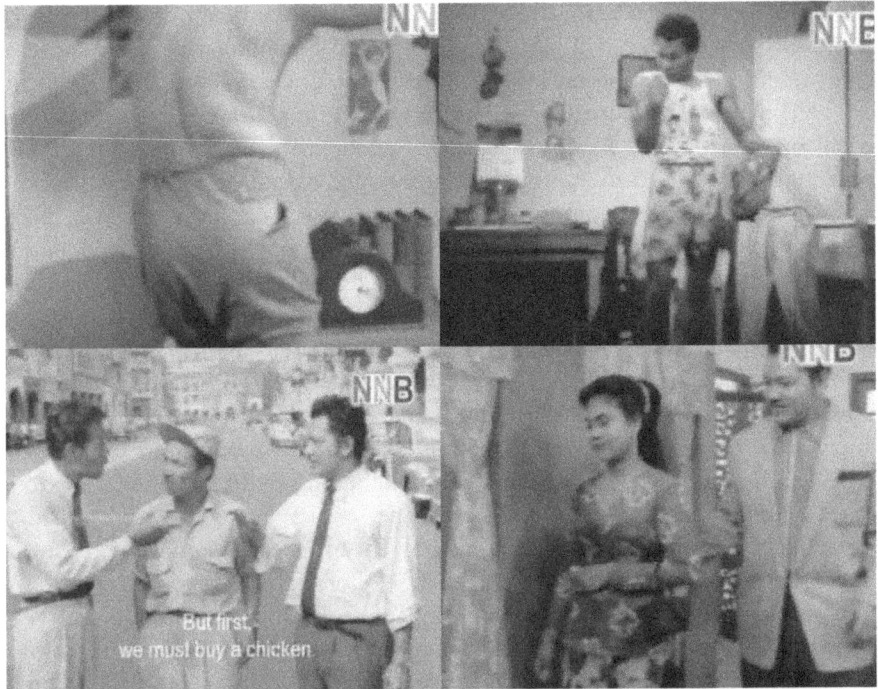

Figure 3.6 Tattered clothing in the kampong, versus formal wear in the city, in *Bujang Lapok*

city, he finally marries his kampong landlady, Cik Normah, who is not concerned about their social and class differences. The kampong community also rallies to help Sudin in his quest to marry Zaiton, the daughter of a wealthy widow next door. Their romance is threatened when her mother insists on a high dowry which Sudin cannot afford. So, together with Zaiton and several villagers, the three friends concoct a plan for Zaiton to steal her mother's ring to pawn and raise money. In fact, nearly the whole village accompanies them to the pawnshop in the city, where they discover that the ring is fake. In the end, Cik Normah appeals to Zaiton's mother on the couple's behalf and the lovers are finally allowed to marry. The primary location in the film is the kampong, which is a common setting in the films of this period. As White observes, the kampongs tend to be depicted through highly stylised sets with obvious painted backgrounds, in comparison to the more realistic-looking outdoor location shots of the city.[41] *Bujang Lapok*'s treatment and deployment of the city and kampong creates a clear contrast between these two spaces. While the kampong is depicted as 'an idyllic space, marked by coconut trees, free roaming chickens and communal living,' the city is 'a noisy space, characterised by traffic sounds, blaring horns and concrete (low-rise) buildings'.[42] This 'is a cold, formal place associated with crime and driven by monetary concerns whereas the kampong is a simpler place where community resides, and the characters can be themselves in their tattered underwear'.[43]

The difference between the city and the kampong is a recurring theme in Ramlee's films,[44] and *Bujang Lapok* may be read as a warning about the potential loss of tradition and values in the face of encroaching urbanisation in Singapore. The contemporaneity of issues raised, emphasis on Singapore locations, performance of a more cosmopolitan Malay culture as well as the hybrid influences apparent in these films, makes it easy to regard the films of the golden age as Singapore films. These are clearly products of their time. However, such narratives as well as those elements that made these films seem so modern and current during the golden age, like setting, costume and music, now seem dated and distant. Even more so are period films, such as *Hang Jebat* and *Raden Mas*, as well as horror films like *Sumpah Orang Minyak*, which were based almost exclusively in rural and kampong settings. These are spaces that no longer exist in Singapore's landscape.

The fact that old films look dated is not, by any means, surprising. What is interesting, however, is that despite early explorations in colour technology, most of these films are in black and white. This makes them seem older than contemporary offerings by other cinemas such as Hollywood, where colour films were already the norm by the 1950s and '60s. Their ageing is accelerated and exacerbated by Singapore's march towards rapid urbanisation and industrialisation that began in the 1960s. The state's urban redevelopment programmes escalated and massively increased in the 1970s and '80s as kampongs were progressively cleared to make way for housing and commercial projects. According to the Urban Redevelopment Authority of Singapore's website, 'between 1976 and 1989, a total of 184 hectares of land were cleared ... [And], Singapore's Central Area was transformed from an area of slums and squatters into a modern financial and business hub.'[45] As such, the Singapore depicted in these films looks nothing like the Singapore of today, except that some of the colonial buildings around the city centre have been preserved. For example, the location of the street scene outside Sudin's office in *Bujang Lapok* has been completely transformed by skyscrapers. The kampong setting in the film which Toh Hun Ping posits was likely shot on location at Kampong Kling, is now the site of Jurong Shipyard (see Figure 3.7).[46]

Not only do the films look like old films, they are also experienced as such. The musical form that was so much a stylistic convention of golden age cinema is no longer practised today. None of the films produced after this period uses this musical style. Indeed, Singapore rarely even makes musical films anymore. The few exceptions are Royston Tan's *881* (2007) and *12 Lotus* (2008), as well as a few of his short films, where the use of the musical form is not so much adherence to a conventional practice as it is consistent with his personal style.

Figure 3.7   Then and now: Robinson Road and Kampong Kling

Changes in the role and use of Malay language in Singapore also contribute to the distancing of these films from the present. Malay, or more specifically Bazaar Malay, was a much more common language among the multiethnic communities in Singapore than it is today. Citing Eddie Kuo's 1979 study on 'Languages in the Singapore social context,' Aye Khin Khin notes that the percentage of the total population that could speak Malay rose from 48 per cent in 1952 to 57.1 per cent in 1972.[47] This far exceeds the number of Malays in Singapore in these twenty years, which was less than 15 per cent of the total population, and reflects the use of Malay as a common language. Aye attributes the significance of the Malay language at this time to several state policies and plans that advocated the use of Malay. For example, Malay was taught as the national language in all schools. All government civil servants had to pass at least the Standard or Primary Two Malay Language Examination for promotion and confirmation, and proficiency in Malay was required for citizenship. Public notices also prioritised Malay over all other languages, and a bonus scheme was introduced in 1965 for teachers who studied the national language.[48] As such, even though Malay films were not usually subtitled, language was clearly not a major barrier in the appeal and popularity of these films as other ethnic groups enjoyed them as well. However, today, proficiency in Malay has fallen below English and Mandarin as a result of changes in Singapore's language policy and the emphasis on bilingual education. English has replaced Malay 'in almost all domains, both formal and informal, and functions as a lingua franca among younger Singaporeans coming from different ethnic backgrounds'.[49] Consequently, while the use of Malay made these films accessible and familiar to an audience in the golden age, the same language is now a barrier to understanding, enjoying and identifying with these films, particularly those that remain un-subtitled. What were formerly films made in a recognisable and familiar language spoken by many have now become foreign-language films to a contemporary local audience.

By the 1970s, Singapore stopped making films inspired by Malay myths, legends or historical tales like the *Sejarah Melayu* or the *Hikayat Hang Tuah*. There were no more period films and the once-popular *pontianak* or *orang minyak* have also disappeared. This is partly because the audience was changing and demanding different kinds of films. The new post-studio films that followed the golden age were also greatly influenced by more contemporary narratives, films and television programmes. The modern and much more Westernised narrative and style of these films from the 1970s, which will be explored in the next chapter, are distinctly different from those that were made in the golden age and constitute a clear departure or break from the past. The period of silence in the 1980s when film production came to a halt exacerbates the distance between the Singapore that is seen and experienced in golden age films and that which was rapidly progressing and developing. When film production was finally revived in the mid-1990s, the films that emerged bore no resemblance to those of the golden age, effectively cementing the distance and fissure between the golden age and the revival as two distinct cinemas distinguished by difference, with little or no connection between them.

Furthermore, the state-sanctioned 'Singapore Story' that begins with its founding in 1819 has become so entrenched and established that events that pre-date it are not only left out of the official narrative but have also become more and more marginalised or obscured over time in the public consciousness. As such, fables like *Bawang Puteh and Bawang Merah*, the legend of Hang Tuah, his magical *keris*, the Taming Sari (a weapon that makes its owner invincible), and his conflict with his best friend, Hang Jebat, or the tale of Raden Mas have become increasingly unfamiliar to the vast majority of Singapore audiences, except perhaps the Malay community where such narratives may still circulate. Indeed, watching films of these stories today gives rise to the feeling that to properly understand them and their resonances requires some knowledge of history, myth, nuances of language and gesture, and their significance.

The lack of familiarity experienced when watching these films, especially among younger local audiences, reflects the historical distance and identifiable difference between the independent, contemporary Singapore of the present and the pre-independent one of the past. This is exacerbated by the lack of availability and access to golden age films. Some prints, like the early *pontianak* films, are now lost, and the substantial body of work that remains is not properly distributed or circulated. Cathay and Shaw released a handful of video CDs in the 1990s but copies of these are increasingly difficult to find and many have no subtitles. They do not exist in more updated forms such as DVDs, so the only ways to view these films are via YouTube, film festival retrospectives or other special programmes. Some of the more popular films are sometimes screened on television during Malay festivals such as Hari Raya but these are few and far between, and usually the same ones get repeated, while others remain obscured. In short, these films are barely visible in Singapore today.

The lack of visibility, added to the contemporary Singapore audience's lack of familiarity with the narrative, thematic concerns, language, style, and even the images of Singapore, have transformed these films from local productions to essentially foreign films, recalling L. P. Hartley's statement that 'the past is a foreign country, they do things differently there.'[50] As such, these films now have a particular historical value as heritage because 'they show us something of the past.'[51] As Uhde and Uhde posit, 'given the inertia of human memory and sentiments, the old times lived on in the movies of the golden age.'[52] Their comment reflects Susan Sontag's view of cinema:

> this youngest of the arts is also the one most heavily burdened with memory. Cinema is a time machine. Movies preserve the past . . . [They] resurrect the beautiful dead; present intact vanished or ruined environments; employ, without irony, styles and fashions that seem funny today; solemnly ponder irrelevant or naïve problems.[53]

However, there is an inherent danger in perceiving films in this way. While period films like *Hang Jebat* may be considered historical films at the time they were made, 'the same cannot be said of the more modern films from that era.' These are not historical films in the sense that 'they were not made to record or document history, nor were they made as period films to enact, capture or recapture that past.'[54] Furthermore, regardless of whether they are period or modern films, they are all fictional narratives, and imbuing them with the value of heritage risks mistaking fiction for truth. As such, 'although these films allow us to travel back in time, they should also not be taken as factual documents or accurate accounts of past reality.' Films 'are biased, fraught and incomplete'.[55] They are artefacts that distort reality, a point that Pierre Sorlin notes Hugo Musterberg had already made as early as the 1910s.[56] However, referencing Siegfried Kracauer, Sorlin also acknowledges that

> in spite of these distortions, it is still possible to deduce from the pictures evidence about the environment, the life-styles ... of past periods. This record has the advantage of being permanent, it could be endlessly rescreened and, ... it could be a means of resisting the passage of time.[57]

As such, while Sontag's 'analogy of cinema as time machine is a tempting one, it is not entirely accurate. Entering a time machine suggests that we can travel back in time through these narratives, but this is not exactly the experience of watching these films because we are ultimately not present in that past time.'[58] This is because, as Thomas Elsaesser and Malte Hagener theorise, 'films ... presuppose a cinematic space that is both physical and discursive, one where film and spectator, cinema and body encounter one another.'[59] So, when watching a film, 'spectators ... inhabit two worlds (the cinematic universe, the diegesis, and their own physical environment and ambient space), suspending one in favour of the other, or shuttling between them.'[60] Therefore, 'it is the lived body encountering the window/frame [of a film] as "container" in which dimensions of time and space are held, that allows one to distinguish a "here" and an "I" from a "there" and a "you".'[61] This recalls what Nataša Ďurovičová considers the film medium's propensity for creating 'perceptual mismatches', that 'double vision' mentioned in the first chapter:[62]

> the complementary attraction of the moving image was that it also rendered one's own place strange, foreign even ... What in literary application of modernism was known as irony, that is, double vision, found its equivalent in cinema's capacity to get a spectator to see his or her self as an Other even while seeing the other as a variant of one's self.[63]

When watching the films from the golden age now, this 'double vision' lies in the spectator's understanding that the Singapore captured in these films is a variant of and different from the Singapore in the present. This 'specter of comparison'[64] in the process of watching likewise recalls the 'consciousness of doubling' that Bauman describes, emphasised by 'the distance between the screen and the viewer that makes conscious the act of watching, of something being performed, much like a theatrical performance would'.[65] Therefore, watching these films from the golden age play before us now, 'we are aware of the time difference,'[66] and the differences between two Singapores: one of the spectator's present and the other captured in the 'container' of the film frame. To extrapolate from what Elsaesser says of history, through these films and in each viewing, the past 'now appears to exist in suspended animation, neither exactly "behind" us, nor part of our present, but shadowing us rather like a parallel world which is un-real, hyper-real and virtual, all at the same time'.[67] Although we recognise what we see as Singapore, we also simultaneously acknowledge that this Singapore is no longer present. As such, the Singapore of golden age films is not only performed through distinctly different conventions, narrative concerns and languages. It is, in effect, (an)other Singapore. It looks like a foreign country, and even Singaporean viewers 'visit it, and the past, like tourists, seeing (an)other Singapore in performance at each viewing'.[68]

NOTES

1. Heide, 161–204.
2. Millet, 38.
3. Timothy White, 'Historical Poetics'.
4. Heide, 197.
5. Millet, 38–9.
6. Ibid., 36–7; Heide, 11.
7. Millet, 37.
8. Prior to Parsi Theatre, more indigenous Malay performance forms such as *wayang kulit* were sponsored and subsidised by patrons, and audiences watched them for free. Mohd Effindi Samsuddin and Rahmah Bujang, 'Bangsawan', 123.
9. Ibid., 125.
10. Heide, 82–4.
11. Ibid., 76.
12. Samsuddin and Bujang, 122.
13. Ibid., 131.
14. These characters are derived from a list provided in ibid.
15. Ibid., 128.
16. Ibid., 130.
17. Heide, 164.
18. Ibid., 163.
19. Ibid.
20. Muhammad, 27.
21. Heide.
22. White.
23. Samsuddin and Bujang, 130.
24. Ibid., 126.
25. White.
26. Ibid.
27. Ibid.
28. Ibid.
29. Timothy White, 'Exactly the Same'.
30. See Umberto Ansaldo, *Contact Languages: Ecology and Evolution in Asia*; Daw Khin Khin Aye, 'Bazaar Malay'; Bao Zhiming and Khin Khin Aye, 'Bazaar Malay Topics'.
31. Aye, 14.
32. Samsuddin and Bujang, 128.
33. Heide, 138.
34. Literally translated, this means 'Is this Singapore?'
35. Hack, 'Malayan Trajectory', 255.
36. Barnard, 70.
37. Margolin, 23.
38. Lim, 'Singapore Cinema'.
39. Ibid., 31.

40. Timothy White, 'P. Ramlee's Cinema', 3.
41. Ibid., 4.
42. Lim, 'Singapore Cinema', 32.
43. Ibid.
44. White, 'Exactly the Same', 6–7.
45. Urban Redevelopment Authority of Singapore, 'Our History'.
46. Hun Ping Toh, 'Bujang Lapok'.
47. Eddie Chen-Yu Kuo, 'Languages', cited in Aye, 13.
48. Aye, 13.
49. Ibid., 16.
50. L. P. Hartley, *The Go-Between*, quoted in David Lowenthal, *The Past*, xvi.
51. Lim, 'Singapore Cinema', 33.
52. Uhde and Uhde, 48.
53. Susan Sontag, 'Film and Theatre', 370.
54. Lim, 'Singapore Cinema', 33.
55. Ibid.
56. Pierre Sorlin, 'Endgame'.
57. Ibid.
58. Lim, 'Singapore Cinema', 33.
59. Thomas Elsaesser and Malte Hagener, *Film Theory*, 4.
60. Ibid.
61. Ibid., 179.
62. Ďurovičová, 'Vector', 90.
63. Ibid., 91.
64. Ibid.
65. Lim, 'Singapore Cinema', 34.
66. Ibid.
67. Thomas Elsaesser, 'One Train'.
68. Lim, 'Singapore Cinema', 34–5.

4. NATION-BUILDING, A NUN AND A BIONIC BOY

Going Global: Industrialisation and Urbanisation

On 9 August 1965, Singapore's Prime Minister Lee Kuan Yew was deeply emotional when he appeared on a televised press conference to talk about the country's separation from Malaysia. He said:

> Every time we look back on this moment when we signed this agreement which severed Singapore from Malaysia, it will be a moment of anguish. For me it is a moment of anguish because all my life ... you see, the whole of my adult life ... I have believed in merger and the unity of these two territories. You know, it's a people connected by geography, economics and ties of kinship ... Would you mind if we stop for a while? [Recording was stopped for the Prime Minister to regain his composure][1]

Four months later, he seemed much more composed and confident in his speech to residents of the Pasir Panjang constituency:

> You know, there is a great deal of strength and stamina in this place. It's the human beings – the skill, the versatility, the expertise, the drive, the relentless pursuit of success and performances – that have made this island what it is. But now, with independence comes independence of action, opportunities to create the conditions for the eventual success of what we want: survival in Southeast Asia, a very turbulent part of the

world, as a separate and distinct people, not absorbed or swallowed up by more backward hordes and bigger hordes.[2]

Indeed, Singapore's survival would be of utmost concern in the years following its independence as the government went about the business of nation-building that, according to Selvaraj Velayutham, is 'a political process of constructing a "nation" and a sense of belonging via the state'.[3] Prior to 1965, the idea of Singapore as an independent political entity was, as Chua Beng Huat argues, an 'absence'.[4] Yet, because Singapore achieved internal self-rule in 1959, the state, as it were, was already formed before independence; it had its own government led by the ruling PAP, national flag and anthem, and head of state in the form of the Yang di Pertuan Negara as well as a prime minister. As such, with independence, what the Singapore government inherited was a state carved out of colonialism, and found itself 'in possession of a state without a nation'.[5] Hence, as Velayutham argues, 'the formation of the Singapore nation is not a natural outcome whereby the citizens of Singapore before or even after independence began to consider themselves as belonging to a shared cultural unit.'[6] Recounting the events leading to and surrounding Singapore's independence in his memoirs, Lee Kuan Yew wrote:

> Some countries are born independent. Some achieve independence. Singapore had independence thrust upon it . . . We had said that an independent Singapore was simply not viable. Now it was our unenviable task to make it work. How were we to create a nation out of a polyglot collection of migrants from China, India, Indonesia and several other parts of Asia?[7]

How they made it work was through a concerted managerial effort on the part of the government. It adopted an 'ideology of survival' founded on the same values as the PAP's ideal of a 'Malayan Malaysia' prior to separation: meritocracy and what Sharon Siddique calls the '4 Ms' – multiracialism, multiculturalism, multilingualism and multireligiosity.[8] Achieving this required a new set of pragmatic values and, in Lee's words, 'a rugged, resolute, highly trained, highly disciplined community. You create such a community, and you will survive and prosper here for thousands of years.'[9] This ideology had three fundamental aspects. The first is the belief that survival requires the 'willingness and ability to adopt a new set of attitudes, a new set of values, a new set of perspectives; in short, on the creation of a new man'.[10] The second is 'producing a tightly organised society', and the third is nation-building.[11]

From the outset, the state faced major challenges. Singapore has a diverse and fragmentary multiethnic population, with a Chinese majority, and it is surrounded by Muslim countries. As observed by W. E. Wilmott:

the Malays in Singapore identified with Malay society and culture on the peninsula and in the archipelago. Because prior to the Japanese Occupation most of the Chinese and Indians considered themselves merely sojourners, no Singaporean identity or sentiment emerged among them. A few Chinese, mainly professionals [...] identified wholeheartedly with the British. Others remained primarily Chinese in their sentiments, and some of these were moved by Chinese nationalism to participate, if vicariously, in the political struggles in China. Similarly, many Indians in Singapore were staunch supporters of the Indian National Congress in its opposition to the British Raj. [...] Most of the English-educated Chinese, on the other hand, did not feel any loyalty to China, whether cultural or political.[12]

Singapore was also still largely an entrepôt, which meant that it was economically still dependent on Malaysia and Indonesia, whose *Konfrontasi* protesting the formation of Malaysia also included Singapore. The urgency to build a new nation, and quickly, led to a series of policies for defence, the economy, housing and education that were designed to achieve specific goals as well as build national cohesion. The years following independence through to the 1980s were formative years that 'marked a shift from colonial rule and domination to a position which was not so much of independence but rather of being "in-dependence" on forces beyond the island state'.[13] These forces were global as opposed to regional, as Singapore sought to attach itself to a new hinterland of larger powers such as the United States.

In terms of defence, 'at the time of independence, Singapore's armed forces consisted of two infantry battalions ... together with one partially mobilised volunteer infantry battalion, a volunteer artillery regiment, an armoured car squadron, some engineers and signals, in all comprising 50 officers and 1000 men.'[14] This was not great news for a small island nation that had just been acrimoniously cast out by Malaysia and was surrounded by regional turmoil. Although Indonesia's Sukarno was losing power by the end of 1965, the *Konfrontasi* he had waged would not officially end until 1966. Added to this was the escalating war in Indo-China and insurgencies in Burma, Thailand and the Philippines. Britain also announced the evacuation of all its forces from Singapore by 1971. It was therefore urgent for Singapore to quickly build a defence force. The government looked to Israel for help, since it was a similar 'small country surrounded by hostile neighbours, which had developed methods to overcome immensely superior enemies in war, and in which compulsory military service in a citizens' force, followed by long-term reserve obligations, had also helped to meld disparate groups into a common national identity'.[15] In November 1965, the Ministry of the Interior and Defence (MINDEF) made plans to develop a small regular army with a larger force of national servicemen. Two years later, legislation was passed to make National Service mandatory; all male citizens of eighteen years of age had to enlist and undergo military training for two years. Thereafter they would continue to serve in the reserve until they were forty, or fifty if they were officers. National service was to serve two purposes: to build a substantial and sustainable army, and function as 'an active agent of national cohesion'.[16] A mission from Israel arrived as early as the end of 1965, and Israeli advisors not only trained the first batch of national servicemen but also remained in Singapore for nearly a decade, 'exerting a strong influence'.[17]

The impending withdrawal of British troops also affected Singapore's economy, since the sizeable workforce employed by the base would soon be jobless. Cool bilateral relations between Singapore and neighbouring Malaysia and Indonesia, and the unravelling of British colonial rule, also meant that Singapore could no longer maintain its historical function as a port city between the region and the West. As Lee Kuan Yew reflected in his memoirs,

> my ... biggest headache was the economy – how to make a living for our people? Indonesia was 'confronting' us and trade was at a standstill. The Malaysians wanted to bypass Singapore and deal direct with all their trading partners, importers and exporters, and only through their own ports. How was an independent Singapore to survive when it was no longer the centre of the wider area that the British once governed as one unit? We needed to find some answers soon, for employment was alarming at 14 per cent and rising. Furthermore we had to make a living different from that under British rule ... We had to create a new kind of economy, try new methods and schemes never tried before anywhere else in the world, because there was no other country like Singapore.[18]

Singapore needed to find a new place in the world, and to help it do so the government sought the advice of Dutch economist Albert Winsemius, who became the state's chief economic advisor from 1965 to 1984. Working closely with Finance Ministers Lim Kin San (1965–7), Goh Keng Swee (1967–70) and Hon Sui Sen (1970–83), these men 'were the architects of what came to be hailed as Singapore's "economic miracle"'.[19] They engineered Singapore's reorientation, 'this time as a regional centre and nodal point in an increasingly interconnected global economy, with an increasingly global division of labour'.[20] So, instead of turning inwards and advocating prohibitive tariffs and quotas to protect its industries and keep out giant multinational corporations, or indigenising business ownership like other newly independent countries in the region, Singapore did the opposite. As Ooi Giok Ling notes, 'between 1965 and 1990, Singapore was the only country in the region which focused so single-mindedly on recreating itself into an international centre for foreign business investors and travellers.'[21]

The aim was rapid industrialisation focused on exports and propelled by Foreign Direct Investment (FDI). To achieve this, the government continued its strategy of rapid industrialisation that was already put in place when the PAP came into power in 1959. At the time, the newly elected government planned to provide

> private enterprise, both of local and overseas origin, all the encouragement and assistance they need, so that they can set up new factories which will create more jobs for our growing population. The Government will not impose restrictions upon foreign investments on the transfer of profits and capital, apart from normal exchange controls.[22]

Citing the same speech, Margolin observes that the PAP had, from its inception, 'sought foreign expertise across the board'.[23] This did not change with independence, but accelerated with new urgency and greater pragmatism. In fact, a number of tax incentives were already put in place to attract foreign investment as early as 1959. These included the Pioneer Industries (Relief from Income Tax) Ordinance, which gave qualifying new companies pioneer status and exemption from taxes for five years, and the Industrial Expansion (Relief from Income Tax) Ordinance, which gave existing firms tax incentives for investing in production output expansion. Companies also enjoyed the very low tax rate of 4 per cent on their profits for ten to fifteen years, instead of the usual 40 per cent. Beginning in 1967, the state focused on what Margolin calls 'the philosopher's stone of rapid economic development . . . in the shape of export oriented industrialisation'.[24] This coincided with the worldwide shift to international division of labour as multinational corporations looked to relocate their operations and assembly factories offshore.

In 1968, legislation was passed to stymie the 'excesses of irresponsible trade unions',[25] to create a disciplined, productive workforce, and to ensure that Singapore was cost-competitive compared to other Asian countries. A new Employment Act reduced the number of public holidays and leave entitlements, extended working hours and restricted overtime and bonuses, while also compensating workers through extending the requirement period for retrenchment benefits, sick leave and more employer contributions to their Central Provident Fund (CPF).[26] The power of the unions was also curtailed by amendments to the Industrial Relations Act that year which eliminated their ability to negotiate over employment redundancies and restructuring. Wages were controlled by recommendations made by the National Wages Council and enforced by the Industrial Arbitration Court, both set up in 1972. So effective were these regulations that Singapore enjoyed its first strike-free year in 1969 and continued to remain mostly so thereafter. Wages for the same level of productivity in the electronics sector were also lower than those in competing countries like South Korea, Taiwan and Hong Kong, and less than one-eleventh of those in the United States.[27]

In 1968, the Economic Development Board (EDB), an agency established in 1961 to plan, develop and supervise initiatives for economic development with private and foreign capital in particular, was also reconfigured to drive foreign investment and meet the needs of post-independence rapid industrialisation. This entailed transferring the responsibility for extending loans to manufacturing industries in exchange for equity share to the newly established Development Bank of Singapore. The bank's president and first chairman was also the chairman of the EDB. Singapore also became the headquarters of the Asian Dollar Market in 1968 and a gold market a year later, surpassing Hong Kong and Beirut.[28] The Jurong Town Corporation (JTC) was set up in 1968 to develop major industrial estates for housing foreign manufacturing companies and factories at a low cost. By 1970, the JTC had established 264 factories employing 32,000 production workers, with more than a hundred new facilities under construction.[29]

Singapore also capitalised on increasing activities in offshore oil exploration in the region and became the support and oil-refining centre for these operations. According to Turnbull, 'Winsemius himself was responsible for attracting the big oil companies, Shell and Esso, and persuading the Dutch giant Philips to set up manufacturing in Singapore.'[30] By the 1970s, Singapore housed as many as thirty oil-exploration companies, with more than a dozen secondary companies such as consultants, diving companies, and construction and specialist engineers. As early as 1970, petroleum already accounted for almost 40 per cent of the country's total manufactured exports, and Singapore was the third-largest oil-refining centre in the world by 1973.[31]

The naval dockyard occupied by the British was given to the state in 1968 in anticipation of the impending full troop withdrawal in 1971. This well-equipped facility became the basis for Singapore's expansion into shipbuilding and enabled it to capitalise on the island's locational advantage and the boom in oil exploration. Singapore launched its own register of ships in 1966, and a national fleet under Neptune Orient Lines two years later. It also permitted foreign ships to register tax-free, 'becoming the first Asian "flag of convenience"'.[32] Shipbuilding and repairing in Singapore almost doubled between 1966 and 1968, in tandem with the boom worldwide. By 1969, its port was the busiest in the Commonwealth, and the country became the major transshipment centre of Southeast Asia following the completion of its container complex in 1972. By 1975, a mere ten years after independence, Singapore's port was the third-busiest in the world after Rotterdam and New York.[33]

While the port enabled Singapore's connection to the world by sea, plans were also underway to do the same in the air. Singapore launched its own airline, Singapore Airlines (SIA), in 1972 and adopted an open-sky policy that enabled equal competition between its own and other international airlines. In return, SIA was able to obtain favourable landing rights in other cities such as London, Tokyo and New York, which increased its competitiveness as an international airline. Plans were also made to construct a new international airport in the less developed area of Changi, to ease congestion in the city and facilitate expansion in air traffic. Changi International Airport was officially opened in 1981. Three years later, a second runway and terminal were completed, significantly expanding the airport's ability to keep up with the growth in air traffic. Besides the key role in providing infrastructural support for the developing and international orientation of the economy, the airport and airline also facilitated increased business and tourist travel to Singapore, either as a final or stopover destination. Today, SIA is one of the top airlines in the world, and Changi Airport one of the busiest. Together, Singapore's port and airport, including its naval fleet and airline, reinforce the young republic's international orientation.

Singapore's dependence on British capital, which constituted 70 per cent of all foreign investments in 1965, dwindled and shifted to the United States, Western Europe, Japan, Hong Kong, Taiwan, Malaysia and Australia. By 1972, a quarter of the manufacturing companies were either joint ventures or foreign-owned. They employed more than 50 per cent of the nation's workforce and accounted for almost 70 per cent of the country's industrial output and 83 per cent of its direct exports. Investments from the United States alone comprised half of the new foreign capital that flowed into Singapore, such that by 1973, America had become Singapore's second most important trading partner after Malaysia. Singapore's economic strategy of rapid industrialisation in the 1960s was so successful that the number of factories more than tripled, while gross domestic product and industrial production expanded annually by 9 and 20 per cent respectively.[34]

In tandem with rapid industrialisation came the extensive urbanisation of the island. Indeed, urban planning and housing development in Singapore between 1965 and 1990 were inextricably linked to its economy's international orientation, not only in terms of building the kinds of infrastructure and support for businesses and industries such as the airport, port, telecommunications and transportation, but also to foster a peaceful population that made for a desirable and productive workforce. Following the withdrawal of British troops, the state inherited the substantial tracts of land that the military had occupied, about a tenth of the island, including prime areas. A Land Acquisition Act passed in 1966 allowed the state to purchase private land below market value. This, together with the state's extensive land-reclamation projects, meant that the government literally had a lot of space to play with, and a free hand to thoroughly restructure and redevelop the island. By the 1970s, the state had become the largest landowner in Singapore, and it conferred power to acquire land for infrastructure and estate development on its various statutory boards, such as the JTC, EDB, Housing and Development Board (HDB), Port of Singapore Authority (PSA), Urban Redevelopment Authority (URA) and Public Utilities Board (PUB).

In the 1960s and '70s, the strategy to urbanise Singapore focused on resettlement. As Ooi notes, this 'national resettlement programme was tantamount to sweeping out of the old colonial spatial order, and in its place, the establishment of a new ordering of land-use development that would be urban and international.'[35] The objective was urban renewal. The city centre would remain as the financial and administrative hub of Singapore, and redevelopment involved turning the space into a 'central business site befitting that of the aspiring world city with its international orientations'.[36] This meant relocating small local businesses and the population residing in the overcrowded city area to the outskirts and other parts of the island to make way for skyscrapers, hotels, shopping centres, offices and other commercial and recreational facilities aimed at attracting international businesses and tourists. Farms, slums, shanties and rural villages were systematically demolished to develop large-scale, high-rise, high-density public housing (or HDB) estates to resettle the population dispersed from these areas, the city centre and old ethnic neighbourhoods. These housing areas were planned to revolve around the other industrial estates that were being built throughout the island, in addition to the one in Jurong, so that residents could live near their workplace. They are self-contained townships, each with its own markets, schools, shopping and community centres, clinics, cinemas and other recreational facilities. Racial quotas, based on the demographics of the population, were put in place to ensure that these estates were multiracial and to prevent ghettoisation. According to Ooi, the building of the estates 'resembled closely an industrial process for mass housing production through which blocks of flats or apartment units were produced in the fastest and cheapest way'.[37]

A home ownership scheme was launched in 1964 to enable citizens to purchase public housing flats at heavily subsidised rates. In 1968, policies were changed to allow people to buy their flats with their CPF savings, which made home ownership easier. Home ownership is a key strategy in fostering a sense of home for Singapore's largely migrant population. By owning a home, they would now have 'a vested interest in national stability'[38] and a stake in the nation's progress. By 1980, 75 per cent of the population lived in HDB flats, a marked increase from 9 per cent in 1960. Today, more than 80 per cent of the population live in HDB flats. As a result of these urban redevelopment schemes, the built-up area of the island increased to 50 per cent between 1965 and 1990, a period that witnessed the most significant physical transformation of the landscape of Singapore.[39] This was a nation literally under construction, and in a big way.

In tandem with urban renewal was the major cleaning and greening of the island that grew out of Lee's quest 'for some dramatic way to distinguish ourselves from other Third World countries. I settled for a clean and green Singapore.'[40] According to him, 'if we had First World standards then businessmen and tourists would make us a base for their business and tours of the region.'[41] So 'to achieve First World standards in a Third World region, we set out to transform Singapore into a tropical garden city.'[42] The plan was to create a clean and green city in three years, beginning in 1967. This included the planting of instant trees along the roads, the building of more parks especially in local neighbourhoods for recreational purposes, and a more efficient system of rubbish disposal and cleaning of drains. New laws required every shop and home to have a dustbin, and stiffer fines were imposed on those who created rubbish and litter. A 'Keep Singapore Clean' campaign was launched in 1968 to 'create a public awareness of everyone's duty to keeping Singapore clean'.[43] In his speech, Lee Kuan Yew said that 'Singapore has become one home, one garden, for all of us ... We have built, we have progressed. But no other hallmark of success will be more distinctive than that of achieving our position as the cleanest and greenest city in South Asia. For only a people with high social and educational standards can maintain a clean and green city.'[44]

The cleaning of Singapore also extended to other aspects like illegal hawkers and 'pirate taxis'. According to Lee,

> we licensed the cooked food hawkers and moved them from the roads and pavements to properly constructed nearby hawker centres, with piped water, sewers and garbage disposal. By the early '80s we had settled all hawkers ... Pirate taxis were banished from roads only after we reorganised bus services and could provide them with alternative employment.[45]

The Singapore River and Kallang Basin, which were essentially sewers for the island, were also cleaned up. As Lee notes, 'since the founding of Singapore in 1819, lighters and barges had plied the river. Their workers lived, cooked and did their ablutions on these vessels.'[46] As a result, the river and basin were overcrowded, filthy and putrid. The vessels and boatyards were relocated to designated outlying areas such as Pasir Panjang, Tuas and the Jurong River. About 3,000 backyard and cottage industries and 5,000 street vendors plying food and other produce along these waterways were resettled in the newly built and better-equipped industrial estates, markets and food centres.[47] Additionally, 8,000 pig farms (with 900,000 pigs) were phased out because of the water pollution caused by their waste. Food fish farms were also closed and relocated offshore, leaving only a few agrotechnology parks and ponds for recreational fishing. Lee opines that 'clean rivers made possible a different quality of life. The value and use of land rose significantly, especially in the city and at sites abutting rivers and canals.'[48] The Kallang Basin has been transformed into a popular location for sun-seekers and watersports, while the low-rise shops and warehouses by the river, such as Boat Quay, have been restored and occupied by high-priced restaurants and alfresco cafes. The massive cleaning operation also improved overall sanitation and hygiene standards that had been deplorable due to slums and overcrowding. In addition, a clean and green Singapore enhanced the impression that the island was well-organised and conducive for business and pleasure.

In keeping with its international reorientation, the state declared that English would be the main language of instruction in 1966. English was perceived as not only an international language and the language of trade, science and modernity but also a neutral one to integrate the various multilingual groups in Singapore. In addition, students must also learn a second language – Mandarin, Malay or Tamil, depending on their race – to preserve their cultural identity. Together with English, these four languages are recognised as the official languages of the state. This bilingual education policy is based on the idea that language is a gateway to and disseminator of culture. While English was pragmatically adopted for Singapore to communicate with the rest of the world, it also led to the fear that Singaporeans would imbibe too much Westernisation through the language. As such, the second language, or 'Mother Tongue', would serve as a cultural ballast to ensure the continuation of Asian values and cultures, and also balance the influence of Westernisation. This creates what Chan Heng Chee and Hans-Dieter Evers refer to as 'a double identity'. According to them:

> each segment of Singapore's population was too distinct and exhibits too strong a cultural tradition to warrant any hope that these traditions would merge into a single cultural identity. The pragmatic solution was to create a double identity: a somewhat subdued cultural identity based on the respective local language and a national identity based on English.[49]

Citing Lee Kuan Yew's speech to school principals in 1966, Turnbull notes that, after independence, Singapore's education system 'was adapted to mould a nation'.[50] Schools were more closely aligned to a national system, emphasising multilingualism and meritocracy. To build an educated and skilled workforce to meet the needs of the growing economy and a developing nation, primary education was compulsory, secondary education focused on science, technical and vocational training, while tertiary institutions concentrated on engineering and business. Furthermore, schools also practised the daily ritual of national flag-raising and -lowering ceremonies that involved singing the national anthem, and reciting the national pledge created in 1966 by the then Foreign Minister, S. Rajaratnam: We, the citizens of Singapore, pledge ourselves as one united people, regardless of race, language or religion, to build a democratic society based on justice and equality, so as to achieve happiness, prosperity and progress for our nation. This daily ritual, according to Velayutham, is 'equally important in educating and espousing the idea of a national community in the minds of young Singaporeans'.[51]

By the 1970s, Singapore enjoyed political, social and economic stability with a high standard of living, double-digit growth rates and nearly full employment, with labour shortages in some sectors of the economy. The state's single-minded efforts at remaking Singapore in its formative years were so successful that by the 1980s, Singapore was one of four Asian Tiger economies characterised by rapid industrialisation and exceptional growth rates. As Turnbull notes,

> the immediate post-independence years were perhaps the most dynamic in Singapore's history, inspiring admiration in many Western countries, who saw the tiny republic living on its wits, seeking a way out of its artificial and precarious position and overcoming apparently insuperable obstacles, while more developed societies floundered in indecisiveness . . . the island and its leadership quickly acquired a reputation out of proportion to the country's size or importance.[52]

What Singapore managed to achieve in less than two decades has been deemed a 'miracle'. The country's transformation has become a model for others and the crux of the Singapore Story, which will be discussed in later chapters. Singapore's international orientation, and rapid industrialisation and urbanisation were not only evident in the physical transformation of the city but also in the mindset of its people as they enjoyed an increasingly urban and Westernised lifestyle. This was exacerbated by the arrival of television, which had a significant impact on Singapore cinema.

A Cinema in Transition

The first monochrome television broadcast in Singapore was in February 1963, followed by regular broadcasts three months later. Programmes were largely imported, particularly from America. Although Singaporeans had always been exposed to Western culture and films, Timothy White argues that 'with television, the ubiquity of Western culture really began; no longer a relatively small part of the cultural mix experienced by Singaporeans, Western images of reality soon became something approaching the norm.'[53] As television became more popular, more and more Singaporeans identified with what they saw in these programmes. According to White,

> This made a crucial difference to the way Singaporeans saw reality in movies. They began to see it more with Western eyes, through which reality lies in the *mise-en-scene* – the objects, the characters, etc. – and not so much in the ideas, emotions, and relationships among people. No longer was it good enough to present mythical stories that expressed feelings, fears, and traditional beliefs through films that suggested the essences, rather than the realistically depicted images, of people, places and things.[54]

Consequently, by as early as the mid-1960s, the black-and-white, Indian-influenced films of the golden age already looked like films from a different era.[55] They were quickly becoming more and more out of sync with rapidly changing Singapore. This resulted in what White describes as 'an unfortunate exodus . . . as Singaporeans began to reject their own movies in favor [sic] of those of Hollywood'.[56]

This exodus, together with other factors such as the rising cost of production and the shrinking market for Malay films, contributed to the decline and eventual closure of Malay Film Productions and Cathay-Keris. While this signalled the end of the golden age, it did not mean that Singapore stopped making movies. The market was now open to more independent film production, which created a post-studio era marked not only by a different mode of filmmaking but also by different kinds of films.

Uhde and Uhde identify this post-studio era as 'the beginning of Singapore national cinema' and one that 'coincides with the demise of the city's predominantly Malay-language film industry'.[57] This era of filmmaking is by no means prolific. A *Straits Times* article identifies only six Singapore films: that is, they were 'made in Singapore by Singaporean producers, using local finance and talent, and aimed at the local market'.[58] These films are very different from those of the golden age and reflect the international outlook and influences of the time. Instead of Malay-language films set in a predominantly Malay Singapore and culture, the films of the 1970s are in English and Chinese, and depict a Singapore that is either Chinese or more international. They are also no longer influenced by *bangsawan* and Indian cinema, and instead of basing their narratives on myths, legends or life in the kampong, these films were largely action features that emulated those of Hollywood and Hong Kong.

This distinct departure from the golden age is apparent in the first of the independent films of the era, *Ring of Fury* (1973), made by Tony Yeow and James Sebastian, who were not known in the world of film production. Instead of black and white, the film was shot in Cinemascope and Eastmancolour. *Ring of Fury* is a martial arts film that pays homage to Bruce Lee, and capitalises on the kung fu craze sweeping Asia and Hollywood at the time.[59] According to Uhde and Uhde, the film 'claims to be the first kung fu action film produced in Singapore and the first film produced in the Malaysia-Singapore region with international distribution'.[60] The narrative centres on Fei Pah, a hawker who is threatened by gangsters when he refuses to pay them for protection. After the gangsters set fire to his house and accidentally kill his mother, he goes to learn kung fu for two years before returning to take revenge. According to Millet, 'the plot certainly sounds like a Bruce Lee or Charles Bronson movie.'[61] The film also featured real martial arts exponents instead of professional actors, which created improvised but very realistic action sequences, even though the cinematography had 'an unavoidable touch of amateurism'.[62]

Millet argues that this film had the hallmarks of a cult film and could have been a landmark film that signalled a new era of filmmaking in Singapore, if it had not been banned in its own country.[63] Film censorship had been strict and highly regulated in Singapore since colonial times. When Singapore attained partial self-government in 1959, film censorship fell under the purview of the Ministry of Home Affairs, which announced its intention to ban all films 'whose primary intent is the glorification or justification of colonialism'.[64] That same year, the government also began a crusade against 'yellow culture' which it believed caused 'the moral degeneration of our young generation'.[65] According to Lee Kuan Yew,

> 'yellow culture' is a literal translation of the Mandarin phrase for the decadent and degenerate behaviour that had brought China to its knees in the 19th century: gambling, opium-smoking, pornography, multiple wives and concubines, the selling of daughters into prostitution, corruption and nepotism.[66]

Then Minister of Home Affairs, Ong Pang Boon, 'ordered a clean-up of Chinese secret society gangsters, and outlawed pornography, striptease shows, pin-table saloons, even decadent songs. It did not harm apart from adding somewhat to unemployment and making Singapore less attractive to tourists.'[67] He also clarified that:

> in the field of publishing, the Government objects strongly to the mixture of sex and sadism, to the presentation of a world peopled by semi-nude and promiscuous women, by the less reputable film stars, by call girls, pimps, gangsters and confidence tricksters. Films and music that, in their own way, encourage 'false modesty and debased tastes' will also come under the Government's severe regard.[68]

Between June 1959 and June 1960, a total of sixty films were banned compared to ten in the same period in the previous year.[69]

Censorship was moved to the Ministry of Culture in 1963 and the minister, Mr S. Rajaratnam, launched a sweeping tightening of censorship to 'clean-up'[70] cinemas. Free film screenings at youth clubs and community centres were banned, as were open-air cinemas, which were perceived as potential venues for gang gatherings. The Twist was outlawed, and films that showed it were banned too. Jukeboxes were also forbidden, and warnings against 'abnormal and corrosive activities such as hippies and flower people seeping through Singapore's society'[71] were made. Tied to the aversion towards hippies, the Ministry of Home Affairs launched an anti-long hair campaign known as Operation Snip Snip[72] in the 1970s. A *Straits Times* article cites a newsletter from the Singapore Anti-Narcotics Association, which points out that long hair on men 'is an attempt at confusion between the sexes ... As exemplified by the hippies, long hair is a symbol of rebellion against the established norms of law and order.'[73] Men with long hair were denied entry into Singapore, and companies were discouraged from employing such people. Those already employed were either sacked, fined or had their pay cut. This applied to the private and public sectors, musicians, entertainers and films. In 1974 alone, 8,172 male civil servants were issued warnings and one was fired.[74] The campaign against 'yellow culture' and long hair only eased in the 1980s,[75] while jukeboxes continued to be banned until 1990.[76]

Among the films that were banned during the strict campaign against 'yellow culture' was Bruce Lee's *Enter the Dragon* in 1973, for being 'too violent and had characters with long hair'.[77] *Ring of Fury* was banned because of its portrayal of gangsterism and valorising of vigilantism, 'very much in the manner of Bruce Lee and even more of Charles Bronson'.[78] According to Yeow, 'the main reason was the element of gangsterism. The government was very uncomfortable that there were gangsters and they were almost conducting their business in the open. That had prompted us to make the film. It was actually an anti-gangster film.'[79] As such, it is ironic that the very qualities that made this film new, distinctive and contemporary as compared to the golden age, also caused it to be banned and remain unseen in Singapore for almost three decades. To date, the film has yet to be commercially released in Singapore.

Two years later, Tony Yeow produced a comedy, *The Two Nuts* (1975), which *The Straits Times* recognised as 'the first local attempt'[80] at a feature-length Cantonese film. Its review of the film, however, was less than great; the film was 'definitely and expectedly not up to par' compared to those from the more established Hong Kong or Taiwan cinemas, even though it 'would be worth seeing if only because it is a truly local film, shot entirely in Singapore.'[81] The review's perspective captures the conundrum of the films of this period. While they strove to copy popular films and genres from more established cinemas like Hollywood and Hong Kong, doing so also led to inevitable comparisons between them. As the films of this period were mostly independently produced on shoestring budgets, and many of the talents from the golden age were no longer working in the industry in Singapore, they lacked the polish and production values of their Hollywood and Hong Kong counterparts.

This is especially evident in the films made by BAS Films International Pte Ltd, a joint venture between the Filipino Bobby Suarez, Malaysian Mohamed Ashraf and Singaporean Sunny Lim. These are regional co-productions that are distinctly internationally oriented and which have come to define Singapore's post-studio cinema. The aim was 'to revive the film industry in Singapore and Malaysia',[82] and even to enter the Hong Kong and American markets.[83] The films were 'not anchored in Singapore's cultural or social background'.[84] Instead they are largely low-budget, English-language action fare modelled on Hollywood films and television shows. According to Millet, they are 'a mishmash of influences ranging from the James Bond and OSS series, and all the B-grade spy movies that followed, to the kung fu wave that came after Bruce Lee. They also drew from the blaxpoitation genre . . . as well as nunsploitation movies' which were popular at the time.[85]

The first of these films is *Bionic Boy* (Leody M. Diaz, 1977). It features Johnson Yap, an eight-year-old karate champion billed as 'Asia's youngest master of martial arts'[86] in the starring role of Sunny Lee. His father is an Interpol agent in Singapore. When the family are in Manila on vacation, father and son thwart an assassination attempt on a Filipino businessman, which is part of a larger scheme by a villainous group sent by a 'family' in New York to destroy the economies of Hong Kong, Taiwan, Malaysia, Singapore, Thailand, Indonesia and the Philippines by threatening the powerful families in these countries. Sunny and his family become the gang's new targets and the gang kills both his parents in a staged accident. Sunny escapes in a critical condition and is saved by a series of operations that give him bionic ears, eyes and limbs. Thereafter, with his newfound bionic powers, Sunny thwarts subsequent attempts to kidnap him, escapes the care of Interpol agents and infiltrates the villains' island base to seek justice for his murdered parents. *Bionic Boy* is obviously influenced by the *Six Million Dollar Man* series, and the film similarly mimics scenes that are iconic to the American programme, such as the surgical operations on Sunny, which recall the same done on Steve Austin, and the slow-motion sequences of Sunny running and jumping.

The film largely takes place in Manila and other parts of the Philippines, and features exotic-looking settings that recall James Bond films. The island location of the villains' lair is also reminiscent of the setting of the tournament in Bruce Lee's *Enter the Dragon*. The influence of the martial arts genre in general is further evidenced in the film's narrative of revenge and its fight sequences, particularly in the 'competition' between Sunny and the multiple martial arts

Figure 4.1   Bell Church in *Bionic Boy*

exponents as he takes them on one by one. Here, the sequence features an array of fight styles that are identified by the costumes rather than the movements of the actors. These include a Japanese fighter wielding a nunchaku, a cowboy wearing a Stetson hat (and wielding a knife, interestingly), and a wrestler in his loincloth. They constitute a mix of generic references to martial arts and action films that are generally international, and more cosmetic than real. Similarly, it is rather difficult to determine the cultural or national specificity of particular settings, or they are confusingly referenced. For example, Sunny goes to a place called Bell Church to offer prayers to his murdered parents. However, the building architecturally resembles a Chinese temple, a view that is reinforced by the interior, with its altars, incense, prayer rituals and chanting sounds (see Figure 4.1). The scenes in this temple-church emphasise the Oriental exoticism of the rituals, trappings and architecture, while the space itself is referenced as a church to generally denote it as a religious site.

The only time the film is 'set' in Singapore is when we first meet Sunny Lee and his family at a martial arts competition. Even so, the space of the sports arena is only inferred as located in Singapore, but is generic enough that it could be anywhere in the world. The villains are racially mixed, with Caucasians, African Americans and others of indeterminate race. However, because the film is also heavily dubbed, all the characters speak in American-accented English, muting their racial, ethnic or cultural identities. So, although Sunny and his parents are Singaporeans, they speak like Americans, as do all the characters in the film, regardless of nationality. The law enforcement organisations that assist Sunny and come to his aid in the end – Interpol and the FBI – are not local but international. These elements obscure *Bionic Boy*'s Asian origins and reinforce its international orientation. The film's close mimicry of action films from Hollywood and other cinemas enable it to capitalise on, and be read and understood alongside, the films that popularised the genre. The strategy of revitalising local cinema by mimicking popular films and genres at the time evidently worked for *Bionic Boy*, if only for a while. It 'was so popular that [they] had a Bionic Boy Ice Cream manufactured by Singapore Cold Storage'.[87]

The second film is *They Call Her . . . Cleopatra Wong* (1978), the best-known of the three, and the only one that actually features locations in Singapore. It is directed by Suarez using the alias George Richardson. Doris Young, who plays the title character, also assumed the stage name Marrie Lee, 'to suggest a connection to Bruce Lee'.[88] Millet notes that Cleopatra may have been named after the blaxploitation film *Cleopatra Jones* (Jack Starret, 1973), and she was presented as 'a sort of Asian sister to [the film's] Tamara Dobson . . . , whose brother would have been Bruce Lee'.[89] This Cleopatra, or Cleo as she is called in the film, is Sunny Lee's aunt and a Singaporean Interpol agent who, according to the film's poster, 'purrs like a kitten . . . makes love like a siren . . . fights like a panther'.[90]

The film opens with Cleo in bed with a man while on holiday in Manila. They are interrupted by a call from her chief, Sims, in Singapore, who requests her return to fight a counterfeiting ring operating in Singapore, Hong Kong and Manila. The film takes place in these three locations, beginning with her return to Singapore. Here, the film features what Millet describes as 'excellent location shots'[91] of Singapore. These are largely tourist sites that the characters pass through, such as the airport, City Hall and Chinatown (see Figure 4.2). Other sites serve as exotic or unique locations to stage action sequences, like the Chinese Garden, which is used for the villa of the local head of the criminal ring where Cleo fights a group of wrestlers, and various parts of Sentosa island, including a cable car chase scene (see Figure 4.2).

As such, although Singapore is featured much more in this film than *Bionic Boy*, it is merely one of three exotic locations that Cleo travels to in her investigation; the first scene in Hong Kong opens with a view of the harbour, complemented with a soundtrack that begins with the sound of a gong followed by suitably Oriental music. Scenes in the Philippines depict terraced plantations, a tribal village and a hilltop monastery, which the criminal ring has taken over to house its counterfeit printing operation.

Figure 4.2 Singapore tourist sites in *They Call Her . . . Cleopatra Wong*

The film's international orientation is also evident in its references, dubbing and casting. Like her nephew Sunny, Cleo also fights gangs of bad guys. However, unlike *Bionic Boy*, these men are not dressed in particular costumes, but are more generically designated as modern-day thugs, except for the local head in Singapore whose costume of jumpsuit and sunglasses clearly references Bruce Lee in *Game of Death*. Like Bond, Cleo also has a modified vehicle – a motorcycle that has a turbo booster and guns in the side carriage. The film is also heavily dubbed, with characters speaking in American-accented English, except Cleopatra, who has a strange British-influenced accent that makes her speech slightly different from the others but which serves no apparent purpose in the narrative. Other Interpol agents assist her in her exploits, especially in the Philippines. The high point of the film takes place in the monastery, which Cleo and the other agents have infiltrated dressed as nuns. They free the real nuns, who were being held hostage, and confront the bad guys (also dressed as nuns) in a long action sequence that features extensive violence and liberal use of slow-motion in the style of Sam Peckinpah's *The Wild Bunch*. Also like *Bionic Boy*, the cast is racially mixed to connote an international flavour: Sims is played by Singaporean Brian Richmond, who is Eurasian and looks Caucasian. The villains are generically Southeast Asian or white. The real nuns are also mostly Asians, but led by the Caucasian Veronica.

The third film is *Dynamite Johnson* (aka *Bionic Boy II*, Bobby Suarez, 1978), which Millet posits may have been titled after another seminal blaxploitation film, *Willie Dynamite* (J. J. Johnson, 1974).[92] This film brings together Cleopatra and Sunny as they team up with Interpol to fight another international crime ring, this time led by the German Herr Koontz. Primarily set in the Philippines, the film does not feature Singapore at all. Once again, the film is heavily dubbed in American-accented English, and features a cast of mixed races and ethnicities, including an indigenous Filipino tribe complete with native costumes and exotic dance, and whose men are called 'braves'.

According to Millet, these films 'left a lasting impression and inspired many'.[93] They achieved cult status, particularly *They Call Her ... Cleopatra Wong*, which made Doris Young 'Singapore's first international female movie star'.[94] Millet also notes that an Australian rock band in the 1990s even named itself 'Cleopatra Wong'.[95] Quentin Tarantino has also claimed that Cleopatra inspired Uma Thurman's character in his *Kill Bill Volumes 1* and *2* (2003 and 2004).[96] Yet, according to White, 'although audiences may have enjoyed these films, it was an enjoyment of these films as camp, not as genuine expressions of Singaporean culture.'[97]

The only exception to these obviously Western-influenced films is *Two Sides of the Bridge* (*Qiao De Liang An*, 1976), directed by Lim Ann and produced by Chong Gay Organisation. Unlike the other players in the industry, Chong Gay was already a distributor and exhibitor in the film business, specialising in imports from Taiwan, Hong Kong and China. It was after the closure of the two studios that the company began to venture into film production. Chong Gay was modelled after the studios of the golden age, but its focus was on the Chinese, not Malay, market. It produced, distributed and exhibited films, and also had a stable of talents made up of Hong Kong experts, with a local crew in training and ten full-time stage actors. With such an ambitious set-up, Chong Gay planned to make three Mandarin films a year. However, it eventually only made a total of three films. The first two, *Crime Does Not Pay* (*Yi Jia Zhi Zhu*) and *Hypocrite* (*Huang Tang Shi Jia*, aka *Family Degeneration*), were made in 1974. They were helmed by its Hong Kong directors and 'thematically unfamiliar'[98] to the local audience. Little is known about these films except that the first was a juvenile crime comedy and did marginally better at the box-office than the second, which was a flop.[99]

The third film, *Two Sides of the Bridge*, is about a young Malaysian man, Yu Fei, who comes to Singapore to work and marry a local girl. To earn more money, he quits his factory job and joins a finance company, where speculating in the stock market leaves him heavily in debt and finally resorting to drug smuggling. The film was made 'mostly by, with and for Chinese locals [and] ... portrays a very "un-Malay" Singapore'.[100] The film's only Malay characters are limited to scenes set in Malaysia, and Yu Fei's friend, Fatimah, speaks Mandarin throughout. As Millet posits, 'this truly reinforced the fact that the Malay days of the movie industry were over, and Singapore cinema was now exploring new avenues in step with a changing society and a new target audience.'[101] The 'Bridge' in the title is the causeway that connects Singapore and Malaysia, and the film also reflects the growing disparity between these two countries, where the former is more business-minded and urbanised and the latter is depicted though a rural village, with a simpler, less hectic lifestyle. Yu Fei's attraction to the glitz of the city and his pursuit of material wealth also highlight the 'very tangible problem in a community undergoing rapid transformation from traditional, isolated communities into a single big metropolis'.[102] *Two Sides of the Bridge* is the only domestically made film in this decade to look inwards and perform a Singapore that is local in flavour, rather than outwards by emulating an internationally popular genre or film. As Uhde and Uhde note, this was 'one of the first screen attempts to deal with a contemporary Singapore issue [,] ... reflecting the experience and mood of the city's dominant Chinese population and its younger generations in particular'.[103] However, despite this, the film did not do well at the box-office and Chong Gay folded eventually as well.

While the changing audience of the time saw reality with more 'Western eyes', White also notes that the Hollywood films they preferred, 'despite their high production values and visual excitement, said little to Southeast Asians about themselves and their culture'.[104] Yet, of the films that tried to capture Singapore, *Ring of Fury* was banned and never locally released, while *Two Sides of the Bridge* and *The Two Nuts* did not resonate with local audiences and have receded into obscurity in public memory. These are not the films that have come to define this era of Singapore cinema. Instead, this post-studio period would be known for *Bionic Boy, They Call Her ... Cleopatra Wong* and *Dynamite Johnson*, transnational productions that are also not 'genuine expressions of Singaporean culture'.[105] They were made to so resemble foreign films that Singapore is either absent or so international that it is foreign. Unlike golden age films which depict a past and embody a cinema that is now seen as foreign, a film like *They Call Her ... Cleopatra Wong* performs a Singapore that is already more foreign than local. As such, it is interesting that these films are seen 'as important historical documents, and as a source of early Singapore nostalgia'.[106] Millet also argues that *They Call Her ... Cleopatra Wong* 'in particular ... is a rare testament to a very scantily documented era for Singapore. The on-location scenes, the fashion styles, the music and the ambience all give this movie undeniable documentary value.'[107] If the BAS films are the only visible artefacts of the period, and define the era, then the value of these films as Singapore films lies not in the presence of Singapore or any accurate depiction of it, but rather their performance of yet (an)other Singapore, one that is either absent or essentially foreign.

Collectively, the films of the period clearly signal that this is a new era of filmmaking that highlights a changing Singapore and audience. The golden age is not only a cinema of the past, but also one that is already emotionally distanced from the Singapore of the 1970s, even though the first film, *Ring of Fury*, was made only a year after the closure of Cathay-Keris. The feeling of newness of this post-studio cinema mirrors the desire for renewal in Singapore as it plunges headlong into nation-building to ensure its survival after independence. The desire to mimic popular films from Hollywood and Hong Kong also mirrors the state's international orientation and emphasis on a global hinterland for survival. This is a cinema that lies squarely between the pre-national cinema of the golden age and the post-national one of the revival in the 1990s. Like Singapore in the 1970s, which is a nation under construction, this cinema is also in transition, between the desire for renewal and departure from the past but not yet fully formed.

Notes

1. Lydia Lim, *Vintage Lee*, 37.
2. Ibid., 39.
3. Selvaraj Velayutham, *Responding*, 2.
4. Beng Huat Chua, 'Racial Singaporeans', 29.
5. Hill and Fee, 18.
6. Velayutham, 48.
7. Yew, 22.
8. Sharon Siddique, 'Singaporean Identity', 563.
9. Kuan Yew Lee, 'Excerpts of Broadcast'.
10. Heng Chee Chan, *Singapore*; quoted in Boon-Hiok Lee, 'Reconciling', 230.

11. Lee, 230.
12. W. E. Willmott, 'Emergence', 592–3.
13. Lysa Hong and Huang Jianli, *National History*, 4.
14. C. M. Turnbull, 307.
15. Ibid., 308.
16. Jean-Louis Margolin, 'Blueprint', 314.
17. C. M. Turnbull, 308.
18. Lee, 23.
19. C. M. Turnbull, 302.
20. Giok Ling Ooi, 'Changing', 324.
21. Ibid., 326.
22. Yang di Pertuan Negara's speech, quoted in Margolin, 305–6.
23. Ibid., 306.
24. Ibid., 317.
25. C. M. Turnbull, 310.
26. CPF is a compulsory social security system of monthly contributions by employers, citizens and permanent residents for retirement or specific use as defined by the CPF Board (such as buying HDB flats or for healthcare).
27. Ooi, 335.
28. C. M. Turnbull, 310.
29. Ibid., 311.
30. Ibid., 302.
31. Ibid., 311.
32. Ibid., 310.
33. Ibid.
34. Ibid., 311.
35. Ooi, 329.
36. Ibid., 329–30.
37. Ibid., 332.
38. C. M. Turnbull, 317.
39. Ooi, 328.
40. Lee, 199.
41. Ibid.
42. Ibid., 201.
43. Lim, 56.
44. Ibid.
45. Lee, 200–1.
46. Ibid., 206.
47. Ibid., 205.
48. Ibid., 207.
49. Heng Chee Chan and Hans-Dieter Evers, 'National Identity', 125; cited in Velayutham, 32.
50. C. M. Turnbull, 303.
51. Velayutham, 33.
52. C. M. Turnbull, 320.
53. Timothy White, 'South East Asia's Hollywood', 4.
54. Ibid.
55. Both Millet and White note that they seem like films from the 1930s: Millet, 71; Timothy R. White, 'Cinema of Southeast Asia'.
56. White, 'South East Asia's Hollywood', 4.
57. Uhde and Uhde, 49.
58. 'Filmmakers'.

59. Millet, 11.
60. According to the writers, the promotional flyer notes that the film was shown in Australia, New Zealand, five European countries, the Middle East, the West Indies and Africa: Uhde and Uhde, 49.
61. Millet, 71.
62. Ibid.
63. Ibid.
64. Lim Kay Tong, *Cathay*, 53.
65. Ibid.
66. Yew, 326.
67. Ibid.
68. 'Light on Yellow'.
69. Uhde and Uhde, 186.
70. Ibid.
71. 'Flower People'.
72. N. G. Kutty, 'Flexible Policy'.
73. 'Long Hair'.
74. 'Shaggy Look'.
75. Siew Hua Lee, 'Less Ado'.
76. 'Jukebox'.
77. Tong, 68.
78. Millet, 71–2.
79. Quoted in Kevin Peter Blackburn, 'Developmental Stages'.
80. Bailyne Sung, 'First S'pore-Made Film'.
81. Ibid.
82. N. G. Kutty, 'Asean Bid'.
83. Millet, 73.
84. Uhde and Uhde, 51.
85. Millet, 74.
86. Uhde and Uhde, 51.
87. Ibid.
88. Ibid.
89. Millet, 75.
90. Ibid., 76.
91. Ibid.
92. Ibid., 74.
93. Ibid., 76.
94. Uhde and Uhde, 53.
95. Millet, 76.
96. Ibid.; Uhde and Uhde, 53.
97. White, 'South East Asia's Hollywood', 4.
98. Uhde and Uhde, 50.
99. 'Filmmakers'.
100. Millet, 72.
101. Ibid., 73.
102. Uhde and Uhde, 51.
103. Ibid.
104. White, 'South East Asia's Hollywood', 4.
105. Ibid.
106. Uhde and Uhde, 53.
107. Millet, 76.

5. NOT SO FOREIGN: THE CASE OF *SAINT JACK*

'A STATE OF MIND'

According to Ben Slater, 'Singapore occupied a particular territory in the Western imagination. A glamorous city of abandon and escape, romance and adventure.'[1] Although this image of Singapore was popularised by the documentary-style film adaptation of Frank Buck's book *Bring 'Em Back Alive* (Clyde E. Elliot, 1932), and Singapore became a popular setting in a number of American films before the 1950s, 'none of the crews . . . had ever left Burbank, California.' The Singapore they created was built on stage sets. Singapore 'wasn't a place; it was a state of mind'.[2]

One of the first films to imagine Singapore is *Across to Singapore* (William Nigh, 1928). This is a silent film about a love triangle between Priscilla Crownshield and two brothers, Mark and Joel Shore. Singapore becomes a setting in the film when Joel and Mark voyage to the island. There, Joel gets involved in a bar brawl, while the drunken Mark is knifed by locals and left behind by his ship. The film's Singapore is a shantytown that is generally Chinese but includes people of other races such as Sikhs and Caucasians. It comprises three main spaces (see Figure 5.1): the port, which is essentially a wooden jetty leading to a dirt road; an ancient Chinese-styled tavern whose patrons are generally Asian – a number of them have turbans, including one who is obviously Caucasian; and a small, narrow, spartan room above the tavern where Mark and a Chinese belly dancer reside after he is injured. This Singapore is obviously a stage set and depicted as an exotic, backward

Figure 5.1 Singapore as represented by the port, tavern and room upstairs in *Across to Singapore*

isle, with strangely attired natives and mixed races. Although the things that happen here forward dramatic action in the film, Singapore is nothing more than a background location.

The Singapore in Jean de Limur's *The Letter* (1929) is a slightly less dingy but still primarily Oriental sea town. It is introduced in the opening sequence as a relatively busy port with locals in bumboats servicing a large ship. The town and streets are filled with Chinese in their loose tops, trousers and hats, Malays in *songkoks* and sarongs, as well as Western sailors in their uniforms (see Figure 5.2). There is also a seedy bar patronised by locals and foreign seamen. Entertainment is provided by a troupe of Caucasian-looking women in ethnic-inspired costumes performing a Balinese-style *gamelan* dance, and an Indian snake charmer complete with flute and huge turban. The bar and streets cast Singapore as a cosmopolitan space where people of various races mingle, while the Asian elements give it a sense of mystery and exoticism.

The film is an adaptation of W. Somerset Maugham's play of the same name, in which Leslie Crosbie, the restless wife of a colonial plantation manager, is accused of killing her lover (Geoffrey Hammond) and blackmailed by his

Chinese mistress. The object of the blackmail is an incriminating letter written by Leslie, which the mistress will return in exchange for $10,000. In the play, the mistress is known only as the Chinese Woman and repeatedly described as 'ignorant'. She is said to speak only Malay or Chinese, even though she has no lines. However, the film gives the mistress a name, Li Ti, and she speaks Chinese-inflected English fluently and frequently. Li Ti is presented as a kind of vamp consistent with other vamps in 1920s Hollywood films, but Oriental (see Figure 5.2). She is not a simple or meek Chinese woman but a rather masculine creature prone to devious glances and sly looks throughout the film. Although both women are manipulative and cunning, Leslie's actions are masked by her angelic looks, enhanced by the halo effect of the backlight (see Figure 5.2), while Li Ti's motives, and Hammond's attraction to her, are explained by her Orientalism. She also runs a prostitution business from a room above the local bar; the women are held in a prison-like cell in the ornately appointed room, but they do not look unhappy. When the two women meet in the room, Leslie is dominated by the overtly Chinese décor of the setting and looks completely out of place. Here, Li Ti verbally belittles and shames Leslie, before flinging the letter to the floor and forcing her to pick it up, saying, 'White woman, Chinese woman feet.' As Leslie does so, Li Ti sneers at her humiliation while the women in the cell join in, pointing and laughing at her (see Figure 5.2). The film's expansion of the mistress' role in the form of Li Ti adds to the mystery and danger encountered by white colonials like Leslie in its performance of Singapore.

In another adaptation of the play, *The Letter* (William Wyler, 1940), Singapore is depicted through a more colonial perspective. This is apparent in the kinds of spaces occupied by the colonials and natives. The first comprises the plantation house, attorney's office and court. The house sits in a kind of tropical farmstead surrounded by lush greenery and coconut trees. It has a veranda, a parrot perched on a fence, rattan furniture and shuttered windows and doors that add to the romanticism of this tropical dream. On the other hand, the office and court are structured, rectilinear spaces that represent order and administrative authority. These spaces are contrasted with the overt exoticism and mystery of 'Chinatown' with its dark, narrow alleys and various inhabitants dressed in Chinese costumes. The mistress resides here in a room above Chung Hi's General Store. The store is crammed with all kinds of strange, exotic things, and serves as a prelude to the room upstairs. In the play, the room is described as:

> a small room in the Chinese quarter of Singapore. The walls are whitewashed, but dirty and bedraggled, on one of them hangs a cheap Chinese oleograph, stained and discoloured; on another, unframed and pinned up, a picture of a nude from one of the illustrated papers. The only furni-

Figure 5.2 Li Ti and Leslie; Leslie dwarfed, humiliated and laughed at by prostitutes in the cell in Li Ti's room

ture consists of a sandal-wood box and a low Chinese pallet bed, with a lacquered neck-rest. There is a closed window, which is at the back, and a door on the right. It is night and the room is lit by one electric light, a globe without a shade.[3]

However, in the film the room is richly decorated with Chinese furniture and ornaments, tinkling chimes, lanterns, and a bamboo screen through which the mistress appears. The smoke from Chung Hi's opium pipe adds to the air of mystery in the room. Here is where Leslie meets the mistress and also where a different kind of justice occurs via the blackmail.

In this version, Hammond's Chinese mistress is mostly silent, but when she speaks it is in a strange Cantonese with a heavy Western accent. She also resembles Li Ti's Chinese imperial throwback with her heavy Oriental-style robes and crown. Unlike the previous adaptation, the mistress only makes a few mysterious appearances and her role is not developed. Wyler's film maintains its focus squarely on the duplicity of its central female protagonist, Leslie. As such, while Li Ti and the earlier film's Singapore are strange and dangerous, the mistress and Singapore in Wyler's version remain in the background as mysterious and unknowable. Although different, both are nonetheless equally exotic variations of Singapore as Orient perceived through the lens of a Western outsider.

The films that follow maintain the view of Singapore as exotic, but the space also becomes a backdrop for romance in films like *The Blonde from Singapore* (aka *Hot Pearls*, Edward Dmytryk, 1941), in which a couple of pearl divers encounter a helpless woman in Singapore and entrust their cache of pearls to her, only to discover that she is actually not what she claims, and *Singapore Woman* (Jean Negulesco, 1941), where a ruined young widow is found drunk in Singapore and is saved by a young colonial who takes her back to his plantation home to sober her up, much to the chagrin of his fiancée. They inevitably fall in love amid rubber plantations, rickshaws and at the Raffles Hotel, which have become recurring tropes in such performances of Singapore, as have seedy bars, streets in various depictions of 'Chinatown' and pearl diving.

In *Singapore* (John Brahm, 1947), Mathew Gordon is a pearl smuggler who falls in love with Linda Grahame in Singapore just before the Japanese invade. Thinking that she perished in an air raid, he goes back to America with a broken heart. Five years later, he returns to Singapore to retrieve a stash of valuable pearls and finds Linda, who now has amnesia and is married to a rubber-plantation owner. This film, like the films before it, also essentially performs Singapore from a Western, colonial perspective. This is apparent in the way spaces are designed to create what the characters call 'the Orient'. These include the hotel, which looks like a typical colonial-tropical setting, the Macau Cabaret, which is chinoiserie by way of Hollywood, where the décor is Oriental and the music and maître d' are French, and the mission, which has geometric screen panels and a circular archway with a pagoda-style tiled roof. Most of these spaces are also mainly occupied by white men and women, while hotel porters, waiters and the airport's policemen are Asians,

THE CASE OF *SAINT JACK*

Figure 5.3   Hotel, Macau cabaret, the mission, street, seedy bar and Rochor Canal in *Singapore*

mostly Chinese. Spaces occupied by locals are much less glamorous, like a seedy bar, the streets and a fishing village identified as Rochor Canal (see Figure 5.3).

The cast are Westerners, and local characters have almost no speaking parts, except for Linda's maid, Ming Ling, and a few others who give directions, answer questions or take instruction. The locals are a rather confusing mix of Malay and Chinese, identified primarily through their costumes: Chinese in mandarin-collared outfits and conical hats and Malay women in headscarves. However, in the fishing village, while the residents look Chinese, some women also wear Malay-style headscarves and sarongs, like Ming Ling. They also seem fluent in Malay, except Ming Ling, who has an odd foreign accent. The title of the film highlights the centrality of Singapore, and the film does strive to create a sense of 'being there' in the opening sequence's aerial view of a waterfront and the use of rear projection as the protagonists travel through the streets in a rickshaw. However, the Singapore in this *Singapore* remains, like the rear projection, just an exotic backdrop for a narrative that could have been set anywhere else.

Cinematic Tourism

By the late 1950s, location shooting had become the norm, or as Slater says, 'the new special effect ... audiences wanted to see stories unfold in real spaces, not just hermetically sealed studio sets'.[4] Location shooting was ideal for the Euro-spy films that boomed in the wake of James Bond, since part of their appeal involved travel to foreign, exotic places. According to Slater, 'the combo of tropical, visual other-ness with widely spoken English, great hotels, food and relative freedom from crime, corruption and political instability (while Indochina is burning), made [Singapore] a perfect location for Asia-set stories.'[5] A number of such movies were shot in Singapore, including *Five Ashore in Singapore* (1967), a French-American co-production about American sailors who get stuck in Singapore, run amok and end up fighting crime together, and *Ring Around The World* (Luigi Scattini, 1966), an Italian-French Eurospy film about a detective whose worldwide investigation ends in a climactic fight scene filmed on location at the Tiger Balm Garden in Singapore. This is a well-known tourist attraction that comprises a circular villa built on a hill in Pasir Panjang surrounded by a vast labyrinth-like landscape of colourful sculptures and scenes from Chinese mythology. Its most famous attraction is the Ten Courts of Hell, which depicts the gory consequences of various sins such as lying, stealing and adultery, and was the source of many a childhood nightmare. The garden was built in 1937 by Aw Boon Haw for his little brother Boon Par. Although they named it Tiger Balm Garden, for the medicated ointment on which the family's fortune was established, the place is also commonly known as Haw Par Villa.

The uniqueness of Haw Par Villa made it a popular location in a number of films like *So Darling, So Deadly* (1966), one of a number of 'Spaghetti and Sauerkraut'[6] films based on the popular German *Kommissar X* series featuring American superspy Joe Walker. This time he is sent to Singapore to investigate a deadly weapon. Its Singapore features a Grand Prix motor race, the Paya Lebar Airport, a drive past the Padang, City Hall, Elgin Bridge, Collyer Quay and Chinatown, a chase scene in the fruit market there, Goodwood Park Hotel, an action sequence at the Haw Par Villa, and an old 'Chinatown' which does not actually exist. Again, here we see a Singapore that is mostly comprised of Caucasians, including the villains, especially in places like the airport and hotel, while the locals are generally just part of other settings as fruit sellers, their customers, workers and people on the streets. To add to the exoticism of the location, the leader of the criminal organisation, the Golden Dragon Society, is a mysterious man in loose Chinese-style robes with a red hood over his face. His accomplice is Li Hu Wang, played by Nikola Popovic dressed as a Chinaman complete with the hat and straggly 'goatee'. There are only three Asians in supporting roles: Lapore, a Malay servant who is Golden Dragon's spy, a mysterious Asian-looking woman who silently appears and disappears, and her 'husband', who turns out to be a Singapore police inspector with a Japanese name, Takato.

All the films capture an older Singapore and not the newly developing one of skyscrapers, housing and industrial estates that was rapidly being built around the island. There are also almost no local actors in the cast. As such, although films like *So Darling, So Deadly* were filmed on location, their Singapores are not very different from those in preceding films. The Singapore they perform is still 'merely a backdrop interchangeable for "the Orient" – an exotic hot zone,'[7] where adventures happen to visitors. Singapore has no 'inner life' or subjectivity.

A film that did attempt 'to deal with [Singapore's] colonial legacy'[8] is *Pretty Polly* (1967). Based on Noël Coward's short story *Pretty Polly Barlow*, the film is about a young English woman, Polly, who comes of age at Raffles Hotel. She arrives in Singapore by ship as her aunt's companion. After her aunt dies, leaving behind her wealth and Raffles Hotel suite, Polly decides to live it up in Singapore. She falls in love with her Indian tour guide, Amaz, loses her virginity, gets contact lenses and a makeover, parties in Bugis Street and ends up at a boozy rave in a large, detached bungalow. Upstairs she discovers reality – a Chinese family making dinner in the confines of a small room and Amaz's spartan accommodation in another. His room exposes Amaz as 'an empty man, a fake Singaporean, fake tour-guide and a fake lover . . .'[9]

In Slater's view, the film 'was a desiccated period piece, representing a Singapore that barely existed beyond the palatial confines of colonial architecture'.[10] Indeed, the Singapore beyond is mainly captured in documentary-style sequences that are interesting digressions but ultimately remain separate from the main narrative. For example, a montage of images shows what Polly sees when she first arrives in Singapore, including colonial buildings, shophouses in Chinatown, laundry hanging off bamboo poles, blocks of HDB flats, a roadside barber, an Indian temple, and street vendors selling fruit. However, these are merely snapshots and impressions that a tourist like Polly would have and the sequence is unbroken by commentary or narrative. As Slater observes, 'throughout, the film can't resist occasionally lapsing into a pure tourist-documentarian gaze, catching images, gestures and reactions of the real locations on the fly, before cutting back to the characters, or even placing them right into the spectacle.'[11] For example, the scene in which Polly gets new contact lenses begins with a sequence capturing a Chinese funeral procession, with the sounds of the ritual's music and its performers, and extreme close-ups of hands clashing cymbals and beating on a drum. A brief whip pan blurs the procession as it passes by, like an unedited moment, as if to suggest some kind of confusion. The film then cuts to Polly blinking profusely on the second floor of a shophouse before returning to a blurry, higher-angle shot of the procession that quickly gains focus. This is obviously Polly's point-of-view, and the film quickly transitions from documentary to narrative when the doctor asks Polly if she is getting used to the lenses. She nods, and looks out of the window. The camera once again assumes her point-of-view to provide a clear high-angle shot of the procession before cutting to street level once again with shots of the details of the cortège and ritual. The film then cuts back to Polly upstairs and the funeral is forgotten. Its sounds fade away as the characters talk about her contact lenses and the film style returns to supporting the narrative action. These documentary-style sequences are emblematic of Polly's encounter with, and so also the film's performance of, Singapore as bite-sized touristic images and locations with no direct engagement. They have no bearing on the narrative and are separated from events and action. Singapore represents the possibility of adventure and a new life for Polly, and her experience of it is as a tourist, accompanied by a guide 'who trades on the false glamour of tourism'.[12]

In Slater's view, *Pretty Polly* is 'not a good film, but it works effectively as metaphor: Amaz is Singapore'.[13] He is the only local character with a significant supporting role and with whom Polly has any tangible interactions. Interestingly, he is played by Shashi Kapor, one of Bollywood's biggest stars of the time. The only other Asian character in the film is Uncle Bob's Chinese girlfriend, Lorelei, whose role is minor. If anything, she merely adds to the sleaziness and fading glamour of the colonial expatriate embodied by Uncle Bob. Played by Trevor Howard, Bob is overweight and past his prime, 'hardly the rugged, sexual adventurer that Coward describes'.[14] According to Slater, 'he represents all that can go wrong if you stay in Asia past your welcome.'[15] Tellingly, as Bob urges Polly to travel with Aunt Eva's money, he says, 'the sun sets on the empire and it gets bloody freezing cold at night.' However, this is as far as the film goes in dealing with Singapore's colonial legacy. Like Amaz the 'fake Singaporean', *Pretty Polly*'s Singapore is also one that is superficial, manufactured for and experienced by tourists. This Singapore could be any other Asian city in the world. The fact that it was set in Singapore is irrelevant because the location has no bearing on the narrative, despite the few documentary sequences.

The similarities between the films of the post-studio era and these foreign productions show that there is no difference in the way Singapore is performed regardless of whether they are made from within or without. The line between inside and outside positions is blurred, problematising the tendency to regard locally produced films as authentic and limit the study of national cinema to such films. Although the post-studio era could be read as a cinema that mirrors the state's international orientation, films like *They call Her ... Cleopatra Wong*'s performance of Singapore is equally as foreign as that of *So Darling, So Deadly*. The strategy of post-studio films was not to look inwards but to appeal to an international market and compete with Hollywood and Hong Kong. Furthermore, the newly independent Singapore was concerned with breaking away from its past and forging a new nation. Whatever sense of identity, consciousness or culture that forging a new nation entailed was, like the nation itself, still being formed. As such, if a film like *They Call Her ... Cleopatra Wong* is authentic to anything, it is to the genres and films it mimics, which make such films equally foreign, imaginary portraits of Singapore as those just discussed above.

The 'quintessential Singapore film'[16]

It is therefore not surprising that, in an era when the country made films that performed Singapore as essentially foreign or absent, the 'quintessential Singapore film' of this period is not a local production. The film is *Saint Jack*, an adaptation of Paul Theroux's book of the same name, and its narrative revolves around Jack Flowers, an American working as a chandler in Singapore with a reputation for supplying ships and foreigners with anything they desire, including girls. Though a foreigner, Jack has lived in Singapore for many years and with that comes local knowledge and familiarity with the locals with whom he does business. He constantly chats and exchanges greetings with locals wherever he goes; he seems to know everyone, and everyone knows him. The narrative is structured in three acts marked by the three visits made by William Leigh, a British accountant from Hong Kong. In the first act, Jack meets William for the first time when he is instructed to pick the latter up from the airport and deliver him to the hotel. Thereafter they go to the Bandung Club, a hangout for ageing expatriates, where Jack meets an American client looking for entertainment. Jack takes him and William to Bugis Street, where they pick up two transvestites (Bridgit and Lily) and proceed to a brothel where the 'ladies' put on a show. Local gangsters constantly tail them, and several locals warn Jack against opening his own brothel. Jack also meets an

Indian prostitute named Monika who becomes his girlfriend. When William's hotel manager is murdered, Jack suspects the local gang. Jack and William promise to meet again when the latter returns the next year.

The second act takes place a year later and Jack has his very own brothel, Dunroamin', which is popular, well-run and well-kept by a group of local employees. Upon his arrival, Jack takes William to the Raffles Hotel for drinks. William is unwell and Jack procures a room for him to rest. Back at Dunroamin' the next day, a gang of local thugs arrive. They kidnap Jack, tattoo Chinese vulgarities on his arms and destroy Dunroamin'. Ever the survivor, Jack spends a drunken night with William at a tattoo shop where flowers are inked over the obscenities.

In the third act, Eddie Schuman, a mysterious American CIA agent, recruits Jack to run an R&R house (Paradise Gardens) for American soldiers on leave from the Vietnam War. However, when Schuman abruptly closes the place, Jack finds himself at a loose end again. William returns for his annual accounting trip and Jack takes him back to the Bandung Club. There, William collapses and dies. Schuman hires Jack to procure evidence incriminating an American senator during his visit to Singapore. Jack tails the politician and takes compromising photos of the senator and a young man in a hotel room. The next day, in anticipation of the money Schuman promised, Jack prepares to leave Singapore. However, he changes his mind and as he crosses a bridge over Boat Quay, tosses the incriminating photos into the river and disappears into the streets of Singapore to the sound of locals greeting him by name.

Saint Jack was shot entirely in Singapore over two months in 1978, with four months on location for pre-production. Based on the mistaken impression that Theroux's book was banned in Singapore, the director Peter Bogdanovich thought that they would not be allowed to shoot on location. As such, it was filmed in 'secret' as 'Jack of Hearts', with the authorities apparently unaware of its theme or source material. The *Los Angeles Times* revealed the deception in an article titled 'Bogdanovich's Singapore Fling'. In it the director admitted he 'just lied: lied about everything.'[17] He said that 'the film is in no way a put-down of Singapore. It's just that we show the low-life as well as the glamour spots ... with our story, I knew we had no chance if we leveled with the government.'[18] This was reported in Singapore's *The New Nation* two weeks later as 'How I fooled them in S'pore [sic]'. The paper pilloried *Saint Jack*'s New York premiere later that year, describing it as a 'raunchy flick' that 'goes into the tired realm of the sexploitative'.[19] It argued that 'the irony of this morality play is that a country and its people, innocent bystanders, are seen by those whose views are clouded by the unmistakable signs of degeneration – their own degeneration – they so vividly portray.'[20] Another article a few months later reported that 'Bogdanovich says it again ... tells *Playboy* why he lied about film.' The director was quoted saying that Singapore is 'a country that is, uh, not free. I suppose no country is, but they were very, very strict about certain things. They're very repressive in terms of sex ... *Playboy* is not allowed.'[21] The article also predicted that 'judging by the nude stills from the film in *Playboy*, *Saint Jack* is likely to go the way of the magazine, – a ban or at least heavy censorship in Singapore.'[22]

This is prophetic because when Warner Brothers submitted the film for release in Singapore in late 1979, the Board of Film Censors banned it for putting 'Singapore in a very bad light by portraying it as a haven for pimps and whores':

> The board and ministry officials who saw the film were aghast at its portrayal of Singapore as a seedy fleshpot of a country, rife with gangsters, pimps and prostitutes ... One scene that raised their hackles particularly – more so than the close-up of two Bugis Street transvestites in a sordid act – showed a Christian burial being conducted within earshot of the firecrackers and symbols of a Buddhist funeral. They objected to the religious imputations and the misrepresentation of a Singapore lacking in religious sensitivity.[23]

The scene in question is William's funeral, which was shot on location at the Bidadari Cemetery. During the sombre service in the chapel, Jack looks out of the window and sees a Buddhist funeral being conducted simultaneously outside. The contrast could not be more obvious. Compared to the desolate and solemn mood of William's funeral attended by the handful of Englishmen from the Bandung Club singing a mournful hymn, the Buddhist chants outside, while still suitably serious and quiet, are punctuated by the clash of symbols and explosion of firecrackers at the end. Interestingly, the Board of Film Censors' objection to the scene is echoed when one of the Bandung Brits is offended by the firecrackers and growls, 'Can't someone stop those bastards?' Jack's Girl Friday, Judy, later explains that it is 'very lucky to make noise'. The scene is deliberately set up to contrast the differences in cultural attitudes and practices. However, the Brit's comment shows the superior attitude and insularity of the colonials, and their lack of knowledge of the culture local to the place in which they have been residing for so many years. Judy's response shows that such an attitude is out of date and no longer relevant in a Singapore that has outgrown its colonial past. In contrast, Jack is a different kind of expat, one who interacts with locals and is familiar with their culture. Yet, despite this, Jack will never be local, and his outsider status is confirmed when he pushes things too far by encroaching on the business of the local thugs by opening his own brothel, and, therefore, has to be taught a lesson.

The film's reception in the West was more positive. It generally received good reviews in the US and Europe, and even won the Italian Film Journalists Award for Best Picture at the Venice Film Festival in 1979.[24] Denholm Elliot, who played William, was also nominated for Best Actor by the British Academy of Film and Television Arts (BAFTA). However, its box-office was moderate, superseded by blockbusters like *Alien* (Ridley Scott, 1979) that were sweeping across cinemas in America. Today, *Saint Jack*'s reputation is dimmed, partly because of the downward spiral of Bogdanovich's career, and the lack of access to the film due to rights issues. It was only in 2001 that the film was finally released on DVD for the first time in the United States. However, the film does have a small cult following, with appreciations from Quentin Tarantino and Wes Anderson, and a kind of 'urban legend' status in Singapore where bootleg videos of it circulate. Singapore's ban on the film was finally lifted in 2006 and DVDs were available about three months later. Even so, copies were hardly flying off the shelves and very few Singaporeans today know of *Saint Jack*.

Given its lack of visibility and a narrative of a white man in a foreign land, it would be easy to dismiss the film as yet another foreign production in Singapore. For example, in Anthony Gunaratne's view,

> Bogdanovich succumbs to the tendency of Western directors to have Western spectators in mind wherever they happen to be shooting: his use of Singaporean locales, though redolent of *film noir* thrillers and not 'inauthentic' per se, does little more than inject some psychological complexity into a somewhat sickly tale of a white adventurer slumming in the Third World.[25]

However, chronicles of Singapore's cinematic history almost always mention *Saint Jack* as an important film of the post-studio period. Main accounts of the development of Singapore cinema, namely the second edition of *Latent Images* and Millet's *Singapore Cinema*, even have separate sections dedicated to discussing the film. Yet the reason for including *Saint Jack* in the history of Singapore cinema is rather unclear. In the first edition of *Latent Images*, *Saint Jack* only receives a passing mention of three sentences, the last of which concludes that it 'does not qualify as a Singapore film since the city was used merely as a backdrop'.[26] However, in the second edition published a decade later, *Saint Jack* is discussed in greater detail in a section of its own entitled 'The Cause Célèbre: *Saint Jack*'.[27] The cause for celebration seems to be that the film won the Italian Journalists Prize for Best Picture. So, 'although not a locally-produced film, *Saint Jack* is nevertheless an important part of Singapore's film history ... an invaluable historical record of the country's past, a veritable treasure of images long lost.'[28] Millet states that the film 'seems to be a seminal movie in the history of cinema in Singapore' because 'it explores the at first unseen aspects of Singapore's multilayered and multifaceted society, and exposes its dark and gloomy – if not sleazy - sides.'[29] He also notes that *Saint*

Jack's interest in the underbelly and independent filmmaking style are characteristics that 'mark the revival of Singapore cinema'[30] in the 1990s. According to Philip Cheah, former director of the Singapore International Film Festival, 'for many Singaporeans, starved of a realist film industry that concentrated on Singapore locations and social mores, the film succeeds in capturing many aspects of Singapore in that era. *St Jack* (sic) thus functions as Singapore's social and visual heritage.'[31] The film does capture a Singapore that the films made by BAS Films International did not, including Bugis Street before it was cleaned up, lower-class Chinatown before redevelopment and uptown Orchard Road at night, offering a visual record of Singapore's landscape and places in the late 1970s. Cheah also says that *Saint Jack* is a 'quintessential Singapore film'[32] and, although he does not explain why, there are several ways that *Saint Jack* could be considered a Singapore film.[33]

Far from the gloating duplicity implied in the local press, Bogdanovich's deception actually reflects an acute understanding of what it meant to make a film in Singapore at the time. Although there were numerous press reports on film crews coming to shoot on location in Singapore, the country's seeming openness to foreign productions was also undermined by its government's extensive campaign against 'yellow culture' and strict stance towards such 'degeneration' in print, film and radio. The most notable of these productions was *Hawaii Five-O,* which had to jump through several administrative hoops before it was allowed to start shooting. So, as Slater says, 'if an innocuous, clean-cut bit of fluff like *Hawaii Five-O* made the Ministry nervous, what hope was there for *Saint Jack*?'[34] As such, Bogdanovich and his team decided to proceed with *Jack of Hearts* as a working title, and the eight-page bogus treatment they submitted was also 'deliberately vague about Chinese gangsters' and portrayed the Chinese 'as positively as possible throughout. The pro-Singaporean sentiments are deliberately heavy-handed and show that the visitors were well aware of the "nation-building" rhetoric of the day.'[35]

Although Singapore had 'absolutely no movie-making infrastructure in place',[36] *Saint Jack* managed to involve extensive local participation in the cast and crew. Bogdanovich wanted the film to be as authentic as possible, and much effort was made to find locals who could fill these roles. They include Tony Yeow, who became the film's unit manager and, through him, other locals for positions like art director and set decorator. Numerous locals were cast in myriad supporting or minor roles, including Gopi, the Indian chandlery worker, Jack's bosses (Big Hing and Little Hing), his *Peranakan*[37] *amah*[38] (Esther) and her *mahjong* friends, his Indian girlfriend (Monika), Girl Friday (Judy) and cook (Jimmy), Wally the Bandung Club bartender, the gangsters as well as assorted extras like prostitutes. They were all non-professional actors, with little or no acting experience. Instead, they are the 'real people' that Bogdanovich wanted for the film, to give it 'a real sense of authenticity'.[39]

Taking the desire for authenticity to the limit, some locals were even cast to play themselves, such as the taxi driver, the brothel madam Diana Voon and some of the working girls. Bridgit Ang, a transsexual famously known as 'The Queen of Bugis Street', not only played herself but also re-created her 'show' for the film, which became the much-discussed performance in the brothel. A number of the Caucasian extras were also cast through connections in Singapore. For example, the numerous American GIs at the Paradise Gardens were students from the local American School and actual navy men whose ships were in Singapore. As such, apart from the roles of Jack Flowers, William Leigh, Eddie Schuman and the Bandung gang, 'practically the whole cast would be making their cinematic debut.'[40] Such an extensive involvement of locals distinctly differentiates *Saint Jack* from previous 'foreign' productions like *So Darling, So Deadly* or *Pretty Polly*.

Furthermore, unlike in the earlier films, the locals are not merely relegated to background decoration in *Saint Jack* but have actual speaking parts[41] that contribute to the narrative or the film's overall tone, mood and attitude. According to Ben Gazzara, 'they were virtually left alone by Peter. When he wanted them to do something, he told them, but he did not try to frame their performances.'[42] As a result, there is a distinct naturalness in the gestures and actions of the local cast that gives the film's performance of Singapore a certain authentic charm and character. This is especially evident in Jack's interaction with the group of locals who follow him from venture to venture. From Judy's matter-of-fact explanation of the firecrackers at the funeral and Dunroamin's Indian security guard's jovial response when caught eating in the kitchen ('I'm a dog, I'm here to bark') to the heartfelt scene when Jack encounters Jimmy, his cook, still cooking with a charcoal stove in a corner of the wrecked Dunroamin'. This is an intimate scene, captured in a two-shot lit by the light of a naked bulb as Jimmy tells Jack what happened and offers him something to eat and drink. His solemn translation of the vulgarities tattooed on Jack's arm causes Jack to laugh at the absurdity of the curses and the situation.

Jack also has a straight-talking *amah*, Esther, whom we first encounter when Jack takes Monika to his apartment in the first act. When asked what she wants to drink, Monika requests tea, to which the *amah* replies, 'No tea. Coffee only.' Monika says, 'I don't like coffee,' and Esther retorts, 'What kind of a girl don't like coffee?' Monika replies, 'This kind of girl don't like coffee.' Jack orders her a Coke and, as the *amah* saunters off to get the drink, she remarks to her friends in Hokkien, 'Boh jiak kopi eh ah . . .'. This last line is literally translated as 'doesn't drink coffee', which is matter-of-fact enough, but the tone she uses is one of mocking amusement, and her friends laugh along with her. Jack's interactions with her are a recurring motif in the film: whenever he rejects her offer of food, she replies, 'You must eat. If not you die, you know?' While the lines themselves do not directly add to the dramatic action, they add

Figure 5.4 Toh, the Little Person

to the overarching groove of a film that captures the local space and inhabitants as easy-going and non-judgmental. As Esther follows Jack from one brothel venture to another, her only admonition is about food and not prostitution or drugs. Even Big Hing and Little Hing, Jack's grumpy and gruff former employers, add to the comic moments in the film. When Jack tells Little Hing not to send any more Australian beef, he claims that the beef is 'No Australia. Prime US.' When Jack retorts, 'Prime your ass. Probably not even Australian. Probably Malaysian,' Little Hing deadpans, 'No cows in Malaysia.' While their individual roles are small, they collectively create a relaxed and laid-back vibe that characterises the film's Singapore. Jack's interactions with them are often funny, breaking the tension in scenes and underscoring Jack's and, by extension, the film's intimacy with this Singapore and its people.

Even the local gangsters, who create a menacing presence at first, are eventually made to look somewhat quirky, particularly Toh, the bespectacled Little Person who leads the carload of goons that descend on Dunroamin' (see Figure 5.4). After they arrive, Toh approaches Jack and asks, 'Would you care to buy some interesting book, Mr Flower [sic]?' 'What are you selling?' Jack asks, and Toh replies, 'Sex material. Swedish.' When Jack does not agree at first, the bigger thugs threateningly start to surround him. Jack relents and says he'll 'take a dozen. How much?' Toh tells him, 'For you. Cheap. We have a large stash in the car. Would you care to choose?' When Jack asks him to 'choose 'em', the Little Person gestures to the magazine in his hand and says, 'Oh Mr Flower, everyone has their own preference in sex. I like this, maybe you don't like.' Tired of the charade, Jack tells the larger thugs, 'All right boys, let's get it over with before I dropkick this little cocksucker down the hill.' As the film cuts from Jack to each of the thugs, tension mounts and is broken when one of his girls pleads on his behalf in Hokkien. Jack tells Esther to take the girl away and the film cuts to Toh, who says, 'I think you should choose your book, Mr Flower.' Jack relents and goes with them. Casting a Little Person as the leader of these gangsters is consistent with the unexpected or somewhat ridiculous villains in Euro-spy films of the period, generating a simultaneous sense of ludicrousness and threat in the situation. Here, the exchange between Toh and Jack is as funny as the threat is palpable. Toh adds to the array of quirky local characters in the film, all of whom in turn collectively lend a peculiar charm and character to the local in *Saint Jack*'s Singapore.

Most of the local characters here speak naturally and in their own voice. Some accents are more pronounced, like Gopi's, Big Hing's and Monika's, but most speak in Singapore English. As K. C. Goh notes in the *Straits Times*, 'more delightful, the capture of authentic Singapore English in all its unadorned glory, as she is spoken.'[43] Jack's *amah* even says all her lines in a distinctively Peranakan accent. As such, what we hear is not only Singapore English but an array of accents and speech patterns that make up the sound of multilingual Singapore – Indian, Peranakan, Chinese – without the overt staginess or affectation of earlier films.

From the outset, *Saint Jack* was not going to be a glossy Hollywood film depicting the more glamorous and touristy aspects of Singapore. Instead, the film seems to have steered clear of the colonial parts of Singapore's built environment. For example, as Slater notes, although the Goodwood Park Hotel was the site for the film's Paradise Gardens, 'the old-school colonial aspects of the [hotel] were deliberately covered up and avoided. Paradise Gardens needed to look like a soulless, modern complex where young men came to get high before being shipped off to die.'[44] New scenes were also being written 'specifically inspired by locations'[45] the crew encountered. The most notable example is Bugis Street, a relatively long thoroughfare that became a red-light district in the 1950s. Here, one could find good food at the many roadside stalls and be entertained by prostitutes who 'were famously good-looking and notoriously ambivalent about their gender'. F. D. Ommanney describes Bugis Street as

> one of the most beautiful streets in the world in its own way, because of the lights and the ever-changing crowds and because of its irrepressible vitality. It is civilised because of its merciful, uncritical tolerance. Nothing matters and the chief sins are not to smile and not to pay.[46]

By the 1970s, Bugis Street was more alive than ever, despite the threat of closure by the authorities. Acquiring the nickname 'Boogie Street', it became a popular destination for tourists 'who wanted to see something spectacular'.⁴⁷ The nightlife, now dominated by flamboyantly dressed transvestites and transsexuals, included 'dancing shows, photo opportunities and a great deal of glitz, glamour and performance'.⁴⁸ There were even postcards of the girls for sale.

Saint Jack is not the first film to have been shot at Bugis Street. As mentioned, *Pretty Polly* features it as well, when Amaz takes Polly to a 'jolly little place called Bugis Street' (see Figure 5.5). The scene begins with documentary-style footage capturing various aspects of the place as Polly and Amaz pass through: the food stalls, a crowd of well-dressed 'women' mingling with foreigners, and touts hawking hats and sarongs. These images establish the scene for narrative action. Longer shots are filled with people and activity, matched by the diegetic noise of chatter and merriment, depicting a vibrant, crowded space. Close-ups of the 'women' especially, add to the sense of compactness of the space but also single them out like curious specimens, encouraging a closer look.

This is 'a jolly little place', as Amaz describes it, and quite a glamorous one too, marked by the film's style as a tourist attraction filled with exotic creatures and ogling tourists like the elderly Brit who lustily adjusts his monocle to better observe a sexily dressed 'woman' and remarks to his companion, 'I say, it's surprising what chappies are wearing these days.' However, the film quickly transitions to focusing on the narrative when champagne arrives at Polly's and Amaz's table and other characters join them. Throughout, these characters primarily interact with each other and not with the locals, who are there merely to add to the background. Without any tangible engagement, Bugis Street is just an interesting location for narrative action that, like the rest of the film, could have occurred anywhere else.

Saint Jack's Bugis Street is also crowded but a visibly less glamorous and frenetic place. As William, Jack and his American client weave through the space to the ambient sounds of cooking, chatting and a rather melodious Chinese song, tables are occupied by locals and foreigners casually having meals. Jack greets the locals, asking after their families and showing a great deal of familiarity with the space and its inhabitants (see Figure 5.6). This is not the same loud and crowded space filled with exotic creatures as *Pretty Polly*'s Bugis Street. Conversations take place at a relaxed pace and tone, matched by the more languid rhythm of fewer cuts and longer takes. Here, the touts sell vibrators alongside other kitsch and the tables display food menus and albums of available girls. However, these are captured as normal and natural, nothing to gawk at, by the casual pace of the scene and manner of the characters as they interact. Even Bridgit's chat with Jack's American client 'must have been a close rendition of her usual Bugis Street patter'.⁴⁹ The film's treatment of this scene is a prime example of its understated style, and spaces are captured as naturally as possible.

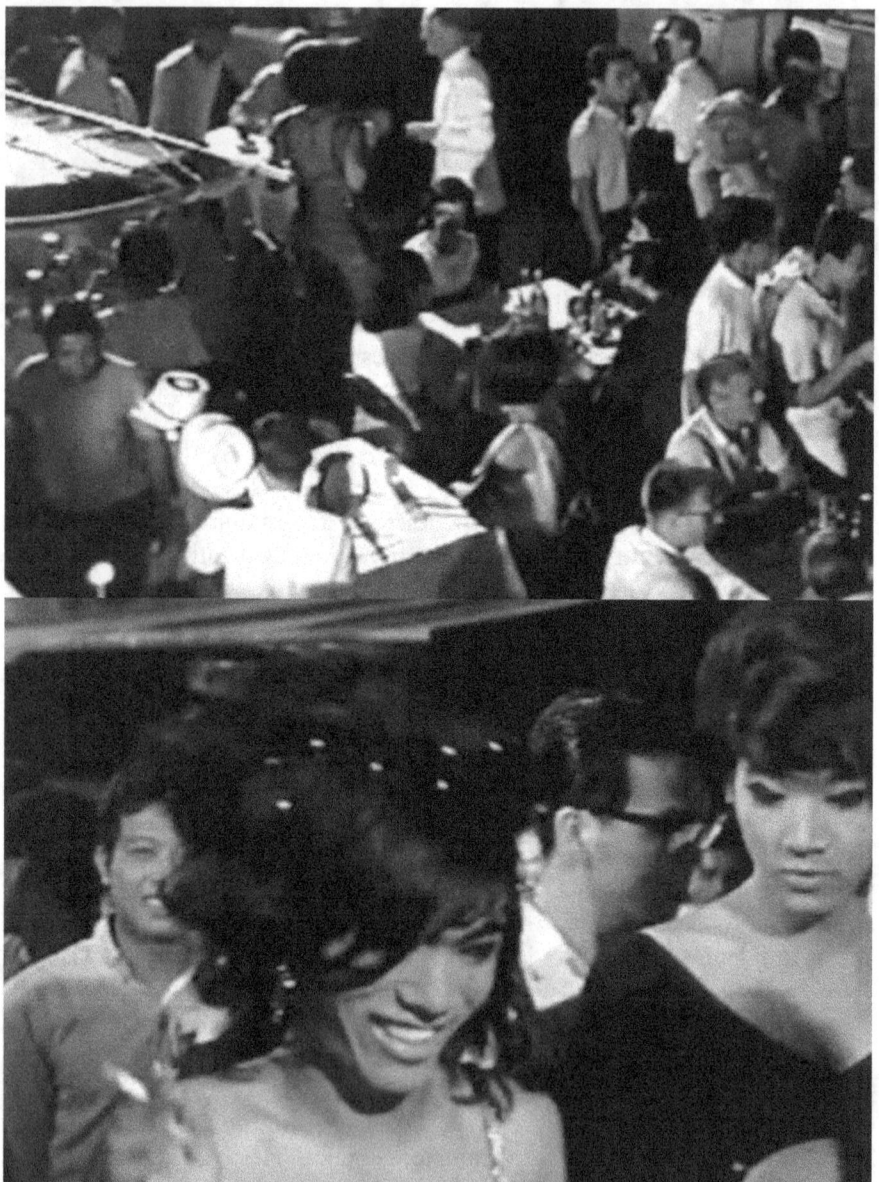

Figure 5.5 Bugis Street in *Pretty Polly*

The most 'stagey' moment in the film is perhaps the nude 'show' in the upstairs bedroom of the brothel. Yet, even here, there is little attempt to sensationalise or eroticise the scene (see Figure 5.7). It begins with Bridgit and Lily setting up for their show. As the theme song of *Goldfinger* begins, Bridgit lies

Figure 5.6 Jack greeting a diner at Bugis Street in *Saint Jack*

on the bed as Lily walks out of the room and back in again, in a translucent kaftan. The dance begins. Despite the theatricality lent by the song, there is a distinct lack of eroticism in this informal performance. It is limited to the rather cramped space between the bed and the window, and we even hear an object clatter to the ground. The camera maintains relatively medium-long shots of the performance, broken by frequent cuts to William, the client and Jack as they look on. These are closer shots that show us their individual reactions – William looks rather amused, the client has his mouth open, while Jack seems rather nonchalant, even bored. Jack even notices the client's wallet on the floor, picks it up and returns it, taking a few seconds off the film's focus on the performance. These cuts prevent the scene from being merely about the performance and integrate it with the narrative development. The reaction shots tell us something of the characters. To William, the dance is one of the many sights he's seen in his first day in Singapore. While he seems to find it interesting, he is not turned on. To Jack, all this is not new, adding to the film's establishment of the extent of his local knowledge and familiarity with the underbelly of Singapore in the first act – this is truly a guy who knows his way around and can get you anything but he is also somewhat tired and cynical about it all. The show is not captured or staged as a polished act to titillate the film's audience, despite the brief glimpse of genitalia. We do not even see it end, as the film follows Jack when he goes downstairs during the performance. The brothel itself is also understated, set in a double-storey house that looks like any other on the street. It is naturally lit and empty, with only a Chinese altar in a corner.

Figure 5.7   Bridgit and Lily's show

The ordinariness of the brothel and the film's casual depiction of Bugis Street and the show cast the so-called underbelly of Singapore as a humdrum world rather than an exotic or erotic one, where picking up transvestites and watching their sex shows are merely mundane and regular occurrences.

Slater argues that *Saint Jack* offers a 'pungent, vivid sense of place. Singapore becomes the first and last major character in the film. *Saint Jack* makes us bear witness to its beauty and its secrets. It has its own journey through the narrative, which is mapped onto several breathtaking moments.'[50] The first is the 360 degree pan opening shot of the old bumboats at the quay and traffic whizzing by the General Post Office, 'patiently waiting for the story to begin' (see Figure 5.8). The second is a 'miraculous vision' of a 'true garden city' in the shot of Singapore at dawn from a hotel window, in which patches of greenery are 'interrupted by the occasional high rise' (see Figure 5.9). The third is the film's final shot of Boat Quay, 'thronging with people and life. A memory of a vanished place. A different city. Jack Flowers walks away and disappears into history'[51] (see Figure 5.10).

These three images mark Singapore's development in the film, corresponding nicely with Jack's own journey in the three acts. The first image recalls those that open many of P. Ramlee's films. This is an old Singapore, that bustling colonial port city marked by the bumboats and the architecture of the General Post Office. Jack is most at ease in this old port city, where he has lived for many years and whose rules he understands. This is how he has thrived as a ship's chandler and pimp. As the film shows us his routine of arriving at the

THE CASE OF *SAINT JACK*

Figure 5.8 Shots in the opening 360-degree pan

Figure 5.9 The 'true garden city'

113

Figure 5.10 The final shot in *Saint Jack*

office, engaging with his grumpy bosses, and taking William and the American client around town in search of entertainment, it is evident that he is an old hand at this. He has done this for a long time, and it shows in his interactions with and reactions to those he meets and what he sees. However, there is also a sense that things are changing with Jack and in Singapore, as evidenced in the menacing presence of the gangsters, repeated warnings he receives about opening his own brothel, and his conversations with William. This is also a Singapore that is shedding its colonial past, as seen in the myriad (British) expatriates who inhabit the Raffles Hotel and the Bandung Club. They are old and clearly past their prime. There are only three left at the plain, drab setting of the Bandung Club, and they are usually drunk and babbling, as if clinging on to some former glory like remnants of a sunset empire. The first act ends with the start of Jack's relationship with Monika and the discovery of William's hotel manager's body in the alley with the distinct sound of piling in the background. Slater argues that this 'dull, metallic thud of pile-drivers . . . became a ceaseless soundtrack' in the film.[52]

The second image captures a Singapore in transition in the 1970s, one that is hurtling headlong into the future as the rural gives way to rapid redevelopment and industrialisation, resulting in a fast-changing landscape. What the film captures is a Singapore in flux, where the old has not yet been completely erased and replaced by the new. This Singapore is a work-in-progress, and this is where Jack consolidates his business and builds his dream establishment with his crew of loyal locals. However, just like the Singapore that is shedding its past, Jack too learns that he cannot do business based on his past. Dunroamin' is destroyed and Jack has to start over with Paradise Gardens and flowers inked over the vulgarities on his arms. Jack, like Singapore, can no longer go back, only forward by doing business with Americans. However, Jack's association with the CIA leads him deeper into moral uncertainty. He is unable to stop the supply of drugs at Paradise Gardens or prevent one of his girls from being beaten by a young GI. As he tails the American senator around Orchard Road at night, the sequence is almost silent, a distinct change from the vibrant sounds of the city and conversations Jack has with people around him. When he slowly approaches the hotel room to take the incriminating pictures, he puts on reading glasses to prepare the camera. Jack is evidently a changed man, no longer young, active or even talkative. Even though he finally takes control of his life and morality once again by throwing the pictures away, Jack is no longer the same.

This corresponds with the nostalgia in the third image for a Singapore that will soon be lost. The Singapore River, crammed with bumboats, will soon be cleaned up. The boats will disappear and the godowns transformed into high-end restaurants and watering holes that will completely transform this waterfront. Indeed, although the film was shot in 1978, it is set in the fictional time frame of 1971. Seven years in a period of rapid development and change is a long time and, as they scouted for locations around the island, the producers were already keenly aware that the Singapore they needed to capture was fast disappearing. As Associate Producer George Morfogen notes, 'it became a race against time for us as we attempted to capture the world of *Saint Jack*.'[53] He also recalls 'having a distinct feeling that places were disappearing at the very moment they were being filmed.'[54] In the film's trailer, Bogdanovich says that 'Singapore is in the progress business, and almost any place we've shot just won't be here in 1980.'[55] Their sense of foreboding is prophetic, as the Singapore of *Saint Jack* does eventually disappear and 'many of the addresses where the crew shot simply don't exist anymore.'[56] Slater's book, *Kind Hot*, lists a number of these in great detail, including the York Hotel, the location of the film's Bandung Club, which has moved to a new location following demolition of the original hotel and the building of a shopping mall on the site. The old bungalow used for Dunroamin' has also been destroyed and a condominium built in its place. Bugis Street has been thoroughly cleaned up and replaced by a massive shopping mall and an underground station. As Slater opines, 'the street may still exist but the place has long since vanished.'[57] Along with the physical world, the vibe and character of *Saint Jack*'s Singapore would also change. The transsexuals and transvestites, of course, have left Bugis Street. Mobile food carts were banned in 1982 and many of the businesses were relocated to specially designated hawker centres. Chinatown has also been drastically altered. Much of it has been demolished and replaced by commercial and residential complexes. Old trades have disappeared, and what little that remains of the old Chinatown has been dressed up for tourists, selling all kinds of kitsch and souvenirs. Slater notes that the city had changed so significantly that when the BBC came to Singapore to film a drama about the Second World War in the early 1980s, key settings could no longer be found and had to be re-created in the UK. Singapore, it seems, 'could no longer convincingly play itself'.[58] Indeed, by the 1980s, Singapore was 'no longer the glamorous, exotic port-city, where cleanliness and efficiency were pleasant side effects of firm state control. Now, clean streets and effective infrastructure were all that was left,'[59] causing William Gibson to describe it as 'Disneyland with the death penalty'.[60] As such, by capturing locations before redevelopment, *Saint Jack* is said to have created nostalgia for an 'old' Singapore.

However, while this may be so, there is also a strong sense that this is a film that could not have occurred anywhere else. The places, and people who inhabit those spaces, do not merely function as background for the narrative but contextualise it and constitute a setting that informs characterisation and supports the narrative. Its Singapore, like Jack, is unique and contradictory, whose complex relationship with the foreign rests somewhere between welcoming and wariness. Here, William and Schuman are the real outsiders, who either have superficial encounters with the country and no real connection to the local, like so many tourists, or exploit it for their own agendas. Jack, on the other hand, inhabits the space like a local. He is comfortable in this setting, easily assuming the role of the middleman who negotiates between the foreign and the local, yet never quite fully becoming either and blurring the boundary between inside and outside positions.

The film similarly inhabits the same position as an essentially foreign film that tried to capture the people and places as naturally as possible to give a sense of authenticity to its Singapore. However, as previously mentioned, authenticity is subject to questions of address –authentic to whom? To the Singapore authorities, the film is considered exploitative, a foreign and inauthentic portrayal of Singapore. However, to its producers, this is the Singapore that they had known. As such it can be argued that this Singapore is not only consistent with a narrative restricted to Jack's perspective and experience, but also authentic to its producers' experience of Singapore. The disparity with which one can regard *Saint Jack*'s authenticity raises an important point. Authenticity is too subjective to be a criterion for considering national cinema. Examinations of national cinema too often depend on authenticity, which privileges views from the inside. If we are to address national cinema in the context of a globalised world and permeable boundaries, where nations are understood as plural, then the valuation of what constitutes national cinema must change as well. Here, there is a difference between representation and engaging the national. As we have seen, Singapore can and has been performed in myriad ways, from the exotic tropical isle to the tourist destination. Yet none of these films has engaged with Singapore with the kind of intimacy that *Saint Jack* has. There is a primacy to its performance of Singapore that makes Singapore not merely a location but a character in the film, one that not only affects the narrative but also develops as the film progresses. This is not a film that could have been made anywhere else. *Saint Jack* is as much about Jack as it is also about a Singapore that was changing and disappearing. It has managed to capture a sense of localness that none of the BAS films ever achieved. So, if the post-studio era of the 1970s performs a Singapore that is foreign or absent, then *Saint Jack* offers us (an)other Singapore, one performed from an outsider's perspective with extensive local knowledge and intimacy, much like the character of Jack Flowers himself.

Notes

1. Slater, 48.
2. Ibid., 50.
3. W. Somerset Maugham, *The Letter*, 117.
4. Slater, 50.
5. Ben Slater, 'Coming of Age'.
6. Slater, *Kinda Hot*, 51.
7. Ibid.
8. Ibid.
9. Slater, 'Coming of Age'.
10. Slater, *Kinda Hot*, 52.
11. Slater, 'Coming of Age'.
12. Ibid.
13. Ibid.
14. Ibid.
15. Ibid.
16. Philip Cheah, quoted in Slater, *Kinda Hot*, reviewers' quotes, i.
17. Quoted in ibid., 169.
18. Quoted in ibid.
19. Quoted in ibid., 174.
20. Quoted in ibid., 175.
21. Edgar Koh, 'Bogdanovich'.
22. Ibid.
23. 'Jack in a Box'.
24. Tied with Georgiy Daneliya's *Autumn Marathon*.
25. Anthony Gunaratne, 'Urban', 171.
26. Uhde and Uhde, 30.
27. Uhde, 53.
28. Ibid.
29. Millet, 77.
30. Ibid.
31. Philip Cheah, 'Singapore', 384.
32. Slater, *Kinda Hot*, reviewers' quotes, i.
33. Ben Slater, 'Saint Jack'.
34. Slater, *Kinda Hot*, 68.

35. Ibid., 99.
36. Ibid., 46.
37. *Peranakans* are Straits-born Chinese whose lineage can be traced back to the fifteenth century, when Chinese migrants settled in Malaya and Singapore and married local (Malay) women. The result is a hybrid of Chinese and Malay cultures apparent in its language, cuisine and dress.
38. *Amah* is a Cantonese term meaning wet nurse, nanny or surrogate mother. It originally referred to the Cantonese women who came via Hong Kong to work as domestic maids in Singapore. However, the term has been expanded to refer to domestic helpers in general.
39. Slater, *Kinda Hot*, 82.
40. Ibid.
41. Ibid., 85.
42. Ibid., 129.
43. Ibid., 182.
44. Ibid., 146.
45. Ibid., 102.
46. Quoted in ibid., 103.
47. Ibid.
48. Ibid., 103–4.
49. Ibid., 142.
50. Ibid., 184.
51. Ibid.
52. Ibid., 190.
53. Ibid., 94.
54. Ibid., 190.
55. Ibid.
56. Ibid.
57. Ibid., 191.
58. Ibid., 194.
59. Ibid.
60. Ibid.

6. ONE PEOPLE, ONE NATION, ONE SINGAPORE

NATIONAL IDENTITY

As a result of the state's focus on rapid industrialisation and urbanisation, Singapore was, by the 1980s, considered by many to be an economic miracle that enjoyed massive growth and stability. By then, it was clear that Singapore had not only survived expulsion from Malaysia but thrived. Economic success created a 'substantial injection of self-definition and national pride'[1] in Singapore. However, there remained the continued perceived threat of 'Westernisation' and the erosion of Asian values, the danger that Singapore was turning into a 'pseudo-Western society' that emphasised individualism and personal freedom, indulged in sexual pleasures and lacked a sense of responsibility to family and society.[2] Furthermore, in this climate of prosperity and rising affluence, the rhetoric of survival that was used to mobilise and unite the people was no longer sufficient or compelling on its own. New imperatives were needed to mould a singular national identity.[3] This 'motivational entropy' led to a series of state-driven policies to 'inject the requisite values into its citizens'[4] and reassert the PAP's political legitimacy by proclaiming 'its version of the nation and to rally Singapore behind it.'[5] The state turned towards 'Asia' for those requisite values to serve as cultural ballast, beginning with the bilingual education policy requiring students to acquire a Second Language (or Mother Tongue) based on their racial identity. In 1981, the existing civics curriculum was replaced by a moral education programme aimed at producing 'good, useful and loyal citizens through inculcation of the desired moral values and social attitudes'.⁶ An English-language programme, *Being and Becoming*, was launched in primary schools along with a Chinese-language syllabus known as *Hao Gong Ming* (*Good Citizen*). Religious Knowledge was introduced in secondary schools in 1982, and became a compulsory subject for Secondary Three and Four students in 1984. Implementation emphasised 'knowledge', not religious instruction, and the options included Bible knowledge, Buddhist and Hindu studies, Islamic religious knowledge and, later, Confucian values. This subject was replaced in 1989 by another civics programme, and the PAP government under the new leadership of Prime Minister Goh Chok Tong configured a set of 'Shared Values' that would become Singapore's National Ideology to counter that ever-present evil of Westernisation and its attendant individualistic ethos. This Ideology 'would identify the *personal* set of values needed to bring about the ideals represented by the five stars on the national flag – namely, democracy, equality, peace, progress and justice – and enshrined in the National Pledge'.⁷ These Values are: 1) nation before community and society above self; 2) family as the basic unit of society; 3) regard and community support for the individual; 4) consensus instead of contention; and 5) racial and religious harmony.⁸ Describing this set of Values as 'a refurbished global systems model',⁹ Hill and Lian argue that they do not depart from the pragmatism of the immediate post-independence era. The state's 'forays into the non-material – in this case, ideological – aspects of nation building, have ultimately been grounded in the pragmatism of the PAP government'.[10]

Yet none of these forays into crafting a national ideology or identity for Singapore has really stuck. Instead, the prevailing impression or identification of Singapore is that it is a successful, affluent nation that is as efficient and clean as it is green. 'Success' has become so ingrained and synonymous with the idea of Singapore that Terence Chong notes the many publications examining the role of state policy in transforming the island from uncertain future to economic miracle, most with 'success' in their titles. These, he argues, support 'the implicit suggestion that success is a faithful companion of nation-building' and central to the Singapore Story, which 'is often narrated as a success story'.[11] According to Henri Ghesquiere, Singapore has become

> a brand name that exudes reliability, excellence and integrity. Singapore and its leaders command respect around the world. The purchasing power of its GDP per person (at around US$50,000) now exceeds that of the United States. Once among the impoverished, powerless and ignored ex-colonies labeled the Third World, Singapore beyond a doubt has become a first-rank prosperous nation.[12]

In his foreword to Lee Kuan Yew's second memoir, published in 2000, Henry Kissinger writes that Singapore had achieved Lee's vision 'of a state that would not simply survive but prevail by excelling. Superior intelligence, discipline and ingenuity would substitute for [Singapore's lack of] resources'.[13] Attributing Singapore's accomplishments to Lee's vision validates the political legitimacy of the PAP government and identifies this vision of a successful Singapore as the state's 'version of the nation'.[14] This is the version that the state rallies Singaporeans to get behind, the reiteration of which continues to assert the party's hegemony. Of particular interest in this chapter is not how such development came to be but rather to uncover the performativity of it, the various acts and gestures articulated and performed by the state to craft a national identity for Singapore as a successful, accomplished and affluent nation.

The Singapore Story of Success

The Singapore Story begins with Raffles' arrival in 1819 and creates a continuous link between the thriving colonial port and the economic miracle of post-independent Singapore, 'making the past seem to lead towards a single correct model for the present, and more ominously, for the future'.[15] However, although the Story officially appeared in 1997, the tendency to invoke that link can be traced back to the early, formative years following independence. For example, in 1967, Lee Kuan Yew mentions

> ... our long association with the British over 150 years which created a community of two million people with one of the highest standards of living anywhere along the equatorial belt, a metropolis of which there is no equal in the equatorial region, born out of British administration, and enterprise, combined with Chinese, Indian and Indonesian industries, skill and drive ...[16]

On 22 March 1968, in his speech inaugurating a series of ministerial broadcasts called 'The Crucial Years', Lee also stated:

> People doubted whether we could survive – two million people, all migrants, or descendants of migrants. The analyses and assessments by political scientists, economists, the experts in newspapers, magazines and scholarly journals – most of them predicted that we would collapse. No natural resources, no viability, no future. Yet, 2½ years later, these critics agree that we have succeeded. They were confounded, because they did not give adequate weight to one vital factor: the human drive, that verve in a determined and a resourceful people who know the terrible consequences of failure.
> ... Singapore is unique. A people of migrant stock have come into their own inheritance. Our forefathers, their labour, sweat, thrift, industry,

> helped to build what we now possess. True, 80% of our citizens are of Chinese origin, and the others of Malay, Indian, Ceylonese stock, not forgetting our Eurasians and European citizens. But we are not a Chinese, nor a Malay, nor an Indian society. Here a distinct community has struck roots.
>
> That saga began on February 19, 1819, when Stamford Raffles came to find a fishing village of 120 Malays and 30 Chinese. He opened Singapore to free competition of all races for the trade and inter-course of the region. Three years later, the population had grown to five thousand, four thousand Chinese and one thousand Indians, Arabs and others.
>
> Our forebears travelled in sailing ships across the Indian Ocean and the South China Sea in search of fortune. They ventured their lives for the pot of gold at the end of the rainbow. They have left two million of us with a great city and a great adventure in nation-building.
>
> ... This is the final chapter in the making of a nation. From a protected trading centre of a vast empire, we must become a self-reliant industrialised nation state responsible for our own security.
>
> ... There was a prosperous and thriving Singapore before the British built their naval and air bases. There will be a throbbing and humming industrial, commercial and communications centre long after the British bases have gone. But for the first time, we must fight for ourselves. This is the acid test. Have we the will to be a nation? Have we the grit?[17]

'That saga' is essentially what would become the Singapore Story, and the speeches not only connect independent Singapore with its colonial past but also make apparent the rhetoric of success embedded in the state's discourse of survival during those crucial years. The message is simple and clear: to survive, Singapore has to succeed. Anxiety for Singapore's future made nation-building the prime objective at that time, and much of the 1970s and '80s was devoted to becoming, as the 1988 National Productivity Campaign slogan declared, 'the Best [it] Can Be'.[18] The fear of failure was the impetus to first project Singapore as a nation that *could* be successful to one that *is*. So, the story of Singapore's survival is essentially the story of Singapore's success. At its crux is the 'great adventure in nation-building', which began at that 'moment of anguish' when Singapore was cast out of Malaysia. This is 'a story of a little island cut from its hinterland and saddled with the challenges of mass housing, high unemployment and an uncertain future'.[19] It tells of 'the Herculean effort to overcome all the odds, and finally the achievement of success. Through hard work, pragmatic policies and sound leadership, the island made the transformation from an "absurd proposition" to a global city.'[20]

According to Chong, the story of Singapore's success is told in two different and often concurrent ways. First is the narrative of material success. This is a tale of rapid transition from colonial port to global financial centre that pays homage to the coherent industrialization and urbanisation processes that have swept across the island over four decades. Housing slums, unsanitary sewerage systems, pig farms and small orchards have been replaced by throbbing satellite towns complete with spanking new plastic malls while the city centre filled with modern skyscrapers to rival those of any global city.[21]

So websites like *Visit Singapore* run by the Singapore Tourism Board tell us that Singapore's

compact size belies its economic growth. In just 150 years, Singapore has grown into a thriving centre of commerce and industry. . . . Singapore is the busiest port in the world . . . [And o]ne of the world's major oil refining and distribution centres . . . It has also become one of the most important financial centres of Asia . . . Singapore's strategic location, excellent facilities, fascinating cultural contrasts and tourist attractions contribute to its success as a leading destination for both business and pleasure.[22]

The *Singapore Education* website, run by the Ministry of Education, believes that Singapore is an ideal 'Global Schoolhouse' because it is

a reputable financial centre, a key regional trading centre, the world's busiest port, and a top location for investment. Often cited as a model for transparency, efficiency and political stability, Singapore has earned recognition from around the world.
. . . The Swiss-based World Economic Forum (WEF) also rated Singapore as the most competitive economy possessing great innovative ability and a solid macro economy . . .[23]

Adding to its argument, the website further states that Singapore's airport 'has for many consecutive years been nominated as the best airport in the world'.[24] It also cites a March 2002 article in *The Economist* which reported that 'Singapore's quality of life [has] surpassed that of London or New York,' making it 'A Multicultural Nation with a High Quality of Life [sic].'[25]

Facts, figures, statistics and numbers are central to the telling of this story, including growth in GDP per capita, home-ownership rates, the size of the country's reserves, and the number of billionaires. They add veracity to the tale that not only makes the story compelling, but 'because it is said that you cannot argue with numbers, their very evocation is often deemed a sufficient, if not convenient, rebuttal to detractors of the city-state.'[26] This sentiment is evident in Kishore Mahbubani's[27] article in *The Huffington Post* titled 'Why Singapore Is the World's Most Successful Society', which begins by asking, 'Is Singapore the most successful society since human history began? Or, to put it differently, did Singapore improve the living standards of its people faster and more comprehensively than any other society?' According to Mahbubani, 'The only way to answer these questions is with empirical data.' So, to make his case, he cites Singapore's growth in GDP per capita from 1965 to 2014, compares this with those of the United States, Philippines and Zimbabwe, and concludes that 'Singapore's per capita income has shot from $500 to $55,000 today, the largest increase any newly independent nation has enjoyed. This spectacular economic success story of Singapore is clearly amazing.' The article also cites UNICEF's James Grant, who 'told me that Singapore's success in another area was even more spectacular. We had reduced our infant mortality faster than any other society, going down from 35 per 1,000 live births in 1965 to 10.90 in 1985.' Other figures follow:

> The OECD ranked 15-year-old Singaporean children number one in the world in a recent global ranking of 'Universal Basic Skills' in mathematics and science. Singapore students also topped the OECD PISA problem solving test in 2012. There are many other areas where Singapore's social standards top the charts.
>
> From the Singapore with slums that I grew up in, we now have the highest home ownership of any country in the world, with 90 percent of residents living in homes they own. Even amongst households in the lowest 20 percent of incomes, over 80 percent own their own homes. Rapidly rising salaries and strong compulsory saving schemes, through the Central Provident Fund, led to this incredibly high home ownership.[28]

Statistics and numbers are reinforced with Singapore's ranking in various areas. Since such rankings are conducted by international organisations and bodies, citing them gives the impression that Singapore's place in these studies is bestowed by others and, therefore, presumably objective. Here, Singapore basks in the reflected reputation and credibility of such studies and organisations. On its webpage titled 'Why Invest in Singapore', the Economic Development Board even has a special section on 'Rankings' as one of the factors that 'makes investing in Singapore the best move into Asian markets'. In terms of economic performance, Singapore is the 'City with one of the best investment potential [sic]. Singapore is consistently ranked as one of the top investment destinations in the world – no. 1 for 18 consecutive years, and no. 2 in 2016.' It is also 'The world's easiest place to do business. The ease of setting up a company in Singapore is a clear advantage when it comes to choosing the best place to do business'; 'Top 2 most competitive city in the world.

Singapore leads the pack among the rest of the global economies when it comes to maintaining its competitive edge.' It has the 'Best business environment in Asia Pacific and the world' and ranks as 'Best global innovation in Asia Pacific and the world. The best-performing Asian country ahead of Hong Kong, Korea and Japan, Singapore excels in the pillars of institutions, human capital and research, infrastructure and business sophistication.' In terms of government, Singapore is 'Top 6 in the world for least corruption in the economy. The Singapore government practises an open and transparent approach when it comes to all business matters' and is the 'Most transparent country in the world. Government policies in Singapore are clear and transparent when it comes to business.' Singapore is 'Top 10 in Asia for most motivated workforce. The mind-set of Singaporean talent is generally positive and makes for a productive working environment.' It is also 'Top 10 in Asia for best skilled labour. Singapore's focus on a knowledge-based economy has led to an influx and growth of skilled labour from around the region and within the city itself,' and 'Top 3 in the world for best labour/employer relations in Asia. The relationship between employee and employer in the average Singapore workplace is the best in the region.' Singapore is also 'Top 2 in Asia for best quality of life. Singapore has been ranked the 2nd [sic: best] place to live, work and play as compared to its neighbouring countries.'[29]

According to Chong, the Singapore success story is also simultaneously told as ideological success. This is a narrative of how myriad migrant ethnicities, with their diverse histories, cultures and religions,

> have been streamlined into broader ethnic categories [Chinese, Malay, Indian and Others] and packaged as one giant construct called 'Singaporeans'. And as 'Singaporeans', we are said to have embraced the ideologies of multiculturalism [including multiracialism, multilingualism and multireligiosity] and meritocracy as sacred principles, without which there would be no success story to speak of.[30]

Again, marking these twin principles as sacred is not a recent tendency, but one that has been reiterated since Singapore's independence, such as in Lee Kuan Yew's 1969 National Day broadcast:

> If we are to overcome our problems we must re-affirm our determination not to allow any citizen to be persecuted because of his race, religion, language, or culture. Four great civilisations have met in confluence here. The British, Malay, Indian and Chinese came and they built a metropolis out of a fishing village near the equator. Eventually, perhaps after several generations, a separate distinct Singapore identity will emerge in which the differences of race, culture and religion will be more than made

up for by similarities in values, attitudes, and a feeling of belonging to one whole.[31]

Tied to multiculturalism is meritocracy, 'a core principle of governance' that is premised on 'equalising opportunities not outcomes and allocating rewards on the basis of an individual's merit, abilities, and achievement'.[32] In his speech at the Raffles Homecoming 2013 Gryphon Award Dinner, Goh Chok Tong, former Prime Minister and now Emeritus Senior Minister of Singapore, summed up the practice of meritocracy in Singapore:

> At its core, meritocracy is a value system by which advancement in society is based on an individual's ability, performance and achievement, and not on the basis of connections, wealth or family background. For Singapore in particular, a meritocratic system, while not perfect, is the best means to maximise the potential and harness the talents of our people to society's advantage.[33]

The idea is to provide a level playing field on which everyone receives an equal opportunity to succeed, regardless of race, language and religion, so that the best will rise to the top in education, business and public administration. Ostensibly, this is a democratic and pragmatic approach to governance for a country that is multiracially constituted and to prevent racial discord that could undermine national stability. Multiracialism and meritocracy have become key tenets to live by in Singapore, influencing state policy, public administration and society at large, reinforced by those institutions and discourses that 'tend toward the regulation or normalization of their subjects.'[34]

A prime example is the national pledge and the ritual act of reciting it: We, the citizens of Singapore, pledge ourselves as one united people, regardless of race, language or religion, to build a democratic society based on justice and equality so as to achieve happiness, prosperity and progress for our nation. According to the National Heritage Board, the late Mr S. Rajaratnam, formerly Minister of Culture and Foreign Affairs, 'believed that language, race and religion were potentially divisive factors and used the pledge to emphasize that these differences could be overcome if Singaporeans were united in their commitment to the country'.[35] The recitation of this pledge was formalised by the practice of standing at attention and facing the National Flag with the right hand raised above the shoulders. This was changed in 1988 to the current practice of placing the right clenched fist over the heart while standing and facing the flag. The pledge is 'an integral part of Singaporean life and is recited by students during [daily] flag-raising and flag-lowering ceremonies as well as on important occasions such as the National Day Parade and National Day Observance Ceremonies'.[36] Each recitation is therefore a ritual commitment to Singapore's multicultural and meritocratic ideology, and quest for success.

The national anthem, 'Majulah Singapura' (Onward Singapore), 'is a musical expression of Singapore's identity as a nation' and usually accompanies the recitation of the pledge, and/or is sung at flag-raising and flag-lowering ceremonies in schools as well as 'occasions of national celebration or national significance'.[37] It is a Malay song, sung by a resident population that is 74.1 per cent Chinese, of which only 0.2 per cent speak Malay at home.[38] In fact, to date only 12.2 per cent of the total resident population speaks Malay at home, which means that to most Singaporeans, regardless of race, language or religion, singing the national anthem is essentially an act in a foreign language. The pledge and the national anthem are performative acts in the form of statements. Based on Butler's description, such statements,

> in the uttering, also perform a certain action and exercise a binding power. Implicated in a network of authorization and punishment, performatives tend to include ... statements which not only perform an action, but confer a binding power on the action performed. If the power of discourse to produce that which it names is linked with the question of performativity, then the performative is one domain in which power acts *as* discourse.[39]

As such, reciting the national pledge and singing the national anthem are acts that reinforce the consciousness of multiculturalism and bind citizens to its significance in Singapore on a daily basis. In addition, Malay is also the language of command in the Singapore Armed Forces. As national service is compulsory, all Singaporean males of eighteen years and above perform to or in this language regardless of whether they actually speak it. Uniformed groups in schools that practise marching drills also use the same commands in Malay. These include the National Cadet Corps, National Police Cadet Corps and the Boys' and Girls' Brigades. So, the use of Malay is not only symbolic but also serves a larger, performative function in constituting the multicultural identity of Singapore that is reiterated on a regular, if not daily, basis. These are, to borrow Butler's terms, 'stylized repetition[s] of acts'[40] that constitute the performance of Singapore as multicultural and democratic.

Such performances are reinforced by the state's policies concerning language, housing and electoral representation that institutionalise and normalise multiculturalism in Singapore. English, Malay, Mandarin and Tamil are recognised as the official languages of Singapore. Malay remains the national language and English continues to be the country's lingua franca. While English is the language of instruction in schools, the other languages are recognised as Mother Tongues and studied as second languages under the state's compulsory, bilingual education policy. Public housing is apportioned based on the ethnic ratio of the population to prevent ghettoisation and ensure a healthy multicultural mix in each estate. Electoral divisions in Singapore comprise Single Member Constituencies (SMCs) and Group Representation Constituencies (GRCs). These are 'demarcated by the Prime Minister by law for the purposes of parliamentary elections and presidential elections'.[41] While an SMC only has one Member of Parliament (MP), a GRC is 'a larger electoral division, both in terms of population as well as physical area' and represented by a group of MPs, at least one of which 'must belong to a minority racial community, either the Malay community or the Indian and other minority communities'.[42] The success of these ideological principles was acknowledged as recently as 21 August 2016, in current Prime Minister Lee Hsien Loong's National Day Rally speech:

> Over 50 years, we have made a lot of progress becoming one people, regardless of race, language and religion . . . Most people believe that race does not influence success; that the interests of one's own race should not come before the interests of other races . . . We did not pretend that race and religion doesn't matter and we worked against the natural flow to expand our common space.
>
> We use English as our common working language. We mixed all races together in HDB estates, so that there are no enclaves or ghettos. We implemented the Ethnic Integration Policy to prevent HDB estates from becoming re-segregated and recite the pledge in schools every day. We also came down hard on chauvinists who try to play up racial sentiments.[43]

However, multiculturalism and meritocracy are not valorised as ideal principles for their own sakes, but rather to ensure social stability as a necessary condition for economic success, which is how the PAP government defines Singapore's survival. As such, when Singaporeans recite the national pledge they vocalise their commitment to 'pledge [themselves] as one united people, regardless of race, language or religion', and to 'build a democratic society based on justice and equality' not merely for the sake of multiculturalism and democracy but in order 'to achieve happiness, prosperity and progress for our nation'. So, the Singapore Story's tale of ideological success is not about multiculturalism and meritocracy per se, but how these twin values are foundations of Singapore's material success. In the same way, Singapore's continued material success also affirms the government's assertion of multiculturalism and meritocracy as core principles on which to build a nation. As previously noted, this same ideology was the basis of the PAP government's syncretised ideal of a Malayan Malaysia versus the UMNO vision of a Malay-centred one. As such, in commemorating its National Day every year on 9 August, Singapore also celebrates how far it has come since that fundamental difference in ideology led to that 'moment of anguish' and the birth of the nation on that same day in 1965.

National Day Parade and Songs

Each year, National Day celebrations culminate in the National Day Parade (NDP), which Lily Kong and Brenda Yeoh posit as 'evidence of the state's efforts at inventing ritual and creating landscape spectacle in order to build up national identity'.[44] Along with other institutionalised rituals involving the pledge, anthem and flag, these parades construct the 'consciousness of being "one people"',[45] and are used by the state 'to persuade Singaporeans of the naturalness of its ideologies'.[46] The scale and spectacle of the NDP also makes it the most visible, state-driven performance of Singapore as success story. This is exactly how the Singapore Tourism Board explains the parade to visitors:

> The Singapore story is well known – how it achieved independence in 1965 amid severe doubt it could survive at all with its tiny size and severe lack of natural resources.
>
> Yet the island succeeded against the odds, deftly navigating its way through stormy waters of domestic turmoil, regional strife and international politics.
>
> It made use of every single advantage it had, emerging on the world stage as a major commercial hub, financial centre and global player – in short, the little country that could.
>
> And in this way, the national narrative has been shaped over the years, a narrative that is retold in varying ways every year during the National Day Parade.[47]

The NDP is organised by the Singapore Armed Forces and begins with a ceremonial parade that involves a flag-raising ceremony, singing the National Anthem, recitation of the National Pledge, the President's inspection of the honour guard, a twenty-one-gun salute and march-past with various contingents of military units from the army, navy and airforce, police, youth, uniformed and sports groups, trade unions as well as schools. It is 'an occasion to show Singaporeans and the world that although the island was small and the population inconsiderable, it had every intention to defend itself against external threats,'[48] and has been a performance of military might since the first National Day celebration in 1966. While modest at first, the parade grew from marching contingents to include a 'demonstration of machinery', with mobile columns of military vehicles such as jeeps, tanks, armoured vehicles and even anti-aircraft missiles, as well as fly-pasts of increasingly advanced military aircraft acquired by the Singapore Air Force.[49] The ceremonial portion of the parade is followed by a celebratory show that includes mass ground performances as well as fireworks and laser displays that have grown more and more spectacular and elaborate over the years.

The 1986 NDP, Singapore's 'coming out party', marked the watershed moment of the nation's twenty-first birthday, 'when by unspoken consensus, Singaporeans left that episode [separation from Malaysia] of their history behind for the last time.'[50] Correspondingly, this was to be 'a Parade with a difference'.[51] Each year, the NDP would have an overarching theme or slogan that embodied the celebrations. For 1986, it was 'Together . . . Excellence for Singapore', and when he launched the theme, then First Deputy Prime Minister Goh Chok Tong said:

> Some Singaporeans may think that this theme is out of touch with today's economic realities. It is not so. The theme of excellence is as relevant today as it is when times are good. Indeed, the biggest threat to Singapore today is for Singaporeans to allow themselves to be overwhelmed by current difficulties and forget about the fundamental values that have brought us here. One of these fundamental pillars is our philosophy of going for excellence in whatever we do . . . Excellence is also the very basis of our prosperity.[52]

The 'current difficulties' he mentioned was the economic recession that hit Singapore's economy very hard, and the theme of togetherness was meant to rally the people and instil a sense of shared belonging to the nation as well as a shared responsibility for its success and future. According to Yeoh and Kong, 'the earlier ideology of survival in its original form was no longer convincing as a means of mobilizing Singaporeans. Instead, the notion of "excellence" was drawn in: to continue surviving, Singapore must excel.'[53] Much state rhetoric in the 1980s emphasised 'excellence', which entails 'unity, commitment to Singapore, productivity, hard work and teamwork'. As Kong notes, the message is simply that 'if Singaporeans can ensure that they have these qualities and mindsets, excellence can be achieved for the country and Singapore may stay ahead of other competitors, if not serve as their role model.'[54] To achieve this, the 1986 parade emphasised the participation of 'ordinary people' and the spectators. According to the *Straits Times*, it would have 'the biggest spectator participation ever'.[55] Such emphasis on spectator involvement was unprecedented in what would be an NDP of many firsts.

This was the first time that a mass recitation of the national pledge was introduced, 'to reflect the stronger involvement of the people'. So, 'a select group of [21] "ordinary Singaporeans" of all ages and from all walks of life, ranging from bus driver to businessman, led a mass dedication ceremony involving everyone present to affirm their allegiance to the "nation".'[56] The ceremonial portion of the NDP was reduced to make way for greater emphasis on the celebratory show. The involvement of Singapore's defence force here would not be martial in tone but geared towards entertainment, 'done with more sophistication, involving skill and dexterity rather than the sheer power of equipment'.[57] There would be, as the *Business Times* promised, 'less parading, more entertainment and more audience participation' at the celebrations.[58] In the years before the NDP was broadcast live on television, contingents and other aspects of the main pageantry would march from the parade grounds through selected streets and neighbourhoods in Singapore, which 'multiplied the effects of spectacle by invading the spaces of everyday life and transforming ordinary streets into theatres of pomp', and enabled this national 'spectacle to move beyond the locus of the ceremonial landscape to the habitations of the people'.[59] In 1986, these route marches were removed 'to enable parade celebrations to be focused entirely on-site at the stadium'.[60] To set the mood, the hour before the ceremonial parade was given to 'audience-loosening' exercises and a performance by local rock band, Tokyo Square. The tone was clear enough. This NDP was not only going to be a party, it was going to be a Singaporean one. So instead of using the standard, foreign tunes for the march-past, locally composed ones were used instead.[61]

The 1986 NDP programme also had as many as nine mass displays, 'the biggest number ever',[62] all designed and named to reflect the NDP theme. They were, in sequential order: 1) 'Pressing On',[63] a mass band-and-flag display by nine hundred students; 2) 'Towards Excellence', a choreographed dance with eight hundred participants forming icons that emphasised 'teamwork and cooperation, ... essential attributes for productivity',[64] accompanied by productivity campaign songs: 'Good, Better, Best' and 'The Best that We Can Be'; 3) 'Unity in Rhythm', a drum performance by 'various ethnic groups making up five circles. Each circle will in turn exhibit its style of drumming and dance movements' before culminating in 'all five groups playing to a common rhythm';[65] 4) 'Spot On', a precision drill display performed by the Singapore Armed Forces Provost Unit who 'tossed their bayonet-tipped rifles as easily as pens, flirting and charming the crowd with their practiced nonchalance'.[66] According to the souvenir programme, this item emphasised 'skill, precision and alertness', 'qualities for a nation of excellence'.[67] Since then, these displays of dexterity and skill as evidence of military excellence have become more and more spectacular;[68] 5) 'From Each His Best', a mass flashcard display of various images by 1,200 participants; 6) 'Fit for Life', a display of rhythmic exercises performed by the Singapore Sports Council; 7) 'Pride', 'a dance display centering on the [Singapore Armed Forces'] productivity slogan Productivity Through Daily Effort. Groups of dancers will initially move aimlessly on the field. But when PRIDE [sic] is introduced, they engage in productive work. They will dance to the song We Serve with Pride';[69] 8) 'A Better

Tomorrow', a song-and-dance number performed by well-known local singers and an array of dancers, and, 9) 'Together Singapore', a 'three-stage finale'[70] involving torchlights, lasers and finally the fireworks, 'pounding, reverberating and drenching the senses with their fire, leaving everyone gasping for more'.[71] Then everyone sang the National Day songs, 'Stand Up for Singapore' and 'Count on Me Singapore'.

Almost every year, a new National Day song is launched to mark the occasion. These were commissioned in the 1980s due to the perceived lack of community singing and local songs 'which everybody knew and could join in'.[72] What was a weakness soon became an opportunity to use songs and group singing to foster solidarity and inculcate a sense of belonging. In 1980, 'a quiet campaign', dubbed Operation Singalong, was launched to promote 'national folk songs' and 'popularise singing'.[73] Then Senior Minister of State and chair of the National Folk Songs Committee, Lee Khoon Choy, viewed this campaign as not only 'one way of building a nation, and it is a very necessary way', but also 'to project a better image of Singapore at international functions' as 'very often, Singapore delegates abroad are hard put to present a song.' According to Lee, during such events,

> when it comes Singapore's turn – there's no song. It is a disgrace to Singapore's cultural prestige and image. They say Singaporeans cannot sing – Singaporeans only know how to make money. They don't care for culture, they're only materialistic. And that's bad![74]

However, the difficulty in finding such songs soon led to the commissioning of 'songs with local themes'.[75] The first of these was 'Stand Up for Singapore' in 1984 for the National Day celebration of twenty-five years of self-government. The lyrics of the song exhorted Singaporeans to 'Do the best you can,' 'Recognise you can play your part/Let it come right from your heart' and 'Be prepared to give a little more' because 'Singapore [is] our home and nation,' so 'Together with determination/Join in like we've never done before/Stand up, stand up for Singapore.' This was followed by 'Count on Me Singapore' in 1986, which assures Singaporeans that 'We have a vision for tomorrow, just believe' and 'We have a goal for Singapore, we can achieve.' So, 'You and me, we'll do our part/Stand together, heart to heart,' because 'We're going to show the world what Singapore can be' and 'We're going to build a better life, for you and me.' So, 'Count on me Singapore/Count on me to give my best and more.' Both these songs reiterate the same NDP theme of participation and contribution to Singapore's future, and singing them at such an occasion makes participants part of the performance.

There are, to date, more than twenty national songs, including 'One People, One Nation, One Singapore' (1988), 'Home' (1998), 'We Will Get There'

(2002), and 'One United People' (2003). Music videos are regularly broadcast on television, while the songs themselves get a lot of airtime on the radio in the run-up to National Day. The songs are also taught in schools so that they have become 'a large part of the children's learned culture'.[76] As such, Kong argues that 'while these songs do not represent "popular music" as the term is commonly understood, they are "popular" in the way in which they are a part of the everyday lives of many Singaporeans.'[77] In 1988, some of these songs were compiled in a package[78] as part of the state's *Sing Singapore* programme led by the Psychological Defence division of the Ministry of Communications and Information. Kong argues that the lyrics reveal the state's hegemonic intentions and reflect its rhetoric, while their anthem music creates a 'civil religion'. One of the strategies is to glorify past achievements and exalt the government.[79] For example, the 1988 National Day song, 'We are Singapore', begins by invoking Singapore's successful survival after separation:

> There was a time when people said that Singapore won't make it but we did
> There was a time when troubles seemed too much for us to take but we did
> We built a nation
> strong and free
> Reaching out together
> for peace and harmony

As Kong argues, such 'appropriation of the past is designed to remind Singaporeans of how successfully the state has been steered from struggling Third World conditions to newly industrialised status and to arouse a sense of pride and loyalty'.[80] Reinforcing this is a chorus that quotes Lee Kuan Yew's 1966 speech – 'This is my country, this is my flag; this is my president, this is my future. I am going to protect it':[81]

> This is my country
> This is my flag
> This is my future
> This is my life
> This is my family
> These are my friends
>
> We are Singapore Singaporeans

Citing Lee's speech connects those 'crucial years' with the present and exhorts Singaporeans to share the same sentiments as the man whose name, face and voice are emblematic of Singapore's struggle for survival and its success. So, pride in the country extends to its founding prime minister and the party he represents, tying Singapore's success to that of its leaders and the state. These lines cement the connection between past and present, survival and success, state and citizenry, and are repeated three more times during the song, serving as one of two choruses. The second stanza crystallises the sense of a shared responsibility towards and belonging in Singapore in words and phrases like 'our homeland', 'we belong', 'all of us united', 'one people', 'together' and 'our common destiny', concluding with the repetition of the lines and sentiments of Lee's speech:

> Singapore our homeland
> it's here that we belong
> All of us united
> one people marching on
> We've come so far together
> our common destiny
> Singapore forever
> a nation strong and free
>
> This is my country
> This is my flag
> This is my future
> This is my life
> This is my family
> These are my friends
>
> We are Singapore Singaporeans

This is followed by the recitation of the national pledge and then singing it as well before finally chorusing, 'We are Singapore/We will stand together/Hear the lion roar./We are Singapore/We're a nation strong and free forever more.' Embedding the pledge in this way makes it literally part of the performance that equates patriotism and nationalism with economic survival and success. These songs, like the national pledge and national anthem, are prime examples of the performative power of discourse to produce what it names and 'confer a binding power on the action performed'.[82]

The 1986 NDP was also the first time that a laser show featured alongside the traditional fireworks display. The parade was held later than usual at 7 pm so that the spectacle of light and fireworks, the climax of the celebration, could be exhibited to full effect against the backdrop of the night sky. Since then, late-evening NDPs have become the norm. In keeping with the theme of togetherness, spectators were also given torches for the first time so that they could participate in the grand finale 'to signify an expression of their support for the aim to build a nation of excellence'.[83] They were 'exhorted to "play their part" so that the nation could "count on them" in the "pursuit of excellence for Singapore"',[84] a message that was especially important given the economic recession. As the *Straits Times* reported the next day, 'as the darkness thickened, the show reached its crescendo. The lasers cut, stabbed and pierced the sky in all directions. The torches went wild, storm-tossed stars in a blank sky.'[85] These 'passive spectators' had been effectively transformed into active participants in the performance, and the result was 'a spontaneous outpouring in unabashed nationalistic flag-waving'.[86] As one spectator-participant said, 'We all had a part to play. We were not here just to watch the prime minister or the contingents.' Another declared, 'After this, one feels like one would fight and die for Singapore.' A hawker who viewed the spectacle on television observed that 'the whole act would not have succeeded if everyone did not do his [sic] part.'[87] Since then, in National Day celebrations over the years, 'the spectators became the parade,'[88] even as the NDP itself became more spectacular, elaborate and populist.

The NDP's themes, songs and items may change from year to year, but they are all orchestrated to elicit a sense of nationalistic pride and belonging among Singaporeans. The entire performance not only reiterates state rhetoric but also its version of Singapore. The NDP is the state's ultimate performance of its Singapore, 'a show of the nation's progress, achievements and aspirations which every Singaporean anticipates and partakes'.[89] As Kong and Yeoh posit, 'alongside this exhortation to exult in pride for the nation is another exhortation: to strive for excellence for Singapore in order that this pride can be sustained.'[90] This is especially evident when the NDP is held at the Padang,[91] an expanse of green surrounded by the buildings that formed the administrative centre of colonial Singapore. This was the site of the nation's first NDP in 1966, an apt appropriation for celebrating Singapore's independence. By the 1980s, the Padang and the colonial structures remained, but the city around them had changed drastically. This location, 'the locus of colonial power and civic pride',[92] is now surrounded by myriad office skyscrapers, world-class hotels and shopping malls. This juxtaposition of past and present, dependence and independence, gives the site significant symbolic value and visual power. Holding the NDP here serves as a visual statement of not only how far Singapore has come, but also once again connects its current success with its glory days as a thriving colonial port city and the beginning of 'that saga' that is the Singapore Story.

Following Butler's argument on the performativity of identity, the nation likewise 'ought not to be construed as a stable identity or locus of agency from which various acts follow; rather [it] is an identity tenuously constituted in time, instituted in an exterior space through a stylized repetition of acts.'[93] So the websites, speeches, the NDP, National Day songs, the Singapore Story and state rhetoric in general do not articulate a pre-existing national identity but rather construct it. They are gestures that perform *a Singapore* – the state's 'version of the nation'. Each site or citation is an act that, as the examples above show, is stylised and repeatable. These acts occur publicly and, through their reiteration over time, have become conventional ways of performing Singapore. In so doing, these conventional gestures have come to constitute Singapore's identity as a nation, reinforced by those institutions, policies and rituals that regulate and normalise its subjects. Therefore, as Singaporeans, 'our identities . . . are the product of these various processes . . . to which we are subject.'[94] These acts and processes have so effectively produced Singapore as successful, efficient, accomplished and affluent that to *be* Singaporean, one must also be successful, efficient, accomplished and affluent; one must perform those gestures to participate in the performance. This has not only created a relentlessly competitive environment but also 'a nation fixated on growth and development',[95] where material success is the hallmark of achievement, or having somehow arrived. Personal success is embodied in the Singapore dream, which from the late 1980s meant acquiring the 'Five Cs' – cash, condominium, credit card, car and country club membership. To achieve this, Singaporeans must excel in school and at work. This means getting good grades, a degree, a high-paying job, upgrading their skills, being productive and generally being 'The Best That [We] Can Be'.

However, according to Butler, 'there always remains a chance within the performativity of identity for dissonant or disruptive gestures by that which such performativity produces as its outside,' because 'in producing the normal, it also produces the abnormal.'[96] For her, such performativity is a force that constitutes by exclusion. Thus, the nation-state's performance of its Singapore also produces what it excludes – (an)other Singapore; the state's performance, while producing success, also produces the lack of success. As the next chapter argues, this other version of the nation is exactly what Singapore's revival cinema produces.

Notes

1. Beng Huat Chua and Eddie K. Y. Kuo, 'New Nation', 6.
2. The *Straits Times* Weekly Overseas Edition (20 August 1988, 4 September 1988, 3 November 1988); cited in Lily Kong, 'Music', 450.
3. Lily Kong and Brenda S. A. Yeoh, 'Construction of National Identity', 219.
4. Hill and Fee, 11.
5. Kong, 450.
6. Teng Cheong Ong, *Report on Moral Education*, 9.
7. Hill and Fee, 213.
8. *Singapore. Parliament, Shared Values*, 1.

9. Hill and Fee, 209.
10. Ibid., 218.
11. Terence Chong, 'Introduction', 1.
12. Henri Ghesquiere, 'From Third World to First'.
13. Lee, 9.
14. Kong, 450.
15. Margolin, 6.
16. Kuan Yew Lee, interview.
17. *Broadcast 1968*.
18. The full slogan is: 'Train Up – Be the Best You Can Be.' US Library of Congress, *Economic Boards* (accessed 30 April 2008).
19. Chong, 1.
20. Ibid.
21. Ibid., 2.
22. The visitsingapore.com website has been replaced by the current YourSingapore.com. Both were run by the Singapore Tourism Board as the go-to site for tourist information on Singapore: 'Singapore Today'.
23. 'Why Study in Singapore?'
24. Ibid.
25. Ibid.
26. Chong, 2.
27. Mahbubani was a President's Scholar and long-serving diplomat whose work in Singapore's Foreign Service includes 'two stints as Singapore's Ambassador to the UN and as President of the UN Security Council in January 2001 and May 2002. He was [also] Permanent Secretary at the Foreign Ministry from 1993 to 1998.' He is currently the Dean of the Lee Kuan Yew School of Public Policy of the National University of Singapore: 'Kishore Mahbubani: About'.
28. Kishore Mahbubani, 'Most Successful Society'.
29. Economic Development Board, 'Facts and Rankings'.
30. Chong, 2–3.
31. *National Day Broadcast 1969*.
32. Donald Low, 'Good Democracy', 48.
33. Hsien Loong Lee, 'Uphold Meritocracy'.
34. James Loxley, *Performativity*, 122.
35. National Heritage Board, 'National Pledge'.
36. Ibid.
37. National Heritage Board, 'National Anthem'.
38. Singapore Department of Statistics, Census 2010, 10–11.
39. Butler, *Gender Trouble*, 225.
40. Ibid., 179.
41. Elections Department Singapore, 'Electoral Divisions'.
42. Ibid.
43. Hsien Loong Lee, 'National Day Speech 2016'.
44. Kong and Yeoh, 214.
45. Ibid., 219.
46. Ibid., 217.
47. 'National Day'.
48. Kong and Yeoh, 224.
49. Ibid., 224–5.
50. Irene Hoe, 'Loveliest'.
51. 'Parade with a Difference'.
52. Chok Tong Goh, 'Speech by Mr Goh Chok Tong'.

53. Kong and Yeoh, 233.
54. Kong, 451.
55. 'Parade with a Difference'.
56. *Souvenir Magazine*, 44; cited in Kong and Yeoh, 230.
57. Kong and Yeoh, 224.
58. Monica Gwee, 'National Day'.
59. Kong and Yeoh, 222.
60. 'Parade with a Difference'; also cited in Kong and Yeoh, 223.
61. Kong and Yeoh, 229–30.
62. 'Parade with a Difference'.
63. 'More Mass Display'.
64. *Souvenir Programme*, 1986, 47; cited in Kong and Yeoh, 233.
65. 'More Mass Display'.
66. Janice Seah, 'The Light Fantastic'.
67. *Souvenir Programme*, 1986, 19; cited in Kong and Yeoh, 233.
68. Ibid., 225.
69. 'More Mass Display'.
70. Ibid.
71. Seah.
72. Suat Lian Tan, 'Let Singapore Sing'.
73. Ibid.
74. Ibid.
75. 'National Day Songs'.
76. Kong, 448; Hilary Winchester, Lily Kong and Kevin Dunn, *Landscapes*, 51.
77. Kong, 448; Winchester, Kong and Dunn, 51.
78. The package includes a *Sing Singapore* book with the lyrics and music of forty-nine songs, two cassette tapes and music videos.
79. Kong, 452.
80. Ibid.
81. 'Pledge to Be Sung'.
82. Butler, *Gender Trouble*, 225.
83. 'Parade with a Difference'.
84. *Souvenir Programme*, 1986, 53; cited in Kong and Yeoh, 232.
85. Seah.
86. Hoe.
87. Hedwig Alfred, 'All Agree'.
88. Kong and Yeoh, 230.
89. *Souvenir Programme*, 1984, 2; cited in ibid., 227.
90. Ibid., 233.
91. Not all NDPs are held at the Padang. Between 1975 and 1984 the parades were decentralised in alternate years. From 1985 onwards, the parades were centralised once again, with the venue alternating between the Padang and the National Stadium, until the latter site was closed in 2007, and demolished in 2010 to make way for a new stadium that opened in 2014.
92. Kong and Yeoh, 220.
93. Butler, *Gender Trouble*, 179.
94. James Loxley, *Performativity*, 122.
95. Pravin Prakash, 'Understanding Meritocracy'.
96. Loxley, 123.

7. REVIVAL CINEMA: 'OTHER' SINGAPOREANS IN (AN)OTHER SINGAPORE

The films of the revival are very different from those of prior periods and this is most obvious in the ways they look and sound. The kampongs or villages of golden age films have been replaced by a new landscape of skyscrapers, Housing Development Board (HDB) apartment blocks and satellite towns that reflect urban, contemporary Singapore. Instead of Malay or American-accented English, the films of this period feature the range of languages and variations characteristic of multilingual Singapore, including Standard English,[1] Singlish (a non-standard, local, English dialect also known as Singapore English), Mandarin and other Chinese dialects such as Hokkien or Cantonese, as well as some sparing use of Malay and Tamil. Emerging after the state's performance of its successful Singapore has been firmly entrenched, it is this idea of Singapore that its revival cinema addresses. As I have previously argued, if the state's version of the nation projects a successful Singapore inhabited by affluent, happy Singaporeans, the films of the revival perform (an)other Singapore populated with 'other' Singaporeans.[2] These are individuals and identities left out of the state's performance and include obvious character types like prostitutes, gangsters, convicts and juvenile delinquents who hover on the fringes of mainstream society. Such characters appear in early films like *Bugis Street – The Movie* (Yon Fan, 1995) and *Mee Pok Man* (Eric Khoo, 1995), and are reflected identities of the marginalised, underbelly spaces they inhabit such as red-light districts, cheap hotels, sleazy bars, dingy coffee shops, dark back alleys and cramped apartments. A brief survey of forty-four Singapore films made between 1995 and 2008 shows that only seven do not have characters who are social rejects, have absent parents, are loan sharks, prostitutes, gangsters, teenage delinquents or disabled. While this may be so, more compelling are the ways that supposedly average Singaporean characters in revival films cannot or fail to participate in the state's version of a successful Singapore. This begins with *12 Storeys* and *Money No Enough*, which are landmark films not only because they are the first films to respectively achieve critical acclaim and commercial success but also because of the ways they influence those that follow, whether consciously or not. As such, this chapter will expand on discussions of these two films in my earlier work to establish a framework for analysis before proceeding to other films that constitute variations of the same counter-performative strategies.

Problematising the Heartland and the Average Singaporean

Most significantly, unlike earlier films, both *12 Storeys* and *Money No Enough* are not set in the underbelly but in the heartland of Singapore. These are generally satellite towns built around public housing apartment blocks constructed by the HDB to improve living conditions, to provide adequate public housing for Singaporeans, and to promote social cohesion and home ownership.[3] These initially simply designed blocks with small, dark, two-bedroom apartments have grown into complete estates of modern high-rise buildings, with architectural features, gardens and facilities like swimming pools and community centres that have become iconic fixtures in the island's landscape. Touted by the HDB as 'one of the most recognised aspects of Singapore living'[4] and 'the cornerstone of Singapore's progress',[5] public housing figures prominently in the state's performance of successful Singapore as 'one of the nation's most renowned achievements'.[6]

The heartland is one of the most commonly recurring settings in Singapore films of the revival. Of the forty-four films made between 1995 and 2008, thirty feature public housing and/or associated heartland spaces such as coffee shops and playgrounds. As the heartland is 'home to more than 80% of Singapore's population',[7] the space is also used to represent the local and ordinary as well as identify characters as 'average' Singaporeans.[8] They are known as heartlanders, one of two categories of Singaporeans identified by former Prime Minister Goh Chok Tong in his National Day Rally speech in 1999. According to him, heartlanders

> make their living within the country. Their orientation and interests are local rather than international. Their skills are not marketable beyond Singapore. They speak Singlish. They include taxi-drivers, stallholders, provision shop owners, production workers and contractors. If they

emigrate to America, they will probably settle in a Chinatown, open a Chinese restaurant and call it an 'eating house'.[9]

The other category of Singaporeans are cosmopolitans whose

> outlook is international. They speak English but are bilingual. They have skills that command good incomes – banking, IT, engineering, science and technology. They produce goods and services for the global market. Many cosmopolitans use Singapore as a base to operate in the region. They can work and be comfortable anywhere in the world.

However, while he acknowledges that 'both heartlanders and cosmopolitans are important to Singapore's well-being', the former are needed for local identity but the latter are crucial to and participants of Singapore's performance of success:[10]

> Heartlanders play a major role in maintaining our core values and our social stability. They are the core of our society. Without them, there will be no safe and stable Singapore, no Singapore system, no Singapore brand name.
> Cosmopolitans, on the other hand, are indispensable in generating wealth for Singapore. They extend our economic reach. The world is their market. Without them, Singapore cannot run as an efficient, high performance society.[11]

Therefore, there exists a problematic distinction between the HDB heartland as the pride of the nation, 'a cornerstone' in the state's performance of success, and the demarcation of its inhabitants, those heartlanders, as essentially 'other' Singaporeans. So, although the heartland is a popular setting in revival films, their heartlanders are characters who cannot rise above their ordinariness and participate in Singapore's performance of success. In some films this is because they are marginalised characters like juvenile delinquents or gangsters. In other films, they are either too poor or lack the proper skills or opportunity to do so. Although *12 Storeys* and *Money No Enough* pre-date Goh's speech, they both problematise the heartland and heartlanders, albeit in different ways.

While officially crafted images depict the heartland as well-developed, multiracial and communal with happy inhabitants, *12 Storeys* 'performs the heartland as underbelly'. It defamiliarises conventional images and contrasts them with its 'reality'.[12] This is immediately apparent in the opening credit sequence, which begins with relatively long takes and still shots of the exterior of an apartment block late at night that alternate with equally dark and empty shots

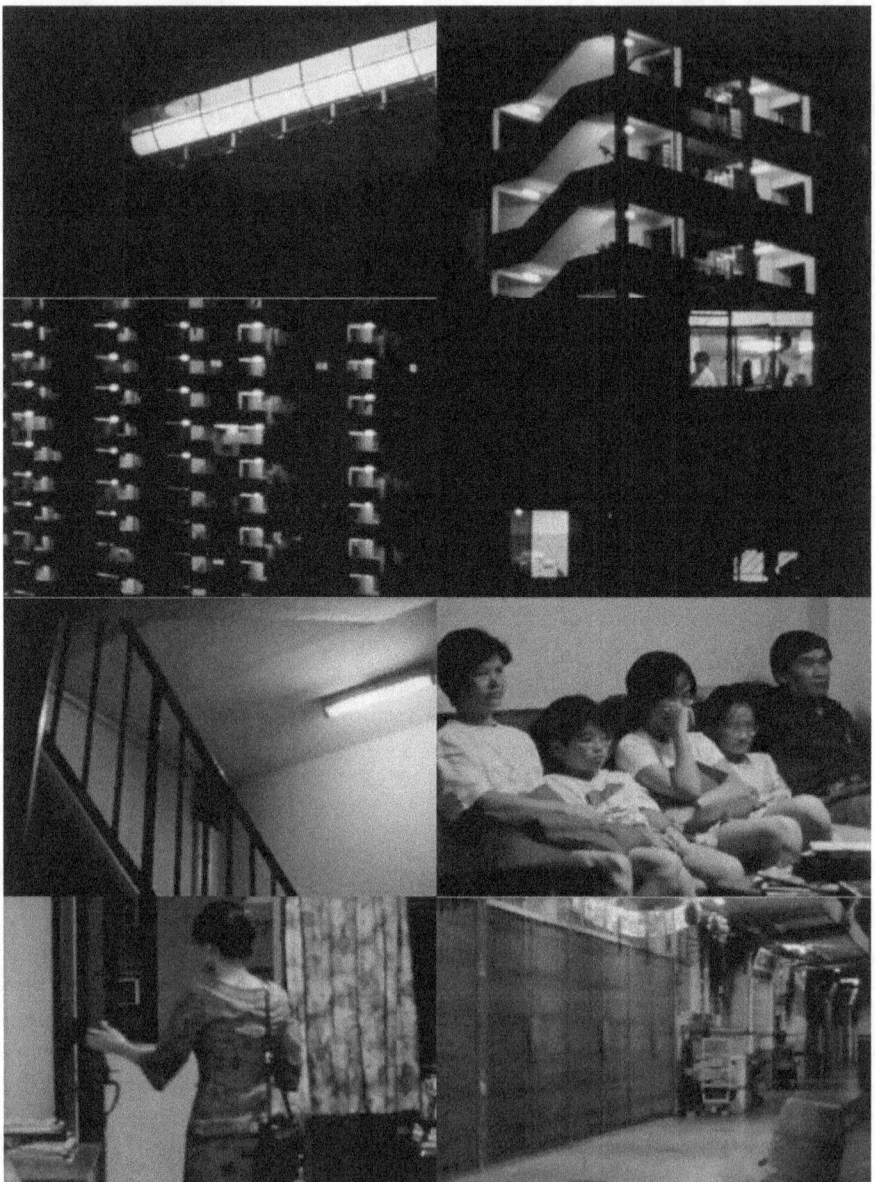

Figure 7.1 Opening sequence of *12 Storeys*

of interior spaces such as the corridor, stairwell and closed shops captured in low-key blue lighting (see Figure 7.1).

The melancholic tune of a solo violin is played throughout, imbuing the images with an overall tone of sadness that affects how we see what we see. So, a frontal view of the block with its neat rows and columns of lit apartments set against the darkness of the night highlights the isolation of individual lights amid the coherence and proximity of their arrangement. Shots that show families and individuals are melancholic and do not depict human interaction. So, although a family watches television together, they do not interact but stare zombie-like at the screen, while the shot itself is still and silent. In another shot, a Singapore Airlines stewardess returns to a dark, small flat, offering a sadder 'reality' that is far removed from the glamorous images of 'Singapore girls' the airline publicises and circulates. The opening sequence casts the heartland as a sterile environment filled with melancholy and loneliness. This is vastly different from what Singaporeans are used to seeing and experiencing, and immediately subverts official articulations of the space.

The credit sequence is broken by the sound of a radio show and bright lighting that suggest the start of a new day as people go about their daily early-morning routines such as jogging, exercising at the public playground and having breakfast at the local coffee shop. However, this more optimistic tone is quickly undermined by a young man's sudden suicide when he jumps from the twelfth storey of a block of flats. Although his death attracts numerous passers-by, only one suggests calling the police. The suicide signals the metaphoric demise of the heartland *as heartland*, marked by inexplicable death and the absence of community. This reinforces the credit sequence's establishment of a different view of the space.

Other images such as family portraits, wedding photos and officially commissioned television commercials promoting marriage and family are also taken to task. Representing happiness and success in the film, these are juxtaposed with the grim 'reality' of its trio of disenfranchised characters who cannot achieve these ideals. Ah Gu, the bucktoothed hawker, seeks marital bliss by marrying a woman from China when he cannot find a local one who will have him. However, she is never at home and refuses to have carnal relations with him. Inspired by television advertisements promoting parenthood, he urges her to have sex only to be forcefully rejected. In response, the lonely and repressed Ah Gu stages 'sex' with a bolster instead. Frequent cuts to wedding photographs of the happy couple in these scenes cement the stark contrast between image and 'reality'. San San is a single, overweight and mostly silent woman whose life is glaringly different from the images she sees on television. These are either romantic scenes or public service advertisements idealising love commissioned by the government-linked Social Development Unit to encourage Singaporeans to marry. However, San San seems doomed to a life of loneliness. She is mocked by men in public spaces like the neighbourhood coffee shop and her only companions are, ironically, the spirits of the young man who committed suicide and her deceased foster mother. Yet, neither of these presences is comforting to her. While the young man's spirit sometimes appears next to her, there is no interaction between them and she does not seem to know he is there. His presence is not comforting but emphasises her isolation and loneliness. Shot/reverse shots between her and the foster mother may cinematically connect the two, but this is deceptive as there is no real interaction or connection between them – San San is seen stoically doing chores while the older woman incessantly calls her names and criticises her. This presence is overbearing and abusive, not maternal, and San San's silence throughout further reinforces her repression. Meng is a schoolteacher who strives to be an ideal citizen and is marked as a representation of the state – he first appears wearing white,[13] with a T-shirt proclaiming 'My block is the cleanest',[14] religiously does the Great Singapore Workout,[15] and frequently cites statistics to make his point. However, he is repeatedly undermined by his inability to control his two siblings, Tee and Trixie, who are left in his care while their parents are away. They are rebellious, preferring to spend time at the movies and clubs than studying. Meng's exhortation on the importance of education falls on deaf ears and differences in opinion lead to escalating arguments that contrast with the film's emphasis on the photographs of this happy family. The deliberate characterisation of Meng suggests the ineffectiveness of a nanny state that has lost touch with its people, making the conflict much more than that across a generation gap. The image of the ideal citizen is further undermined by Meng's perverse obsession with Trixie and her virginity expressed through point-of-view shots of his sister's body, for example, and the way he lovingly caresses her toothbrush. He is exceedingly interested in her sexual conduct and finally loses control when he discovers that she is no longer a virgin. In the end, Meng trashes the public playground in a drunken rage and is arrested.

Although the three main characters live in the same block of flats, they do not interact with each other and barely share the same space. For example, Meng and San San are in the same space only once – the playground – but do not see or acknowledge each other (see Figure 7.2). The shot is framed with a long slide in the middle which splits the screen, visually separating the characters and dividing the otherwise unified setting. As such, the spaces they occupy, while contiguous, are disconnected, highlighting the irony of close proximity.

These three stories may share the same narrative space of the film but they are told as juxtaposing fragments of separate vignettes that are woven together but do not impact each other. They are only connected temporally as events that happen at the same time, and thematically as stories of pain and repression. These are not shared emotions but are experienced and told individually in the same way that the characters themselves lead separate lives in a single block of flats.

The film ends by returning us to the image of the block of flats, creating circularity in a narrative that problematises images in general and the image

'OTHER' SINGAPOREANS IN (AN)OTHER SINGAPORE

Figure 7.2 Meng and San San in the playground

of the heartland in particular by offering another 'reality', another performance of the heartland as a counter-performative strategy. The heartland of *12 Storeys* is characterised by pain and repression. Instead of social cohesion and community, it is an ironically fragmented space that isolates and separates, where close proximity exists without reciprocation but enhances loneliness and alienation instead. As such, the film not only 'creates a different performance of the heartland, but also causes it to perform differently'.[16] In essence, what the film has produced is (an)other heartland in (an)other Singapore, constituted by 'other' Singaporeans who are either left out or fail to be a part of Singapore's success.[17]

Unlike *12 Storeys*, *Money No Enough* may not directly challenge the image of the heartland, but its narrative nonetheless problematises the deployment of the space as shorthand for the local and the ordinary.[18] Its three main characters, Keong, Ong and Hui, are friends, heartlanders who seemingly have very different lives. Keong is a successful executive who, with his new, lavishly renovated flat, good job and fancy car, seems to be living the Singaporean dream. However, the reality is that he has financially overextended himself to create the appearance of success. Problems arise when the stock market crashes and he is passed over for promotion due to his lack of qualifications, computer illiteracy and poor language skills. Impulsively quitting his job further exacerbates the situation but he vehemently refuses to give up symbols of success like the widescreen television, as his wife suggests. Out of frustration, she leaves him, and the banks repossess all the trappings of his former lifestyle. Ong, on the other hand, is an opportunistic contractor who is not well-educated but also aspires to live the affluent Singapore lifestyle. When one of his plans to make a quick buck fails, he is forced to hide from loan sharks. Hui, a coffee shop assistant, is the least educated and successful of the three and spends all his money gambling. However, Hui becomes more conscious of his disadvantages when he is unable to afford medical care for his ailing mother or a lavish funeral for her when she dies, and is insulted by his richer siblings. As such, although the title suggests that the issue is not enough money, 'it is not merely the shortage of money that is a problem but the lack of it in consumerist, affluent Singapore.'[19]

Keong, Ong and Hui may speak Mandarin, but they are generally Hokkien-speaking characters who use the latter language for informal, everyday conversation, especially among themselves. Hokkien is also frequently used for jokes and comedy. In contrast, Mandarin sounds more formal, such as in the first scene in the coffee shop during which the serious conversation about flag burning begins in Mandarin but lapses into Hokkien as it becomes more comic. Mandarin is also primarily used in the office or heard on the news. Keong converses with his wife in Mandarin, which casts their relationship as more tense and formal than the camaraderie he shares with the Hokkien-speaking Ong and Hui. *Money No Enough* was the first film to prominently use Hokkien, or dialects in general for that matter, and doing so imbues a sense of localness that Mandarin does not. This contributed significantly to the film's popularity and box-office success but also contradicts the state's bilingual education policy and privileging of Mandarin. In the 1980s, aggressive 'Speak Mandarin' campaigns were launched, exhorting Singaporeans to 'Speak Mandarin and not Dialects'. Dialects were simultaneously banned from television, radio and print media. In schools, Mandarin was also designated as the second language for Chinese students. As such, the film's particular use of Hokkien performs a localness that defies state-driven causes.

Singlish and Standard English also have similarly performative functions. Singlish is used in informal conversations especially between characters of different races, such as when Keong and Ong negotiate with a Malay salesman to buy a television. On the other hand, Standard English marks characters with higher education or social standing, like the clearly English-educated Jeremiah Adolpher Lee. Keong is mocked by his daughter when he cannot pronounce 'hippopotamus'. He also loses his promotion to Jeremiah and is unable to find another job because, as one interviewer tells him, 'to succeed in Singapore, you must know English and computer.' Hui, on the other hand, is unable to understand it at all, as is evident in the comic scene in which the three friends fill in forms to register their company. Hui does not know what to put under 'S-E-X'. Ong deliberately misleads him and says that, for himself, it is three times a week, while for Hui it is once in a while. Standard English is not only a marker of socioeconomic mobility but is also seen as a foreign language to these average Singaporeans that must be acquired like computer skills or higher education. As if to expand on the unnaturalness of Standard English, Keong calls Jeremiah an 'Ah Qua' (a local, derogatory term for gay or transsexual) and envisions him in drag in a daydream/nightmare. Yet, although Keong casts Jeremiah as a sexual other in this film, it is he who is left out and essentially marginalised in the job market because of his lack of Standard English.

The characters' lack of proficiency in English and the relative ease with which they speak Singlish is consistent with observations on the role of both dialects in Singapore. English may serve as lingua franca but Singaporeans are not encouraged to identify with it. It is not designated as a Mother Tongue in the bilingual system for any race, including Eurasians who, unlike the Chinese, Malays or Indians, have no official language or common tongue.[20] Ironically, the result of using English for inter-ethnic communication was not greater proficiency in the language but the development of Singlish instead. Singlish became such a common language of communication that by the 1990s it was celebrated in books, on television and websites, and used in informal and creative writing, particularly for localised dialogue or humour. However, in 1999, the government launched the 'Speak Good English Movement' to promote Standard English and discourage Singlish.[21] The perception was that Singlish was 'bad' or 'broken' English and should be eliminated for several reasons: 1) Singapore could not 'go global' with it; 2) it was associated with ghettoisation; and 3) it was proof and cause of the decline in the standard of English in Singapore. Standard English, on the other hand, was seen as integral to and a barometer of Singapore's success and economic prosperity.[22] In his National Day Rally speech that year, then Prime Minister Goh Chok Tong said:

> Our schools must teach Standard English, and our children must learn and speak Standard English. Most of our pupils still come from non-English-speaking homes. For them, English is really a second language, to be learnt almost like a foreign language, and not their mother tongue. For them to master just one version of English is already quite a challenge. If they get into the habit of speaking Singlish, then later they will either have to unlearn these habits, or learn proper English on top of Singlish. Many pupils will find this too difficult. They may end up unable to speak any language properly, which would be a tragedy.
>
> We learn English in order to communicate with the world. The fact that we use English gives us a big advantage over our competitors ... to become an engineer, a technician, an accountant or a nurse, you must have Standard English, not Singlish.[23]

As a result, the title character of the popular television series *Phua Chu Kang*, whose appeal was precisely because he spoke only Singlish, was urged to go back to school 'to improve his English'.[24] Heated arguments over the value of Singlish as it pertains to Singapore's identity continue to this day. In 2002, a television advertisement for *Talking Cock: The Movie* was banned for 'excessive use of Singlish'. The film itself was given an NC-17 rating to prohibit children under 17 from watching it because of Singlish and not sex, violence or profanity.[25] Proponents of Singlish argue that it is authentic and an essential part of Singapore's uniqueness; eliminating it 'denies to Singaporeans (as with the other dialects) something of themselves that is recognizably their own'.[26] Although *Money No Enough* pre-dates the 'Speak Good English Movement', its use of Singlish and Hokkien not only give the film a distinctly local flavour; they are also markers of difference and otherness in characters who speak it, especially in relation to those who speak Mandarin and Standard English. Singlish and Hokkien are 'other' languages spoken by 'other' Singaporeans.

Furthermore, the film's depiction of the need for qualifications and upgrading of skills contradicts official narratives about the success and desirability of Singapore's workforce and bilingual education system. If Keong represents the average Singaporean executive, then his inability to get ahead shows that Singapore's workforce is evidently not as well-trained or educated as state articulations project. Keong, Ong and Hui are not merely average Singaporeans seeking the Singapore dream. They are average Singaporeans who are trapped by their ordinariness and doomed to being average. Although they eventually start a successful carwash business together, they still do not have enough money by the film's conclusion and find themselves in the same predicament they were in at the beginning. As the circular narrative of the film implies, these 'other' Singaporeans are forever caught in the perennial cycle of striving but never arriving. Therefore, while their carwash business may show that one does not need to have a degree or speak English to be successful, their continued lack of money in the end also suggests that striving to achieve the Singapore dream is not the same as participating in the state's performance of success; they may strive for the Singapore dream but remain excluded from the state's performance of success.[27]

If the characters in the film are average Singaporeans then this average is vastly different from that which the state's performance suggests. While Singapore's public housing development is an integral part of the state's performance, films like *12 Storeys* and *Money No Enough* show that the people who inhabit the space are either far from successful or unable to participate in the rhetoric of success. Therefore, the heartland is disengaged from the state's performance and redeployed as a site for counter-performance in these films. If the state's performance projects a successful Singapore inhabited by upwardly mobile, happy Singaporeans, both *12 Storeys* and *Money No Enough* project a different Singapore through a heartland populated by heartlanders who are essentially 'other' Singaporeans. In doing so, they establish 'a set of stylized acts that, as a relational force and by virtue of their repetition in subsequent films, continue to disrupt the state's performance of successful Singapore as a unified, homogenous national identity'.[28] So, although revival films frequently use the heartland as a setting, their heartlanders are often characters who cannot rise above their ordinariness and participate in successful Singapore. For example, in Royston Tan's semi-documentary *15*, the two groups of fifteen-year-old boys who play themselves are rebels, truants and gang members. They extort money at playgrounds and indulge in fights, pornography, tattoos and piercings. Here, the heartland is counter-performed as a cold, unsympathetic and futile place of lost innocence and private pain. Although the second set of boys venture further afield to famous (tourist) places such as the old Parliament House, the Central Business District, Chinatown and Orchard Road, the film depicts their presence and actions in these places as acts of rebellion that reject rather than claim or take over these spaces.[29] Kelvin Tong and Jasmine Ng's *Eating Air* also features juvenile delinquents whose inability to participate in the state's performance of a successful Singapore is rendered in the liminal and transitory spaces they occupy, such as the expressway tunnel, the Central Business District, empty rooftops and construction sites, Boy's cluttered home and the figments of his imagination. These spaces are borrowed only for the moment as the characters pass through but never fully inhabit them.[30] I have discussed these two films more fully elsewhere and only provided a summation of my analyses here to enable the rest of this chapter to discuss other work by other directors, namely *Singapore Dreaming* (Colin Goh and Woo Yen Yen, 2006) and *Singapore Gaga* (Tan Pin Pin, 2005).

Unravelling the Singapore Dream

Like *Money No Enough*, *Singapore Dreaming* is about striving for the Singapore dream of the Five Cs – cash, condominium, credit card, car and country club membership. The film revolves around the Loh family – Poh Huat, his wife, their son, Seng, and daughter, Mei. It opens by immediately contrasting the dream of material wealth and the 'reality' of the average heartlander Singaporean. The first shot is a close-up of Poh Huat in sunglasses and smoking a cigarette as he lounges poolside to the sound of lapping water and birds chirping in the background. This tranquil image is quickly interrupted by the credit sequence of shots that depict the familiar view of Singapore as an energetic, bustling modern city as it goes about its business – the Singapore River with the Merlion, the Esplanade, passing boats reflecting off the glass façade of a high-rise building, crowded escalators, masses of mostly young

Figure 7.3 Poh Huat's reality

people on the move and on the phone, a traffic jam, an MRT train going into a station and people counting money. Accompanying this sequence is the start of a Hokkien song about a young, single lady of '17 going on 18' who sees a 'fair and handsome' young man. The film then cuts back to Poh Huat in a medium shot that reveals he is lounging in a shirt and pants, which are incongruent with the setting. His phone rings as the background song fades and the ensuing conversation reveals that Poh Huat is heavily in debt. After the call, he stands up, picks up his briefcase, faces the pool and moves his arms as if he is swimming (see Figure 7.3). After a few strokes, he stops and walks out of the frame. The contrast between the luxury of the space and Poh Huat's attire, behaviour and dialogue reflects the disparity between the dream of the condominium and the reality of financial debt. If Poh Huat was dreaming in the first shot of the film, then this subsequent scene reveals his reality.

This scene is followed by the second sequence of shots set in a heartland neighbourhood market as the song continues. We see a rooster, vendors selling eggs and scaling fish, hawkers preparing their food, various elderly folk, including one in a wheelchair, and Mrs Loh buying groceries. It ends with an establishing shot of a HDB estate that serves as the backdrop for the film's title (see Figure 7.4). The continuation of the song connects the two sequences, reinforcing the sense of routine common in both. However, the differences between the images create a contrast between city and heartland, where the former is urban, youthful, wealthy and successful, and the latter is rustic, ageing and associated with small businesses, reflecting Goh's speech about cosmopolitans and heartlanders. Including common tourist images of Singapore

Figure 7.4   Title shot in *Singapore Dreaming*

in the city sequence also implies that this space is the face of the nation while the heartland, in contrast, is its reality.

The heartland as reality is further emphasised by the cramped confines of the Lohs' flat, the cluttered common corridor and the constant nuisance of urine in the lift as the film unfolds. The non-diegetic Hokkien song in the city sequence is not natural to the space and what it represents, and the dissonance disconnects the aural from the visual. On the other hand, the song seems more appropriate to the parochial space of the heartland, making this space the source of this music. As such, if the city sequence reflects the heartlander's dream of belonging to or associating with that space, the dissonance implies the unnaturalness of such desires. The rest of the song in the heartland sequence wonders 'Oh when will the gentle man bring the spring wind so flowers can bloom/I see someone at the door/I open it to see who it might be/but I only see the moon laughing at me/I have been deceived by the wind.' Like our introduction to Poh Huat, the song reinforces the difference between dream and reality. The implication here is that the image of the city, the face of the nation, is also as insubstantial as a dream.

The start of this film immediately juxtaposes two different views of Singapore associated with the contrast between Poh Huat and his wife. Their humble home in the heartland identifies them as average Singaporeans, and the different Singapores in the opening sequence can be read as each character's perspective or experience of the nation. Poh Huat's resembles the state's version of successful Singapore – the bustling city with its attendant mobility and affluence. The film introduces him as an average Singaporean who desires to participate in that success through achieving the Singapore dream of the Five Cs. He is a legal clerk who hordes boxes of clippings of dream houses and cars. He goes into debt to send his son, Seng, overseas for further education so that the family can become upwardly mobile and succeed. While the opening may show that Poh Huat has not yet arrived, subsequent scenes suggest his dreams are on the verge of coming true. Seng has completed his studies and is coming home. Poh Huat himself wins the local lottery of $2 million, finally has credit cards ('Bloody bank! They've turned me down my whole life but now I'm rich, they give me so many!') and is invited to join an exclusive country club. In other words, he is poised to achieve the Singapore dream of material success. His wife's perspective comprises the mundanity of the heartland and the home, and the film articulates this as a limited one in terms of space and ambition. She is mostly seen in the home and her sphere of action is restricted to that space and neighbourhood. She does not have the same material desires as her husband or children. When her husband gives her diamond earrings, it is a source of discomfort in more ways than one. She is first troubled by the present as her ears are not pierced. Although she eventually pierces them and wears the earrings while doing laundry, the jewellery is out of place in the humble setting of her home, simple costume and chores. She also winces as she takes them out to apply medication to the wound. Her concerns are related to the family and home. Throughout the film, she constantly plies her family with herbal tea and reminds them to drink it. Towards the end of the film, she reveals that when she was young, she loved to sing and even won a singing competition in her hometown in Muar, Malaysia. However, after coming to Singapore and marrying Poh Huat, 'Every morning I'd wake up and all I'd know is to wipe the tables, mop the floor, go to the market, cook and make herbal tea. I never sang again.'

The contrast between Poh Huat and his wife is reflected in the juxtaposition of the film's English and Chinese titles against the HDB heartland in the background (see Figure 7.4). The English title is *Singapore Dreaming*, but the Chinese title is *Mei Man Ren Shen*, which means a perfect, contented or fulfilling life. The difference pits the ideal of the Singapore dream against that of a contented life. On one hand, this can be read as reflecting the difference between Poh Huat and his wife. On the other hand, while achieving the Singapore dream is also supposed to lead to contentment, the film reveals that these are conflicting, not complementary, ideals. The characters not only fail to achieve the dream (hence still dreaming), but the quest to do so leads to unhappiness all round. Poh Huat may have won the lottery but he dies shortly after in the car park of the country club just before his membership interview. Ironically, he only gets a big house and car after he dies, in the form of paper offerings that are burnt as part of Taoist funeral rituals. His investment in Seng also does not pay off because his son is only interested in making a quick buck, instant gratification and the trappings of success rather than working for it.

Seng fails a job interview because his diploma is from an unknown university. To cover it up, he claims he wants to set up his own business. Poh Huat gives him the money to do so, but he ends up leasing a Porsche instead. Later, he also reveals that he did not actually graduate. Seng never achieves anything in the film and finally loses everything, including the Porsche. Perhaps Poh Huat should have invested in his daughter, Mei, instead. Unlike her brother, she is hard-working and responsible but stuck in a dead-end job with an employer who takes her for granted and treats her like a servant. However, like her father, she also dreams of a better (material) life and upgrading to a condominium, which strains her relationship with her husband Keong, an unsuccessful insurance salesman who does not earn enough to help her fulfil this dream. In the end, although the couple reconcile, she remains trapped in her job until her mother gives her $300,000 from Poh Huat's winnings and she is now able to do whatever she wants. Even though she has a more hopeful ending than her brother, Mei never gets to buy a condo. Instead, she seems to have found fulfilment in family, reiterating the conflicting ideals of the Singapore dream and a contented, meaningful life.

Like the city as the face of the nation, the film also associates the Singapore dream with the Chinese notion of 'face' or '*mian zi*', which is 'a reputation achieved through getting on in life, through success and ostentation'.[31] It has to do with self-aggrandisement and ego, and 'can be borrowed, struggled for, added to, padded'.[32] Poh Huat sees his ability to send his son overseas as an accomplishment and an investment in the quest to achieve the Five Cs, which is the ultimate ego boost. So he tells Seng to 'make sure you get a good job! That way you can repay us. Then I can retire and move to a condo and get out of this low-class place where people urinate in the elevator! It really stinks!' Later he says, 'Now you come back, you can't play the fool anymore, ok? What if you end up selling insurance like [Keong]? Don't make me lose face.' The implication here is that if Seng does not get a good job, he will lower his father's esteem in the eyes of others. When Seng wants to start a business instead, Poh Huat gives him more money than requested because 'If you want to do business, you got to do it big! Don't do small-time business! You'll only make me lose face!' Here, 'face' is tied to making it, achieving the Singapore dream, or at least the appearance of it. The latter is certainly the case for Seng. When his girlfriend confronts him about the Porsche, he retorts that 'Nowadays people look at what car you drive, what house you live in, what university you go to. If you want to make it you've got to look like you've already made it.' Both Poh Huat and Seng, who is also known as Jeffrey outside the family, are very conscious of dressing up. They both wear suits to their respective membership and job interviews. Interestingly, Poh Huat is repeatedly seen stripping off his work clothes as soon as he is home, which is reminiscent of Ramlee, Sudin and Ajiz doing the same in *Bujang Lapok*. Similarly, *Singapore Dreaming*'s contrasting depiction of the city and heartland also recalls the earlier film's distinction between the city and kampong. However, whereas *Bujang Lapok* is concerned with the erosion of tradition and community values as the city encroaches on the kampong, in *Singapore Dreaming* the heartland is seen as a limiting space which heartlanders like Poh Huat and his children wish to leave. Hence, the desire for a condo.

The backdrop of the heartland in the title shot is, therefore, telling. This is where average Singaporeans reside and these are the people who, like Poh Huat and his children, want to achieve the Singapore dream. However, as much as they wish to leave the heartland for a better life, they never do, except Mrs Loh, who literally leaves the space and returns to Malaysia at the end of the film. As she does so, she looks back at the corridor and sees Poh Huat's ghost, still dressed in the suit, drinking herbal tea and forever stuck in the heartland. Seng is also finally trapped in the flat as he evades debt collectors and is allowed to continue living there by his mother. Like the characters in *Money No Enough*, Poh Huat and Seng are heartlanders who may strive for the Singapore dream but never achieve it and remain left out of the state's performance of successful Singapore. In fact, the film seems to suggest that as heartlanders they are forever doomed to remain in that 'low-class' space, as the only ways to achieve a meaningful life are to be contented with what you have or physically leave Singapore altogether.

The film's use of Hokkien is also performative. This is apparent not only in the opening sequences, but also to mark characters like Poh Huat and his wife. His use of the language is crude and reflects the crassness and limitations of a heartlander who will never be the cosmopolitan that the Prime Minister describes. While Mrs Loh understands Mandarin, she only speaks Hokkien, casting her as the least educated and upwardly mobile character. As such, Poh Huat constantly disparages and dismisses her as ignorant. She is also left out of conversations that lapse into English or Singlish. Mrs Loh's linguistic limitations differentiate her from the rest of her family, who easily switch between dialect, Mandarin, Singlish and Standard English, reflecting also her difference as one who does not aspire to achieve the Singapore dream. So Hokkien is used to mark her as an 'other' Singaporean, reinforced by the fact that she is actually Malaysian. Although she emerges as the wisest character of them all, there is no triumph or valorisation in the end. The quest for the Singapore dream has ruined her family and her departure shows that a contented life is only possible by opting out and leaving the city behind.

Reframing Performance and Performing Alternatives

Singapore Gaga is 'a 55-minute paean to the quirkiness of the Singaporean aural landscape,'[33] and comprises a collection of performances by local individuals or communities. They include popular ventriloquist Victor Khoo and his puppet Charlee; Margaret Leng Tan, a celebrated pianist; the accomplished harmonica player Yew Hong Chow; as well as different buskers like Melvyn Cedello, Ying and Liang. However, the film's aural landscape also includes other stories and sounds that do not fall within conventional definitions of performance, such as the voice of MRT announcements; dialect newsreaders; madrasah students cheering and singing in Arabic and English at their sports day; a group recalling Latin songs from their school days; an elderly man singing communist songs from his past; and even the ambient noises of Little India. The film also captures these moments in the same way that it does the more conventional performances. It does not distinguish between types of performances, but instead weaves them together as intersecting stories that segue into one another, which the structural logic of the film reveals is not random but deliberately considered, captured and connected.

Singapore Gaga begins with an explosion of fireworks followed by Melvyn singing Freddie Fender's 'Wasted Days and Wasted Nights' at an empty MRT station at night. The song then serves as a sound bridge as the film cuts to an aerial view of Singapore from the interior of an airplane. As the plane lands at Changi Airport, 'Wasted Days and Wasted Nights' gives way to the stewardess' in-flight announcement: 'Welcome to Singapore, ladies and gentlemen. And to all Singaporeans and residents of Singapore, a warm welcome home.' The plane's arrival at Changi Airport not only locates the film in Singapore but also makes Singapore as much a subject of or character in the film as the others. However, the contrast between the celebration and Melvyn singing 'Wasted Days and Wasted Nights' in an empty station establishes a rather desolate or even cynical tone right at the start. This continues as the plane lands to another sound bridge of the song's lament: 'Why should I keep loving you?/When I know that you're not true./Then why should I call your name?/When you're the blame/for making me blue.' The lyrics frame the arrival and also undermine the in-flight announcer's warm welcome to Singapore. The opening is thus a warning that the Singapore we are about to see is neither warm nor welcoming.

This is obvious in the first full performance we see in the film, which is Ying's. Although Ying earlier introduced himself as an internationally known, national treasure, his performance of the Skater's Waltz goes unnoticed by the people around him. The film highlights this difference between his view of himself and how others see, or rather do not see, him, with multiple shots of Ying performing in the foreground as people in the background sweep by (see Figure 7.5). It also captures the difference in perception and use of the space. To Ying, the underground passage is a performance space, but to the crowd it is merely a transitory and functional one. As the pace of the song increases, the film matches its rhythm and beat with quick cuts to crowds of people walking

Figure 7.5 Ying's performance

by, going up and down escalators, and Ying performing. These are interspersed with close-ups of hurrying feet and Ying's clogs as he taps to the music. The editing thus creates a visual vibrancy that joins in with and celebrates the robust performance. So, even though the people around Ying ignore him, the film clearly does not.

The performance ends when a station official gestures Ying to leave. As he does, the energy of his act and the film's visual style are replaced with the relative monotony of still shots and ambient sounds, emphasising how dull the space is without Ying's lively performance. It shows that performances like Ying's add vibrancy and texture to Singapore's soundscape, if only it was perceived and regarded as such. This segment suggests that the fault lies with us, the people in the crowd who do not pay any attention to his dedicated performance. However, Ying's story is picked up again later on when he talks about how he was arrested for performing without a licence, followed by a scene of a passer-by asking him if he has a permit. This later scene raises the state's role in defining what constitutes performance through regulation and licences that literally permit some performances and not others. It also makes one wonder how such decisions are made. This first complete performance establishes several thematic strands that develop as the film unfolds: 1) how everyday spaces and sounds can be reframed via or as performance; 2) how performance is regarded, legitimised and celebrated, especially when it occurs in unconventional and everyday spaces; and 3) the potential and opportunity for a more inclusive definition of performance in Singapore. These strands comprise the film's overarching argument that an alternative soundscape exists and constitutes an alternative performance of Singapore.

The next scenes feature an elderly man singing a song from his time in the communist army, and people singing 'Happy Birthday'. Here the film presents us with other circumstances in which performance can occur, i.e. at home. Although the space is informal, the film captures and frames the ex-soldier's singing of the communist song as a kind of performance as well – he sings to the camera as if it is his audience, suggesting his consciousness of performing. The birthday song is contextualised by the familiar occasion of such celebrations, where singing is not usually considered or marked as performance. Yet linking these with Ying's earlier act causes a reframing of what could be defined as performance. The film suggests that such acts can occur in multiple spaces and be considered as performance if they are framed as such.

The birthday celebration is followed by an interview with Margaret, who recalls how she was lambasted for her first performance of John Cage's $4'33'$ in Singapore. However, a decade later, after she was recognised and acclaimed in America, she performed the piece in Singapore again. This time it was 'a real homecoming', as people 'were literally lining up to have pictures and CDs autographed'. When asked how it feels to be welcomed now, she replies, 'Oh, it warms the cockles of my ageing heart.' This is followed by Liang, singing her $1 tissue song outside an MRT station to attract customers but, like the other buskers in the film, she is ignored by the people around her. This depiction of Liang connects her with Melvyn and Ying, and their stories are also linked with Margaret's as common experiences of lack of recognition and legitimacy.

The film then shows us three different scenes, all tied to the context of school: 1) Victor and Charlee performing in a school auditorium filled with little children laughing, cheering and singing along; 2) the madrasah school's sports day; and 3) the group of men singing their Latin song. However, while Victor and Charlee have all the trappings of a conventional performance (stage, audience and the space of the auditorium), the others do not. The sports day occurs in a stadium, while the ex-classmates sing their song at one of their homes. As such, while one is considered a performance, the other two are not, begging the question: why not? As if to reiterate its point, the film then shows us Margaret's performance of John Cage's $4'33'$ with a toy piano in the void deck of a HDB flat (see Figure 7.6).

This performance is shown in its entirety – 4 minutes and 33 seconds of silence, as Tan's hand slowly moves from one end of the keyboard to the other. The music itself is Cage's commentary on how everyday sounds are musical if

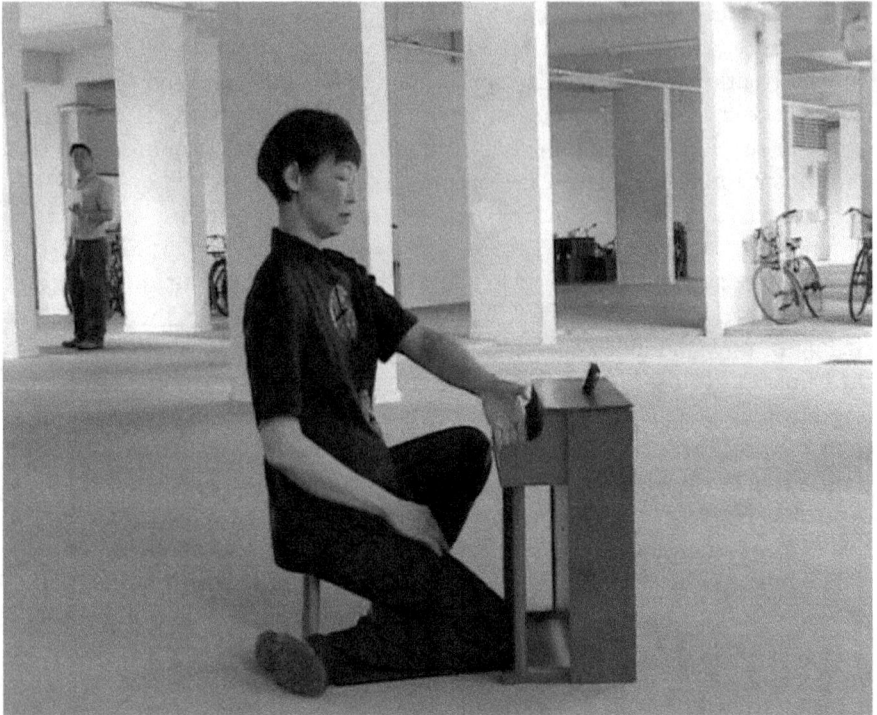

Figure 7.6 Margaret performing *4'33'* in the void deck

we would only stop to listen to them as music or art. It is a conscious emphasis on sounds of the environment, which, in this case, is that of the void deck that is usually taken for granted and not considered on a daily basis, much less as music or art. Yet the void deck is not a usual venue for such a performance, and staging it thus deliberately causes the high art form of Cage's music to relate to its relatively low cultural environment, transforming this everyday space into a performative one. In so doing, the sounds of this environment are reframed as music. This staging of *4'33'* is consistent with the way the film as a whole consciously causes spaces like the MRT station, school, stadium and home to perform and be perceived differently.

This is carried through to the next segment about Juanita, the voice of MRT announcements. Here, the range of sounds the film explores extends to include language. Juanita discusses how certain station names like Lavender are pronounced and why she has chosen the proper English version (Lair-vender) to the local, Singlish one (Ler-vender); she is from Raffles Girls' School, one of the top institutions in Singapore, and her principal was 'a stickler' for 'perfect English' so 'there is no way to go wrong with that kind of training.' The film's depiction of Juanita is as interesting as it is also deliberate. She is the only character in the film whom we do not see. Instead she remains a disembodied voice that overlays a black screen or images of people in the MRT trains, sitting, chatting, sleeping or staring into space. This creates the contrast between the considered crafting of the announcements by someone who takes her work seriously and the nonchalance of commuters to whom the sound is part of the environment. Although the announcements are part of Juanita's work, the commuters do not see it as art, and the film's refusal to show us who she is ensures that she remains unrecognised.

The immediate transition from one woman to another, as well as the difference and similarities between them, connects and overlaps their stories. Juanita and Tan are obviously well educated and speak proper English, and their stories emphasise the common theme of lack of recognition. However, while Margaret Leng Tan is certainly a bona fide performer, her art is celebrated and her rendition of Cage's music is staged *as performance* in the film, Juanita's work is depicted as and relegated to ambient noise and part of a commuter's daily experience. This difference not only continues to develop the film's positioning of everyday sounds as performance, it also begs the question of whether we require performance to be framed thus in order to be regarded and celebrated as such.

The film's sequencing of these stories and performances causes each to flow into and inform the other to gradually build a portrait of Singapore through characters and sounds. They connect and resonate to create an internal logic and structure in the film that suggests that what is considered performance is subjective and arbitrary. The film shows that performance can occur anywhere, in a variety of contexts and spaces. This recalls Marvin Carlson's view of performance:

> the recognition that our lives are structured according to repeated and socially sanctioned modes of behavior raises the possibility that all human activity could potentially be considered as 'performance,' or at least all activity carried out with a consciousness of itself. The difference between doing and performing, according to this way of thinking, would seem to lie not in the frame of theatre versus real life but in an attitude – we may do actions unthinkingly, but when we think about them, this brings in a consciousness that gives them the quality of performance.[34]

What *Singapore Gaga* offers is a more inclusive definition of performance. By making us see these acts and activities not conventionally considered as performance alongside those that are, the film not only causes these spaces and contexts to perform differently but the space and context of Singapore as well. In short, *Singapore Gaga* causes us to see a different Singapore by producing one that is lively, vibrant, multifaceted and multicultural. So, if *Singapore Gaga* is a celebration, then what it celebrates is difference. This is the dominant and simpler reading of the film that is problematised by the repetition of the sense of wasted opportunity and marginalisation as a result of lack of recognition.

At the end of her segment, Juanita says that she wants 'to be recognised by the industry but not by the passengers ... No, there's no need to. It's good for them to know there's a voice that comes on air and tells them, gives them instructions and all that.' The film then shows us an example of such an instruction. Juanita's announcement, 'Your attention please. Eating or drinking is not allowed in the stations and trains. Thank you for keeping the stations and trains clean for the comfort of all passengers' is heard as the film once again shows us the bored faces of the commuters on the train. The end of this segment reframes Juanita's story and makes hers the voice of order and control.

This is the last we hear of Juanita, as the film cuts to the noise and bustle of Little India where diegetic sounds of traffic and passers-by compete with announcements of a bus' destination through a megaphone and in a local accent. This obviously contrasts with Juanita's preference for proper English. However, this new scene and sound reinforces the reframing of Juanita's story at the end of her segment. The noise of Little India and localness of the woman's accent now denote the everyday, while Juanita's voice and instructions take the position of the formal and official, even the elite because of the use of proper English.

As the film cuts to the interior of a passing taxi, dialect news from its radio takes over from the ambient sounds of Little India and becomes the soundtrack as the vehicle passes through the space. This creates a clear separation between interior and exterior, foreground and background. The choice of sound and space here raises racial implications. This is a Chinese sound laid over an Indian space, and could be read as a framing of the minority Indian community through the perspective of the dominant Chinese. Then the distinction between the interior and exterior implies the coexistence and separation of Indians and Chinese, of majority and minority races in Singapore, while the foregrounding of one sound, the Chinese news, causes the marginalisation and literal disappearance of others.

However, what we hear then takes on a different significance as the film transitions from the dialect news in the taxi to its source – the newsreaders in the studio. Their story reveals their dedication to reading the news in various dialects to preserve these languages that are fast disappearing as a result of Singapore's choice of and emphasis on Mandarin over dialect. With this story, the news report that was first marked as the sound of the dominant Chinese now becomes that of marginalised languages, connecting the newsreaders with the other stories of lack of recognition but also emphasising the resulting marginalisation and potential loss of these dialects as a consequence of state policy.

The sense of wasted opportunity is reinforced with the story of how the more complex instrument, the recorder, was chosen by the Ministry of Education because of its associations with the West, while the simpler harmonica was rejected because it was tied to the East. The segment creates a clear contrast between the two instruments by showing us multiple instances of Yew Hong Chow beautifully playing the harmonica, while the recorder never emits more than a few shrill sounds. In fact, the segment ends with Yew's soulful rendition of 'Home on the Range' on the harmonica. The choice of this Western song refutes the perception that the harmonica is associated with the East, and the performance itself shows us what exactly has been lost as a result of the state policy.

In the build-up to the end, we see the ex-communist soldier singing another song from his past ('Look at our mighty heroes/China will not fall'); the madrasah students at the stadium singing an Arabic song about Singapore ('Stand up Singapore/On this big day of celebration/Live it up Singapore like a shining star'); and Victor and Charlee, who says, 'I've been around for fifty years, even older than Singapore. All of you know me. In fact, I am to Singaporeans what Mickey Mouse is to Americans. So why is it that after fifty years of being a true Singaporean, I have never received my National Day Service award? Why?' Put together in this way, these scenes are cumulative expressions of patriotism that cement the film's questioning of Singapore's marginalising of these people and communal activities through suppression (communist history, dialects), alternative policy (the harmonica) and failure to recognise their achievements (Victor and Charlee, and Margaret).

These expressions of patriotism are pitted against the spectacle of the 2003 National Day Parade in the scene that follows (see Figure 7.7). As military planes fly past with the Singapore flag, the people in the stadium wave their own little flags that give way to lights as night falls. Interspersing these images are cuts to an inflatable Mount Everest being erected in the middle of the stadium to the sound of the announcers' repeated urging to 'Stand up Singapore'. Dramatic music takes over as a man climbs to the peak of the finally inflated mountain and waves the Singapore flag. The film then cuts to a wider shot depicting the mountain in the foreground with a much larger Singapore flag in the background. In between are the scores of performers in their choreographed colours and positions, and the vast crowd of cheering spectators in the stands. This is the climax of the film but it is immediately undermined by the sound bridge of Melvyn singing 'Wasted Days and Wasted Nights'. The beginning of the song overlaps with the last image of the National Day Parade before the film cuts to the lonely busker at the MRT station, which is nearly deserted save for a few commuters who once again ignore him as they pass (see Figure 7.7).

Bookending the film with 'Wasted Days and Wasted Nights' creates a circular narrative in which the ending references itself as a logical conclusion of

Figure 7.7   National Day sequence and Melvyn at the station

the beginning. The opening clearly locates *Singapore Gaga* as a film about Singapore held together by the song's sad tone and theme of wasted opportunity. It is, in essence, a performance of Singapore that celebrates the marginalised, forgotten or unrecognised individuals and communities who find small ways to resist order and control, mainly by stressing their individuality against the monolith of 'nation'. In the process, it shows us what Singapore could be through its presentation of an alternative soundscape, even as it also laments the opportunities that are lost and wasted in its final fade to black.

The films discussed here are not unique but typical examples of the kinds of films that constitute Singapore's revival cinema, creating a corpus that projects another view, another narrative, another performance of Singapore. Regardless of whether they are about the underbelly or the marginalised, these films perpetuate the existence of 'other' Singaporeans in (an)other Singapore. Together, they comprise an unconscious but collective attempt at not only presenting an alternative performance but also owning or reclaiming representation. These voices clearly contradict and complicate state-driven representations of the nation; collectively, they articulate a plurality that resists homogenising, state-driven narratives. Singapore cinema is not a nationalistic cinema. Instead, the presence of the 'other' Singaporean highlights the paradox/tension that underpin nationalism and national cinema. By performing (an)other Singapore, these films highlight the performativity of the state's version of the nation because they deliberately perform a counter position and enact a different performance. Collectively, these films have created a Singapore cinema that exemplifies those dissonant gestures Butler describes, which disrupt the performativity of the state's own performance of Singapore by the creation and repetition of the 'other' Singaporean in (an) other Singapore.

Notes

1. I adopt Andrea Fraser Gupta's usage of the term 'Standard English' as the main dialect of English used globally 'with a small number of minor regional differences, most of which are lexical': Andrea Fraser Gupta, 'Singapore Standard', 59.
2. Lim, 'Coming'; 'Counterperformance'; 'Singapore Cinema'.
3. 'HDB was set up in 1960, at a time when a large number of people were still living in unhygienic, potentially hazardous slums and crowded squatter settlements packed in the city centres': Housing Development Board, 'Background'.
4. Housing Development Board, 'About Us'.
5. Housing Development Board, 'A Stake in the Nation'.
6. Housing Development Board, 'Public Housing'.
7. Housing Development Board, 'History'.
8. Lim, 'Singapore Cinema', 24.
9. Media Division Ministry of Information and The Arts, 'National Day Speech 1999'.
10. Lim, 'Singapore Cinema', 26.
11. Ministry of Information and The Arts, Media Division.
12. Lim, 'Counterperformance', 189.
13. White is associated with the People's Action Party because its members are usually dressed in this colour at ceremonies like the National Day Parade.
14. To encourage Singaporeans to take care of their environment, the HDB launched a series of competitions for the cleanest block of flats.

15. The Great Singapore Workout is a series of exercises put together by the government to cultivate a healthier nation.
16. Lim, 'Counterperformance', 190–1.
17. Lim, 'Singapore Cinema', 24.
18. Ibid., 26.
19. Lim, 'Coming'.
20. Lisa Lim, Anne Pakir and Lionel Wee, 'English'.
21. Gupta.
22. See ibid.; Lim, Pakir and Wee; Tai Ann Koh, 'Rice'.
23. Ministry of Information and The Arts, Media Division.
24. Ibid.
25. Hwee Hwee Tan, 'War'.
26. Koh.
27. Lim, 'Singapore Cinema', 25–6.
28. Ibid., 29.
29. Lim, 'Counterperformance', 196–200.
30. Ibid., 192–6.
31. Chin Hu Hsien, '"Face"', 45.
32. Ibid., 61.
33. tanpinpin.com, 'Singapore Gaga'.
34. Carlson, 4.

8. SINGAPORE CINEMA IN SINGAPORE

In 2013, Anthony Chen's *Ilo Ilo* made waves for being the first Singapore film to win the Caméra d'Or at the Cannes Film Festival. Among other awards, it also bagged the Best Supporting Actress, Best Original Screenplay, Best Picture and Best Director prizes at the Golden Horse Awards, beating such heavyweights as Wong Kar Wai (*Grandmaster*), Johnnie To (*Drug War*), Jia Zhangke (*A Touch of Sin*) and Tsai Mingliang (*Stray Dogs*). Chen was quickly hailed as the 'man of the moment' and 'poster boy for Singapore cinema', and the film's success was deemed 'a significant turning point in Singapore films' for giving the nation's cinema international visibility and attention.[1] This was nearly twenty years after Eric Khoo's *12 Storeys* first put Singapore on the map through the critical acclaim it received at Cannes and other festivals. Yet the differences between the two films are not as marked as the two decades may suggest. The 'other' Singaporean in (an)other Singapore that augured the revival is still very much alive in *Ilo Ilo*.

Still Talking about the Heartland

Like the films before it, *Ilo Ilo* is also about heartlanders. This time, the narrative revolves around the Lim family trying to get by during the Asian financial crisis in the 1990s. Teck is a tempered-glass salesman whose pitch is stymied by faulty samples and his inability to connect with English-speaking clients. He has substantial stock market losses and also loses his job, all of which he keeps from his wife, Hwee Leng, who struggles to cope with her pregnancy, housework and the threat of retrenchment. Their son, Jiale, is a mischievous boy who misbehaves to get attention and is strangely obsessed with keeping clippings and records of lottery draws. Added to this is the family's newly hired Filipino maid, Terry. Upon arrival, she has to surrender her passport to Hwee Leng, and Jiale is immediately hostile. He hates the idea of sharing his room with her and refuses to sit next to her at the dinner table. He also deliberately puts an unpaid item in her bag at the stationery store, causing alarms to sound when she runs out of the shop after him. She is caught and interrogated but only let off when a security tape reveals what Jiale has done. Unused to the Singaporean, heartland practice of hanging laundry on bamboo poles outside the flat, she drops one. As she rushes to retrieve it downstairs, she witnesses someone falling from the roof of the building. Taken together, Terry's initial experience of Singapore via the heartland and its heartlanders is harsh and unpleasant. The heartland is depicted as not only foreign and inhospitable but also a place for death and suicide, recalling other similar instances in films like *12 Storeys* and *15*.

Jiale eventually bonds with Terry and replaces the child she had to leave behind in the Philippines. On the other hand, she becomes his surrogate mother in place of his real one, whose cast-offs she is given to wear and lipstick she secretly uses. Jiale even prefers Terry's cooking and company to his mother's. The centrality of this relationship is reflected in the film's Chinese title, *Ba Ma Bu Zai Jia*. Literally translated it means father and mother are not at home, and the film could be read as a commentary on absent parents whose roles are performed by the maids they hire. However, the film's English title references Terry's home town in the Philippines, which is never shown because the entire film is set in Singapore. So, the absent Ilo Ilo, which signifies Terry's home and the sense of belonging that comes with it, is replaced with the reality of the Singaporean one she now finds herself in.

However, these substitutions are, in the end, flawed. Despite their bond, Terry is ultimately not Jiale's mother. When the school principal threatens to expel Jiale for hurting a schoolmate, and both his parents are unreachable, Terry intercedes on his behalf, repeatedly referring to him as 'my boy'. She is eventually asked to wait outside when Jiale's real mother arrives and summarily put in her place when Mrs Lim tells her, 'You are not his mother. I am.' Similarly, Terry never really finds a sense of belonging with the Lims or in Singapore. Teck, forgetting that they now have a stranger living in their home, continues to walk around in his underwear. When he encounters Terry in the living room, they are both shocked. He quickly covers himself and apologises to her. Over time, she does get used to living with the Lims, and bonds with Jiale especially, but her place in the family is clear. As a foreign domestic helper she may live with them but will never actually be family. As such, at Hwee Leng's mother's birthday, Terry is made to sit by herself outside the private room of the restaurant as the family celebrate inside. Her isolation is also emphasised in spaces outside the home. For example, when she goes to Lucky Plaza, a shopping mall where most Filipinos usually hang out in Singapore, she is captured alone and apart from her fellow citizens. The other Filipinos she interacts with, such as the neighbour's maid and the girls at the hair salon, are acquaintances, not friends.

Other substitutions are equally problematic. For example, after Teck hurls Jiale's Tamagotchi device out of the car window, he gives the boy real chicks to care for as a replacement and the family end up slaughtering them for food. Instead of finding comfort in the home and family, Hwee Leng seeks it among strangers at a seminar peddling hope 'within yourself' as 'opportunities in crisis'. She buys the videos and signs up for a ten-day course, only to find out later that it was all a scam. Teck gets a job as a security guard to replace the one he lost. However, he ends up breaking the eggs in the warehouse during one of his rounds and loses that job too.

As a result of inadequate substitutions, the characters are all displaced. Terry lives with but is not family and cannot find a sense of home in Singapore. Teck's role as head of the family is undermined by his employment and financial woes. Hwee Leng feels threatened by her maid, and Jiale's place as the only child is destabilised by the impending arrival of a sibling. Likewise, the film's narrative of a family on the verge of breaking down, whose members are unhappy and struggling with individual issues, also subverts the image of a happy, upwardly mobile middle-income family in Singapore, which is what the Lims represent on the surface. Like the heartlanders in *Money No Enough* and *Singapore Dreaming*, the Lims are caught in the struggle to survive and succeed but never do. There are no solutions to problems in this film but futility and the perennial cycle of coping. Their family car, which keeps breaking down, is scrapped and they cannot afford a new one. They cannot sell their HDB flat because they will not be able to get a good price for it in such an economy. Hwee Leng does not allow Teck to start a bubble tea business because she thinks he is incapable of doing business. In the end, Terry has to leave because the family can no longer afford a maid. In a desperate bid to prevent this, Jiale buys lottery numbers in the hope of winning some money. However, although he had previously successfully predicted winning numbers for his teacher, he fails to do so this time and Terry is sent home.

Like in *12 Storeys*, family and proximity do not beget reciprocity or intimacy. Family members are disconnected from each other and unable to communicate or share their individual worries. Conversations between characters are usually about the business of everyday life. Connections are found in small moments instead, such as Terry and Jiale laughing and having fun together or when Teck asks Terry if she is ok when he sees her in tears after a phone call home. In return, she keeps his smoking habit a secret. However, such moments are limited to Jiale's and Teck's interactions with Terry and do not occur between the family members themselves. So, while we see Jiale and Teck individually connecting with Terry, we do not see father and son having the same intimacy. There are also no happy interactions between husband and wife or mother and son. So, these pockets of connection in the film do not make up for the emotional distance within the Lim family. They also do not add up to tangible or real knowledge of each other. Towards the end of the film, Teck is surprised when Terry asks for a cigarette as he does not know she smokes. When she has to leave, Terry does so rather matter-of-factly while the heartbroken Jiale grasps a lock of her hair as if holding on to her. She leaves behind her Walkman with a tape of Filipino songs that she once shared with Jiale, and he listens to it at the end of the film as he awaits the arrival of the new baby in the hospital. Yet, like the many flawed substitutions in this film, these cannot adequately replace Terry's absence in the boy's life. Although father and son finally have a moment when they share the earphones to listen to the song together, their connection is still conducted via the absent Terry and the items she left behind.

So, although *Ilo Ilo* is a recent film, its narrative of the hard life of heartlanders is not new but familiar. Its average Singaporean family is as disconnected and troubled as those in prior films, and its heartlanders are likewise 'other' Singaporeans. As such, it would seem that two decades after the revival, the heartland continues to figure prominently as a site for counter-performance, and Singapore cinema is still addressing the state's version of the nation.

Variations

Like *Ilo Ilo*, Tay Ping Hui's *Meeting the Giant* (2014) is also about the experience of foreign residents in Singapore. Based on the true story about Singapore's practice of using foreign talents in its sports teams, the film is a fictionalised account of a group of basketball players from China who are offered scholarships to come to the country and compete for a place on the national team. Their experience of Singapore is not unlike Terry's. Like so many other Chinese nationals, one of its main characters, Chen Hang, has left his village in China to study in Singapore. However, his experience of the local school is hostile and alienating. The students make fun of him, are jealous of his basketball skills, refuse to pass him the ball and play a malicious prank to deliberately injure him. Even though he leads the school team to victory, he remains isolated from his teammates at the celebration dinner. The scene is captured in a time-lapse sequence reminiscent of the coffee-drinking scene in *Chungking Express* (Wong Kar Wai, 1995), with Chen Hang eating in slow motion in the foreground and the camaraderie of other team members articulated through a faster speed in the background (see Figure 8.1). The disjunction between foreground and background separates the spaces and experiences, effectively

Figure 8.1 Celebration dinner in *Meeting the Giant*

isolating Chen and emphasising his experience of the dinner as a subjective, lonely event. He is not only different and experiences the celebration differently, he is also left out by his team and isolated by cinematic style. The treatment of this scene highlights the film's narrative focus. Whereas films like *I Not Stupid* deal with the influx of foreign talents by presenting them as sub-par, culturally clueless and only here to take jobs from locals, *Meeting the Giant* offers a view from the other side – that of the foreigners themselves and their experience of Singapore.

Chen Hang may have come to Singapore to better his prospects but his life here is a hard one. He lives in a small room with his mother, has no money for a phone and struggles with the pressure to keep his grades up. He finds a greater sense of belonging when he joins the basketball team comprised of Chinese nationals like himself as part of the programme to enhance Singapore's sporting strengths by importing foreign talents. However, this group of Chinese players is isolated and their sphere of action is mostly limited to the apartment they share and various basketball courts in which they play. They all struggle with homesickness and the pressure to be a great team. Their friendship is later jeopardised when they are forced to compete with each other for a place on the team. In the end, though a few are selected, only one player ends up staying in the team. Chen Hang goes to study overseas, one returns to China and joins the national team in his home country, and another takes a part-time job to survive in Singapore. Only Singapore does not change, as is evident from the news report that the women's basketball team will be conducting the same programme. The film clearly problematises the state's policies on importing foreign talent in general and such sports programmes in particular by focusing on the cost to and sacrifices made by those who come to Singapore. It humanises the experience of foreign talents and, in so doing, offers a different perspective of an equally other Singapore.

Tan Pin Pin's documentary *To Singapore with Love* (2013) also adopts an external perspective. It is 'shot entirely outside the country, in the belief that we can learn something about ourselves by adopting, both literally and figuratively, an external view.'[2] The film comprises a series of interviews with former student leaders, activists and members of the Malayan Communist Party who fled Singapore in the 1960s, '70s and '80s to escape detention without trial and have since been living in exile in the UK, Thailand and Malaysia. In the film, they discuss their reasons for leaving and 'what Singapore still means to them today'.[3] Woven together through Tan's associative style of narration, their stories can be cumulatively read to offer 'a glimpse of a Singapore that could have been'.[4] This is also perhaps why Singapore's Media Development Authority (MDA) banned the film and classified it as Not Allowed for Ratings (NAR). In the Authority's assessment,

> the contents of the film undermine national security because legitimate actions of the security agencies to protect the national security and stability of Singapore are presented in a distorted way as acts that victimised innocent individuals. Under the Film Classification Guidelines, films that are assessed to undermine national security will be given an NAR rating.[5]

Although Tan subsequently appealed the rating, the MDA upheld its decision to prohibit the film, causing much uproar and debate. Cries railing against the state's suppression of alternative accounts and refusal to allow its people to discuss and form their own opinions on 'an aspect of our nation's history that is rarely discussed in the public sphere'[6] were met with further statements by the government emphasising the film's obfuscation and whitewashing of facts.[7] Addressing the ban, Tan Pin Pin argued that

> I was also hoping that the film would open up a national conversation to allow us to understand ourselves as a nation better too. I am therefore very disappointed that my film is banned. By doing this, MDA is taking away an opportunity for us Singaporeans to see it and to have a conversation about it and our past that this film could have started or contributed to. It is vital for us to have that conversation on our own terms, especially on the eve of our 50th birthday. We need to be trusted to be able to find the answers to questions about ourselves, for ourselves.[8]

However, her statement also emphasises the emotional rather than political aspect of her film:

> They talk about why they left, but they mostly talk about their lives today and their relationship with Singapore. They show us the new lives they have created for themselves . . . The focus is on their everyday lives . . . their feelings for Singapore are intense and heartfelt, albeit sometimes ambivalent, even after so long away. Those feelings (more than the circumstances of their exile, or even the historical 'truth' that led to such exile) are what my film predominantly focuses on . . .⁹

This is apparent the film's depiction of its subjects. Although there are some like Tan Wah Biao who continue to question democracy in Singapore and Said Zahiri who still believes that the nation is suppressed, the film as a whole humanises its interviewees by capturing them as rather average and innocuous individuals going about their lives in their homes and businesses rather than as dangerous dissidents or threats to national security. For example, Han Juan Thai, who was accused of being a chauvinist and inciting violence, is shown at home in the UK cooking lunch and playing with his children, reuniting with his mother in Johor, Malaysia and connecting with family members through a video call as they celebrate his mother's birthday in Singapore. Most poignant is the image of Han standing on the Johor beachfront looking across the narrow straits to Singapore, conveying the pain of being so near yet so far from home. We also see Ang Swee Chai, who had followed her activist husband, Francis Khoo, into exile in London, reuniting with family and friends in Malaysia. Her story also evinces the cost of activism in Singapore, which is displacement and estrangement from the emotional comfort of home, family and friends. As she says, 'Making a stand is expensive. Supporting those who make a stand can be just as expensive.' In addition, what comes across in the scenes of those who left Singapore in the 1960s is how ordinary and old they are, particularly the hunched figure of Yap Wah Pin, the wrinkled faces and liver spots of Hee Jin and his wife emphasised in close-ups and their frailty in the final long shot of the elderly couple walking slowly away (see Figure 8.2). These images of Mr and Mrs Hee are contrasted with the black-and-white photographs of them in communist army uniforms. Their discussion of that time as communist fighters in the Malayan jungle is rather surprising and incongruous with how they now appear.

All these individuals are obviously also other Singaporeans whose voices have been marginalised and silenced by the state and their continued exile. Furthermore, depicting them as rather ordinary people presents an alternative view of these exiles and undermines the state's portrayal of them as dangerous 'individuals . . . involved in violent and subversive actions to advance the

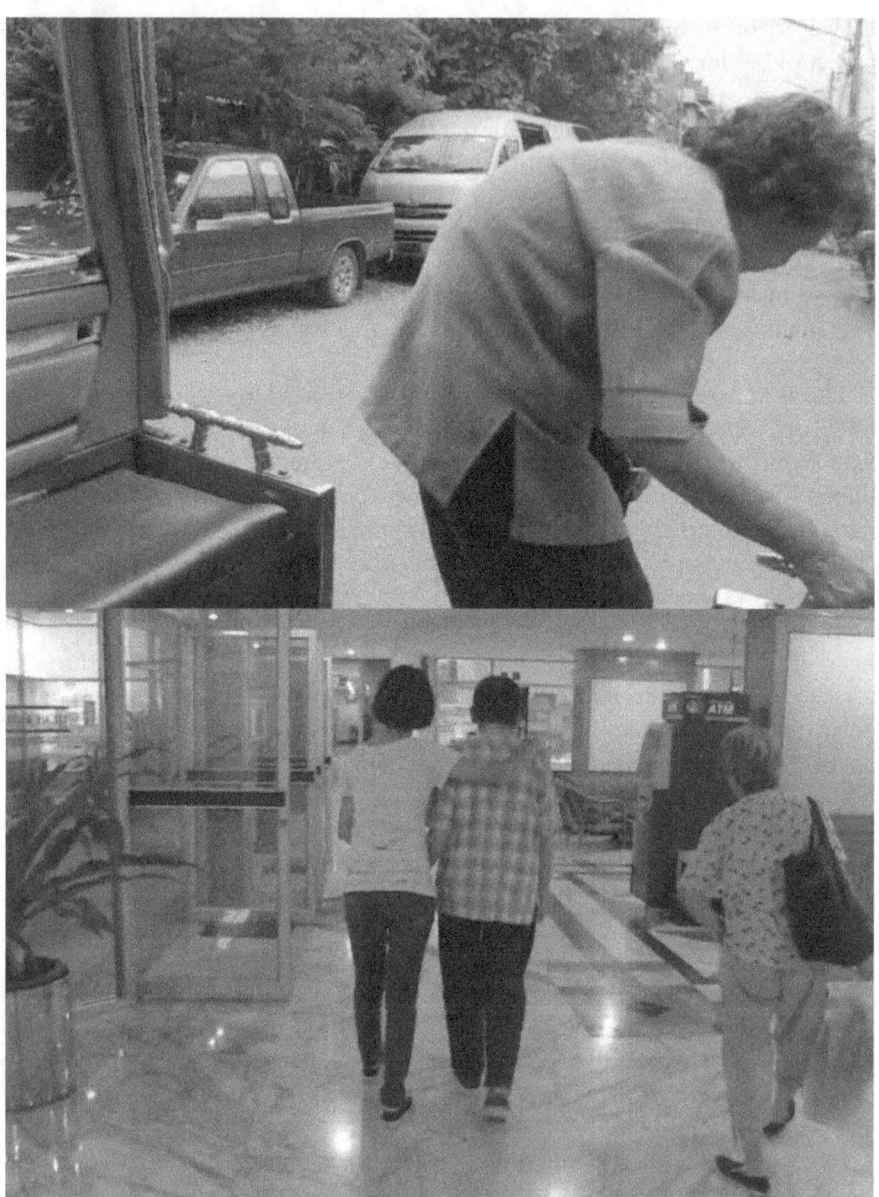

Figure 8.2 The hunched Yap Wah Pin and long shot of Hee Jin and his wife

CPM's agenda, and had posed a serious threat to the security of Singapore and the safety of Singaporeans'.[10] As such, *To Singapore with Love* follows the trend of prior revival films by featuring other Singaporeans and enabling them to tell their stories. In so doing, the film produces yet (an)other Singapore though its narrative. Its Singapore is one that is unforgiving and does not tolerate political dissension and opposition but also inspires deep love and connection from those who still long to return.

SG50 AND OTHER SINGAPORE STORIES

In 2015, Singapore celebrated its fifty years of independence with a year-long programme of activities collectively organised and branded as SG50. According to the official website, www.singapore50.sg, 'SG50 is a nationwide effort to celebrate our country's 50th birthday in 2015. That's a huge milestone – 50 years of independence! This is a momentous event for Singaporeans to reflect on how far we've come together as a nation and people.'[11] A number of films released that year commemorated the milestone in their own ways and are explicitly about Singapore. These include *1965*, *A Long, Long Time Ago Parts 1 and 2*, *In The Room* and *7 Letters*.

The last is an omnibus of individual short films made by seven prominent local filmmakers that celebrates

> those personal stories among us – each 'letter' is intricately interwoven with our memories, experiences, joys and woes ... This will be more than just another film. *7 Letters* is our story. It is our hope that through it, you too will be inspired to reflect on your connections with this place we call home.[12]

Each short centres its reflection of 'home' via the past or a connection to it. Some are set in a past time such as the setting of the kampong in 1975 in Jack Neo's *The Girl*, an Indian family's questioning of where they belong amid the impending withdrawal of British troops in K. Rajogopal's *The Flame*, and the quiet connection between a young Chinese boy and an elderly Malay woman in the heartland in the 1980s in Royston Tan's *Bunga Sayang*. In others, 'home' is informed through memory and loss. Eric Khoo's *Cinema* re-creates a *pontianak* film that connects past and present. First, it is presented as the film that we the audience view, before becoming a film-within-a film enjoyed by a diegetic, animated kampong audience in the past. Finally, it is played on a small television for elderly, nursing home patients who stare impassively at the screen (see Figure 8.3). Among the audience is one of its crew members and watching the film triggers his subsequent journey across town to once more take his place on a set where the old multiracial cast and crew have gathered to 'make' the film. For him, home is 'on the film set, [where] race, language and religion did not matter'. Khoo's short is a nostalgic tribute to the golden age even as it also laments its loss and traces exactly the fate of these films today.

CELLULOID SINGAPORE

Figure 8.3 The *pontianak* film in three ways: as the film we watch; viewed by diegetic audience; and on television

The remaining three films in the collection explore the past by evoking Malaysia, thus referencing the long history between these two countries. In Tan Pin Pin's *Pineapple Town*, an adoptive mother's search for her child's birth mother leads her to Malaysia twice; first, to a rest stop where she discov-

Figure 8.4 The little girl with the Pineapple statue captured via passing car

ers the woman's circumstances but does not actually meet her, and a few years later when she takes the young child to her 'tummy mummy's' home town of Pekan Nanas, the Pineapple Town of the film's title. Both journeys are borne out of the mother's desire for her adopted child to know where she came from. Yet the child herself is a stranger to what would have been her home town. She visits Pekan Nanas as a tourist who poses for photos with the town's giant pineapple. This is how she is finally captured through the interior of a presumably local car passing by in the last shot of the film (see Figure 8.4). The girl's past, like Singapore's, is tied to Malaysia, and her lack of connection with the space and what it represents corresponds with the distance and difference between these two countries in the present as well.

Boo Jun Feng's *Parting* explores the intersection of past and present when an elderly Malaysian returns to Singapore to find his lost love, only to discover that too much has changed. He neither finds her nor connects with the Singapore in the present, which is disorienting and unfamiliar to him. All he is left with are the fragments of memory endangered by the onset of dementia and reflected in the debris of the now-defunct Tanjong Pagar railway station that once connected Singapore and Malaysia. Kelvin Tong's *Grandma Positioning System* centres on a family's dependence on the grandmother's directions to guide them to her husband's grave in Johor, Malaysia. There, she also gives her husband directions to help his spirit navigate back to their home in Singapore. As the city has changed so much, she painstakingly describes each of the places that have altered or disappeared so that he would not get lost or disoriented. When they return the next year, the grandmother has passed on and, without her, the family cannot find their way out of the cemetery despite the maps and car's navigation system. They end up back at the grave, where they take turns to give the grandparents directions to their new home. This family ritual is about remembering as the directions force the characters to emotionally navigate memories embodied in the places that once had meaning to them but which, like the departed, have now disappeared. The ending concretises this with a montage of old black-and-white photos of those very places, such as the causeway, the old Ford and soy sauce factories, and favourite hawker stalls. That this has to be done every year also implies the rapid rate at which Singapore changes, whereas the Malaysian cemetery remains the same. Evoking Malaysia to commemorate Singapore's fiftieth birthday is not surprising, since this nation was born as a consequence of separation. However, unlike the state's version of SG50, which celebrates how far Singapore has come, what these films emphasise instead are loss and disconnection as a result or effect of progress and development.

Eric Khoo's *In the Room* is the filmmaker's 'own little tribute to SG50'.[13] Here, Singapore is embodied by the film's fictional hotel, The Singapura, as evidenced by the use of the country's Malayised name (see Figure 8.5). According to Khoo, the hotel was inspired by the actual New 7th Storey Hotel that was the tallest building in Singapore when it was built in the 1950s: 'it was like a landmark and was grand with great parties on the top floor, but in its last ten years of its existence it became a shit hole. It just became sad then it was demolished.'[14] The narrative comprises a series of vignettes about the activities and experiences of characters who occupy the transitory space of room 27 from the 1940s to the '90s and beyond. The intention is

> to show the progress. Each story shows the passing of a different decade, which is also represented in the room's changing soundscape and interior. Moving down the timeline, we will experience the roaring 50s and the swinging 60s, along with the movement towards social liberation and changing perspectives towards sex. By the 1990s, the Singapura has become a budget hotel, a cheap stop for lost souls on the road.[15]

The film begins with 'Rubber' in the 1940s. Shot in black and white, two men, a colonial expat and a local businessman who are also lovers, discuss the implications of the British surrender on Singapore, their relationship and individual lives in what seems to be the last time they will meet in the room. The story of the '50s, 'Pussy', features a flamboyant stripper teaching a group of neophytes the power of the vagina, which she ends up wielding to subdue the leader of a gang of thugs. This story is, according to Khoo, a 'tribute to Rose Chan, this famous stripper from Singapore'[16] during that time. In 'Listen', the vignette of the '60s, a local band uses the room to celebrate the new year and their song making it to number one on the charts. It reflects the heyday

Figure 8.5 The Singapura

of local music at the time and is Khoo's take on one of the more popular groups – The Quest. To cement the reference, one of The Quest's members, Vernon Cornelius, appears in a cameo role as the film's band manager.[17] Next is 'Change', which is about a Thai couple who are in Singapore for one of them to undergo a sex-change operation. It is set in the '70s, a time when Singapore was a popular destination for such operations.[18] The prevalence of a large Japanese expat community in Singapore in the 1980s is reflected in 'Search', in which a Japanese housewife has an afternoon tryst with her local boy toy in their regular room. The next story, 'First Time', is set in the '90s and is about a pair of South Korean tourists – a young woman escaping from unfulfilling sexual relationships and her male best friend. This is not only their first visit in Singapore but also the first time that she experiences her orgasm.

Each story thus represents a decade and is set against the context of the respective period. However, this is not a conventional account of the country's history. This is not the Singapore Story by any stretch of the imagination, and the film does not re-enact milestone events such as the merger or separation. Instead, each story offers an alternative view of the decade within which it is set from variously inside (local) and outside (foreign) perspectives. For example, while the 1990s is a decade when the state cements its performance of successful Singapore, what the film offers instead is the young South Korean woman's rather scathing perspective of the country when she says: 'I want to be somewhere as unromantic as possible, a place like this city. No history, no art. Sterile like a hospital. With so many strict laws.' Her view of Singapore is reinforced by the shot of a newspaper article about a local political dissident being released from detention. Furthermore, as all the stories are about sex, *In The Room* presents a Singapore story experienced through a range of sexual encounters.

However, because much of the film is limited to the room, the narrative of the film can also be read as the history of The Singapura, which is pit against that of Singapore as a kind of parallel, alternative account. As time passes, and Singapore progresses, the hotel correspondingly deteriorates, such that after the 1990s it becomes a dingy, decrepit space occupied by vagrants, foreign workers and sleazy sexual encounters. This is captured in a montage sequence that alternates between the gradual deterioration of the space and the people who inhabit it. It is only at the end that we see 'Singapore' beyond the confines of the room in The Singapura. This Singapore exists in an undisclosed future and is imagined as a dark, soulless, space reminiscent of Fritz Lang's looming *Metropolis* (see Figure 8.6). In this foreboding and pessimistic image of Singapore's progress, the alternative history of this once-grand hotel is no longer relevant and already forgotten as The Singapura becomes an underbelly space, dwarfed by the futuristic structures of a sci-fi future.

(An)other Cinema

In 2008, I wrote that 'it is somewhat ironic that the very element that augured the revival of Singapore films, this "other" Singaporean, is also the same element that has come to not only characterize Singapore films in general but also resulted in its position as the "other" cinema in Singapore.'[19] Nearly a decade later, this situation has not changed. Although the formation of the Singapore Film Commission in 1998 marks the state's recognition and support of local film production through funding grants and infrastructure, production output remains relatively small compared to larger cinemas such as China or South Korea. Between 1995 and 2016, Singapore produced 215 theatrically released films, which is an average of 9.8 films per year. The industry high was in 2008 with seventeen films.[20] In contrast, South Korea produced fifty films in 2016 alone.[21] What this means is that there are fewer local films to be screened in the cinemas, especially when compared to the regular slate of international films available to movie-goers, primarily from Hollywood.

Access to and visibility of local films in Singapore remains an issue. Prior to the 2000s, film exhibition in Singapore was a 'bipolar world'[22] of commercial films in major commercial cineplexes, namely those run by Golden Village, Shaw, Cathay, Eng Wah and Filmgarde, and non-mainstream fare in alternative venues and events such as the Singapore Film Society, the Singapore International Film Festival and the Goethe Institute. Since then, the number

Figure 8.6 Singapore's sci-fi future

of alternative venues and activities has increased with the emergence of The Arts House's Screening Room, the National Museum's Cinémathèque, The Substation, Sinema Old School, the Alliance Française, The Projector, various festivals and programmes like the Singapore International Film Festival and

The Substation's Moving Images film programme, and repertory theatres run by major film exhibitors such as Golden Village's Cinema Europa and Cathay's The Picturehouse.[23] However, while the opening of more alternative venues suggests increasing interest in non-mainstream films in Singapore, the polarisation between mainstream and arthouse remains.

Singapore's revival cinema is largely an independent cinema and produces fewer films that would be considered commercial or mainstream. There are basically two so-called mainstreams in Singapore. The first is cinematic, where the mainstream comprises commercial films primarily from Hollywood and other, usually big-budget, productions from Hong Kong, China or South Korea. This is where Hollywood blockbusters like *Captain America: Civil War* (Anthony and Joe Russo, 2016) and *Rogue One* (Gareth Edwards, 2016) dominate alongside *The Great Wall* (Zhang Yimou, 2016) and *Train to Busan* (Yeon Sang-ho, 2016). The second is the Chinese television mainstream that has been dominated by dramas and programmes produced by the only broadcasting company in Singapore, MediaCorp. Its long history in domestic television programming can be traced back to the 1960s when it existed as Radio Television Singapore, a department of the Ministry of Culture. Radio Television Singapore became a statutory board in 1981 and was renamed the Singapore Broadcasting Corporation. It was eventually corporatised as the Television Corporation of Singapore (TCS) in 1994, and later privatised as MediaCorp TV Singapore Pte Ltd in 2001, under the MediaCorp group of companies. With this history comes a wealth of experience in producing local programmes for television, particularly variety shows and drama serials for its Chinese-language channel, Channel 8. These local productions have been very popular with domestic audiences since the 1980s and constitute a significant portion of MediaCorp's programming. They remain, to this day, the cornerstone of the company. As such, at the time of the revival, Singapore did not have a film industry but it did have a very mature television industry that already had its own talents and stars.

It is from this firm base in television production that MediaCorp's explorations into the medium of film emerged as a natural consequence. Raintree Pictures was formed by the then TCS in August 1998 for the distinct purpose of venturing into the business of film production, and its products were very closely tied to its parent company and television. This is apparent in the two kinds of films Raintree produced. The first are local productions based on popular television characters or featured television stars. Prime examples include *Liang Po Po: The Movie* (Teng Bee Lian, 1999), which is based on the immense popularity of the title character played by Jack Neo and made famous through Channel 8's long-running Chinese variety programme *Comedy Night*, and *One Leg Kicking* (Eric Khoo and Wei Koh, 2001), which featured a stellar cast of local comic talents like Kumar, Hossan Leong, Mark Lee, Jack Neo,

Mosses Lim and Gurmit Singh, as well as numerous Jack Neo films from *I Not Stupid* in 2002 to *Money No Enough 2* in 2008. The second type of films that Raintree produced are what it called 'borderless' films. These are co-productions with other cinemas, particularly Hong Kong, that featured well-known Hong Kong directors and actors. Examples include *AD2000* (Gordon Chan, 2000), *The Eye* (Pang Brothers, 2002) and *Infernal Affairs II* (Andrew Lau and Alan Mak, 2003). Singapore stars were initially cast in major roles such as Fann Wong in *The Truth about Jane and Sam* (Derek Yee, 1999). However, the lack of popularity of these films eventually saw local talents taking on smaller roles like Tay Ping Hui in *Infernal Affairs II* before disappearing altogether. Later Raintree co-produced films such as *Painted Skin* (Gordon Chan, 2008) had no local actors. As such, these films are not generally regarded as Singapore films but Hong Kong ones, despite Raintree's involvement. Raintree's films are commercial ones with elements that are tried and tested, especially on TV, or already 'proven' box-office hits. Although Raintree stopped making movies in 2012, it was through this company that Singapore's mainstream film production emerged as an offshoot of television, comprised largely of Chinese-language films directed by Jack Neo.

Neo makes an average of one film a year and is the only filmmaker to date who consistently makes films for a general, mass audience and whose films are usually box-office hits. Other ventures into this market by other filmmakers are less frequent and successful. So, while the film industry does make commercial films, they constitute a small sub-set of the larger mainstream market of Hollywood blockbusters. The bulk of Singapore's films are more arthouse than mainstream. They circulate in festivals rather than local major cinemas. As such, the usual venues for watching Singapore films in Singapore are at alternative venues. Viewed through film exhibition practices, Singapore cinema is generally positioned as an alternative to the mainstream that is primarily dominated by Hollywood films.

Furthermore, the existence of these alternative venues has also been short-lived, succumbing to the pressures of 'high rents, online viewing – both legal and illegal – high marketing costs and unappealing locations forced on them by their low-profit margins'.[24] Cathay's The Picturehouse was converted to a commercial venue in 2011 and is now 'an arthouse-focused brand name, The Picturehouse Selection'.[25] Sinema Old School was closed in 2012 and has become an organisation that jointly hosts alternative film screenings with Golden Village. Golden Village's Cinema Europa has also been phased out and is no longer listed on the company's website. Only those that are housed within larger, multipurpose venues and organisations supported by public funding, like the National Museum's Cinémathèque and The Arts House's Screening Room, have survived.[26] Instead, 'the major chains now screen these works without the need to slap on the "arthouse" label which, in recent years, has lost its prestige value and may in fact deter those who associate it with dullness and pretension.'[27] While this seems to ameliorate the dichotomy between arthouse and mainstream, and works in favour of the largely arthouse style of Singapore films by improving access to them, being screened in major theatres does not necessarily lead to significantly improved viewership. Screenings of arthouse films at these major venues tend to be more limited than mainstream ones. For example, despite being hailed by the local press, *Ilo Ilo* had a modest local release of fifteen prints in major theatres compared to Jack Neo's more commercial *Ah Boys to Men 2*, which had forty-four prints. In contrast, *Ilo Ilo* opened in eighty cinemas in Paris and was the number five top-grossing film there in 2013.[28] This suggests that a film like *Ilo Ilo* has a larger market and is more popular among audiences abroad than domestically.

Local films also do not have the same budget as Hollywood films and so are not as heavily marketed or publicised, leading to a lack of visibility and information about these films in the domestic market. Furthermore, most films are not able to recoup their production costs at the local box-office. For instance, in 2006, of the ten films released that year, only one was profitable – Jack Neo's *I Not Stupid Too*.[29] Even the much-acclaimed *Ilo Ilo* was reported to have taken in only SGD$500,000, SGD$200,000 short of its SGD$700,000 production budget, after a two-week run.[30] It was nearly two months later before the film crossed the million-dollar mark after a special re-release and extended screening in Singapore.[31] The seventeen films released in 2008 collectively made SGD$15,269,752.4,[32] which is less than 10 per cent of the SGD$152,732,730 net total of box-office receipts in the major cinemas in Singapore that year.[33] Of these seventeen films, only *Money No Enough 2* made it to the top ten grossing films of the year.[34] Between 2003 and 2016, only eight locally produced films were in the top ten grossing films of the year. With the exception of Royston Tan's *881* in 2007, the rest of these films were made by Jack Neo. To date, *Money No Enough* is also the only Singapore film to have made it to the top five grossing films of all time in the country, a position it held for nearly a decade between its release in 1998, before it was out-grossed in 2008.[35] In comparison, since 2004, nine of the top ten grossing films in South Korea have been South Korean films.[36] These figures show that, apart from occasional hits primarily by Neo, Singapore films are evidently not as popular in cinemas in Singapore, and the primary diet of local film-goers is comprised of Hollywood films that dominate the box-office. It may be the case that local films are viewed elsewhere, such as online or on DVDs. If this is so, then Singapore cinema continues to be positioned as an alternative cinema viewed through alternative platforms. This will not change even if viewership of local films through these alternative modes and venues surpasses that of the major theatres.

This situation is exacerbated if we include the films of the golden age and post-studio 1970s, which are not only much less visible and accessible than those of the revival but also perform Singapores that are foreign or far removed from the nation today. They are regarded as films of the past, historical artefacts occasionally encountered at film festivals and in retrospective programmes but which otherwise remain obscure and unknown to the general local audience. As such, whether it is lack of access, visibility and/or interest, Singapore cinema as a whole has not only produced other Singapores, it is also an(other) cinema in Singapore.

Conclusion

The films discussed above clearly continue to engage the nation by performing other Singapores filled with other Singaporeans. These counter-performative acts have, over time and by virtue of their repetition, become normative in Singapore cinema to the extent that 'they are in the end nothing but their repetition.'[37] Viewed in this way, Singapore films from the 1990s onwards seem to invariably tell the same story. If so, then what is the point? Is national identity, like gender, also 'an assignment which is never quite carried out according to expectation, whose addressee never quite inhabits the ideal s/he is compelled to approximate'?[38] If the addressees of a nation's identity are its citizens then Singaporeans too can never fully inhabit either the ideal of the state's successful Singapore(an) or the alternative of the other Singaporean performed in its cinema. The other Singaporean counters and exposes the desire to succeed and acquire the material dream of the Five Cs as performative gestures. However, the other Singaporean is also a performative gesture that engages an imagined Singaporean who tries to embody or enact those desires to participate in the state's version of a successful Singapore. If the battleground is identity, as I suggested at the start of this book and elsewhere, then neither the state's nor cinema's performances can fully address, depict or represent the nation because

> performativity describes this relation of being implicated in that which one opposes, this turning of power against itself to produce alternative modalities of power, to establish a kind of political contestation that is not a 'pure' opposition, a 'transcendence' of contemporary relations of power, but a difficult labour of forging a future from resources inevitably impure.[39]

Viewed thus, Singapore's revival cinema's counter-performance of state rhetoric is 'not a "pure" opposition'. By exposing the performativity of the state's rhetoric, Singapore cinema also implicates and exposes itself as performance. Indeed, if national identity is 'real only to the extent that it is performed',[40] then attempts at performing the nation, whether state-driven or cinematic, should not be viewed dialectically 'but as impure, implicated and interacting performances that stage and re-stage the nation as process'.[41]

The multiple Singapores produced by the films across the three periods studied here attest to the notion of nation as process. As Singapore has transitioned from its attachment to larger political entities to a more self-determined sense of itself as a nation, so too has its cinema evolved from a transnational beginning to a greater national consciousness or imperative. In this sense, like nation and identity, celluloid Singapore is not singular but a composite of multiple Singapores in multiple films through multiple periods. If films are not just texts but performances as well, then, when viewed through the lens of national cinema, what they perform is the nation. While nations may be said to produce their cinemas, cinemas also produce nations. While nations are, as Chakravaty says, 'inevitably diverse and plural',[42] such plurality and diversity is also apparent across time and timeframes, as the examinations of the three periods and various ways of considering the films as Singapore films here show. This book is not about Singapore cinema per se, or Singapore, but both. There are, of course, more films and issues that can be discussed than space here or time permit. The question of how a cinema is national is a complex, ongoing one, and what *Celluloid Singapore* offers is essentially a 'way of seeing as' where cinema and nation are viewed and understood in tandem. In doing so, this book hopes to have forwarded the discussion by cultivating a different understanding of both Singapore and its cinema.

Notes

1. Dylan Tan, 'Basking'.
2. Pin Pin Tan, 'Tan's Statement'.
3. Pin Pin Tan, 'To Singapore with Love'.
4. Ibid.
5. Info-Communications Media Development Authority, 'Nar'.
6. 'Filmmakers''.
7. See Nur Asyiqin Mohamad Salleh, 'Parliament'; Nur Asyiqin Mohamad Salleh, 'Exiles'.
8. Tan, 'Tan's Statement'.
9. Ibid.
10. Salleh, 'Parliament'.
11. 'Sg50 Frequently Asked Questions (Faq)'.
12. '7letters.Sg'.
13. Ray Yeh, 'Reworked'.
14. Amir Ganjavie, 'Interview with Eric Khoo'.
15. Ibid.
16. Yeh.
17. SINdie, 'In the Room'.
18. 'In the 1970s and '80s, hospitals in Singapore accepted numerous sex change patients from abroad, with foreigners making up around half of all surgeries performed, while the rest were locals and Malaysians': Meng Choo Chan, 'First Sex Change Surgery'.

19. Lim, 'Coming'.
20. 'List 1991–2016'.
21. 'South Korea 2016'.
22. Jan Uhde and Yvonne Ng Uhde, 'The Substation', 210.
23. Ibid., 219.
24. John Lui, 'Tough Luck'.
25. Ibid.
26. Ibid.
27. Ibid.
28. Boon Chan, 'Audience?'
29. 'List 1991–2006'.
30. Chan, 'Audience?'
31. John Lui, 'Ilo Ilo'; 'Ilo Ilo Facebook'.
32. 'List 1991–2016'.
33. 'Cinema Attendance'.
34. 'Top 10'.
35. 'Top Grossing'.
36. 'All Time'.
37. Loxley, 124.
38. Judith Butler, *Bodies That Matter*, 231.
39. Ibid., 241.
40. Butler, 'Performative Acts', 526.
41. Lim, 'Counterperformance', 201.
42. Chakravarty, 223.

WORKS CITED

'Cinema Attendance in Singapore'. Accessed 4 March 2017. https://www.imda.gov.sg/~/media/imda/files/industry development/sectors/media/4 - cinema attendance since 1990 - 2015.pdf?la=en.

'History Sg: Indonesia Announces Konfrontasi (Confrontation)'. Accessed 4 March 2017. http://eresources.nlb.gov.sg/history/events/126b6b07-f796-4b4c-b658-938001e3213e.

'Kishore Mahbubani: About'. Accessed 5 May 2017. http://mahbubani.net/about/.

'Sg50 Frequently Asked Questions (Faq)'. www.singapore50.sg. Accessed 12 June 2015. https://www.singapore50.sg/SG50/About.

'Ilo Ilo 爸妈不在家's Facebook Page'. 5 December 2013. Accessed 7 January 2015. https://www.facebook.com/iloilomovie/posts/732357440116167.

Souvenir Magazine, *The Straits Times*, 6 August 1986.

'Filmmakers'&Arts Community's Statement Re: Mda's Ban on Tan Pin Pin's "To Singapore with Love"'. 10 September 2017. Accessed 9 January 2017. https://www.facebook.com/notes/filmcommunity-sg/filmmakers-arts-communitys-statement-re-mdas-ban-on-tan-pin-pins-to-singapore-wi/1494957707417453.

'National Day Songs', *Singapore Infopedia*. 11 March 2015. Accessed 24 September 2016. http://eresources.nlb.gov.sg/infopedia/articles/SIP_2015-03-11_165927.html.

'Pledge to Be Sung as Part of New National Song', *The Straits Times*, 20 June 1987. Accessed 23 September 2016. http://eresources.nlb.gov.sg/newspapers/Digitised/Article/straitstimes19870620-1.2.28.14.aspx.

'Singapore's Top 10 Grossing Movies by Year from 2003'. 31 December 2016. Accessed 2 February 2017. https://www.imda.gov.sg/~/media/imda/files/industry development/sectors/media/3 singapores top 10 grossing movies by year from 20032015.pdf?la=en.

'Light on Yellow', *The Straits Times*, 23 June 1959. http://eresources.nlb.gov.sg/newspapers/Digitised/Article/straitstimes19590625-1.2.66.aspx.

WORKS CITED

Broadcast by the Prime Minister on 22 March, 1968, Inaugurating a Series of Ministerial Broadcasts, Entitled 'the Crucial Years'. Ministry of Culture, 1968.
'Lim Warns of Flower People, Yellow Culture', *The Straits Times*, 13 January 1968. http://eresources.nlb.gov.sg/newspapers/Digitised/Article/straitstimes19680113-1.2.14.aspx.
The Prime Minister, Mr Lee Kuan Yew's National Day Broadcast. Ministry of Culture, 1969.
'Long Hair "Mark of a Rebel"', *The Straits Times*, 22 June 1974. http://eresources.nlb.gov.sg/newspapers/Digitised/Article/straitstimes19740622-1.2.102.aspx.
'"Shaggy Look Doesn't Pay" Message Driven Home', *The Straits Times*, 12 December 1975. Accessed 23 June 2016. http://eresources.nlb.gov.sg/newspapers/Digitised/Article/straitstimes19751212-1.2.48.aspx.
'Filmmakers Who Tried and Failed in Singapore', *The Straits Times*, 29 November 1980. http://eresources.nlb.gov.sg/newspapers/digitised/article/straitstimes19801129-1.2.154.11.2.aspx.
'Jack in a Box That Won't Be Popping out on Big Screen', *The Straits Times*, 14 January 1980.
'Jukebox Ban Off', *The New Paper*, 15 July 1991.
'No Claim Made on P. Ramlee's Works', *The Straits Times*, 7 May 1999.
'P. Ramlee's Works Belong to Us, Says Kl', *The Straits Times*, 6 May 1999.
'Singapore Today'. 2005. Accessed 25 February 2005. http://www.visitsingapore.com/sections/articles/3c/1,1177,222,00.html.
'Why Study in Singapore?' 2005. Accessed 24 February 2005. http://www.singaporeedu.gov.sg/htm/sis/sis01.htm.
'7letters.Sg: Foreword'. 2015. Accessed 7 April 2017. https://7letters.sg/ - FOREWORD.
'National Day'. Singapore Tourism Board. 2015. Accessed 16 August 2016. http://www.yoursingapore.com/festivals-events-singapore/cultural-festivals/national-day.html.
'Singapore's Top 5 Grossing Movies of All Time'. 2016. Accessed 8 February 2017. https://www.imda.gov.sg/~/media/imda/files/industry development/sectors/media/2 - singapores top 5 grossing movies of all time 2016.pdf?la=en.
'Statistics: All Time'. 2017. Accessed 10 May 2017. http://www.koreanfilm.or.kr/jsp/news/boxOffice_AllTime.jsp?mode=BOXOFFICE_ALLTIME.
'Statistics: South Korean Films 2016'. 2017. Accessed 1 May 2017. http://www.koreanfilm.or.kr/jsp/news/boxOffice_Yearly.jsp?mode=BOXOFFICE_YEAR&selectDt=2016&category=ALL&country=K.
'More Mass Display Items on N-Day', *The Straits Times*, 12 July 1986.
'Parade with a Difference', *The Straits Times*, 12 July 1986.
'List of Singapore Movies (1999–2006)'. December 2006. Accessed 1 December 2016. https://www.imda.gov.sg/~/media/imda/files/industry development/sectors/media/1 box office information for singapore films 19912006.pdf?la=en.
'List of Singapore Movies (1991–2016)'. March 2017. Accessed 1 May 2017. https://www.imda.gov.sg/~/media/imda/files/industry development/sectors/media/1 box office information for singapore films 19912015.pdf?la=en.

Alfred, Hedwig. 'All Agree It Was the Best Ever', *Straits Times*, 10 August 1986. Accessed 7 July 2014. http://eresources.nlb.gov.sg/newspapers/Digitised/Article/straitstimes19860810-1.2.4.13.
Aljunied, Syed Muhd Khairudin. 'Films as Social History – P. Ramlee's "Seniman Bujang Lapok" and Malays in Singapore (1950s–60s)', *The Heritage Journal* 2, No. 1 (2005): 1–21.

187

Anagnost, Ann. *National Past-Times: Narrative, Representation and Power in Modern China* (Durham, NC: Duke University Press, 1997).
Anderson, Benedict. *Imagined Communities: Reflections on the Origin and Spread of Nationalism* (New York: Verso, 2000).
Andrew, Dudley. *Concepts in Film Theory* (Oxford: Oxford University Press, 1984).
Andrew, Dudley. 'Time Zones and Jet Lag: The Flows and Phases of World Cinema', in Nataša Ďurovičová and Kathleen Newman (eds), *World Cinemas, Transnational Perspectives* (New York: Routledge, 2010), 59–89.
Ansaldo, Umberto. *Contact Languages: Ecology and Evolution in Asia Contact Languages* (Cambridge: Cambridge University Press, 2009). Accessed 24 January 2016. EBSCOhost. eBook Collection (EBSCOhost).
Aye, Daw Khin Khin. 'Bazaar Malay: History, Grammar and Contact' (National University of Singapore, 2006). Accessed 24 January 2016. scholarbank.nus.edu.sg. http://scholarbank.nus.edu.sg/handle/10635/15028.
Barnard, Timothy. 'The Ambivalence of P. Ramlee: *Penarek Beca* and *Bujang Lapok* in Perspective', *Asian Cinema* 13, No. 2 (2002): 9–23.
Barnard, Timothy P. 'Decolonization and the Nation in Malay Film, 1955–1965', *South East Asia Research* 17, No. 1 (March 2009): 65–86.
Berry, Chris. 'From National Cinema to Cinema and the National: Chinese-Language Cinema and Hou Hsiao-Hsien's "Taiwan Trilogy"', in Valentina Vitali and Paul Willemen (eds), *Theorising National Cinema* (London: British Film Institute, 2006), 138–47.
Berry, Chris and Mary Farquhar. *China on Screen: Cinema and Nation* (New York: Columbia University Press, 2006).
Bhabha, Homi. 'Introduction: Narrating the Nation', in Homi Bhabha (ed.), *Nation and Narration* (London: Routledge, 1990).
Blackburn, Kevin Peter. 'Developmental Stages of Singapore Cinema'. Accessed 18 May 2016. http://www.hsse.nie.edu.sg/staff/blackburn/Singapore.htm.
Butler, Judith. *Bodies That Matter* (New York: Routledge, 1993).
Butler, Judith. *Gender Trouble: Feminism and the Subversion of Identity* (New York: Routledge, 1999).
Butler, Judith. 'Performative Acts and Gender Constitution: An Essay in Phenomenology and Feminist Theory', *Theatre Journal* 40, No. 4 (December 1988): 519–31.
Carlson, Marvin. *Performance: A Critical Introduction* (New York: Routledge, 1996).
Chakravarty, Sumita S. 'Fragmenting the Nation: Images of Terrorism in Indian Popular Cinema', in Mette Hjort and Scott Mackenzie (eds), *Cinema and Nation* (New York: Routledge, 2000), 222–38.
Chan, Boon. 'Where Is the Audience?' 14 September 2013. Accessed 6 May 2016. http://www.straitstimes.com/singapore/where-is-the-audience.
Chan, Heng Chee. *Singapore: The Politics of Survival 1965–1967* (Singapore: Oxford University Press, 1971).
Chan, Heng Chee and Hans-Dieter Evers. 'National Identity and Nation-Building in Southeast Asia', in Peter Chen and Hans-Dieter Evers (eds), *Studies in ASEAN Sociology: Urban Society and Social Change* (Singapore: Chopmen Enterprises, 1978).
Chan, Meng Choo. 'First Sex Change Surgery'. Accessed 7 April 2017. http://eresources.nlb.gov.sg/infopedia/articles/SIP_1828_2011-08-04.html.
Cheah, Philip. 'Singapore: Starting Over', in Aruna Vasudev, Latika Padgoankar, and Rashmi Doraiswarmy (eds), *Being & Becoming: The Cinemas of Asia* (New Delhi: Macmillan, 2002), 380–91.
Chong, Terence. 'Introduction: The Role of Success in Singapore's National Identity', in Terence Chong (ed.), *Management of Success: Singapore Revisited* (Singapore: ISEAS Publishing, 2010), 1–20.

WORKS CITED

Chua, Beng Huat. 'Racial Singaporeans: Absence after the Hyphen', in Joel S. Kahn (ed.), *South Asian Identities* (Singapore: Institute of South East Asian Studies, 1998), 981–1001.

Chua, Beng Huat and Eddie K. Y. Kuo. *The Making of a New Nation: Cultural Construction and National Identity*, Working Paper No. 104 (Singapore: National University of Singapore, Department of Sociology, 1990).

Discovery Communications. *The History of Singapore: Lion City, Asian Tiger* (Singapore: John Wiley & Sons, 2010).

Ďurovičová, Nataša. 'Preface', in Nataša Ďurovičová and Kathleen Newman (eds), *World Cinemas, Transnational Perspectives* (New York: Routledge, 2010), ix–xv.

Ďurovičová, Nataša. 'Vector, Flow, Zone: Towards a History of Cinematic Translation', in Nataša Ďurovičová and Kathleen Newman (eds), *World Cinemas, Transnational Perspectives* (New York: Routledge, 2010), 90–120.

Economic Development Board. 'Facts and Rankings'. 2016. Accessed 20 July 2016. https://www.edb.gov.sg/content/edb/en/why-singapore/about-singapore/facts-and-rankings/rankings.html.

Education, Ministry of. *Launch of National Education*. moe.gov.sg, 2004.

Elections Department Singapore. 'Types of Electoral Divisions'. Government of Singapore. 21 April 2016. Accessed 20 July 2016. http://www.eld.gov.sg/elections_type_electoral.html.

Elsaesser, Thomas. '"One Train May Be Hiding Another": Private History, Memory and National Identity', *Screening the Past*, No. 6 (1999). Accessed 10 March 2010. http://tlweb.latrobe.edu.au/humanities/screeningthepast/reruns/rr0499/terr6b.htm.

Elsaesser, Thomas and Malte Hagener. *Film Theory: An Introduction through the Senses* (New York: Routledge, 2010).

Ezra, Elizabeth and Terry Rowden. 'General Introduction: What Is Transnational Cinema?', in Elizabeth Ezra and Terry Rowden (eds), *Transnational Cinema: The Film Reader* (New York: Routledge, 2006).

Fee, Michael Hill and Lian Kwen. *The Politics of Nation Building and Citizenship in Singapore* (New York: Routledge, 1995).

Fernando, Jeremy and Tan See Kam. 'Singapore', in Mette Hjort and Duncan Petrie (eds), *The Cinema of Small Nations* (Edinburgh: Edinburgh University Press, 2007), 127–43.

Ganjavie, Amir. 'When a Room Is No Longer Just a Room: An Interview with Eric Khoo'. 2015. Accessed 7 April 2017. http://filmint.nu/?p=16612.

Ghesquière, Henri. 'From Third World to First: Singapore's Success'. Accessed 17 June 2014. http://www.nzcpr.com/wp-content/uploads/2013/12/Report-on-Singapores-Success-from-third-world-to-first.pdf

Goh, Chok Tong. *Speech by Mr Goh Chok Tong, First Deputy Prime Minister and Minister for Defence, to Launch the 1986 National Day Celebrations Theme at the Island Ballroom, Shangri-La Hotel on Saturday, 21 June 1986 at 10.00 Am*. www.nas.gov.sg: National Archives of Singapore, 21 June 1986.

Gunaratne, Anthony. 'Urban and the Urbane', in Robbie B. H. Goh Goh and Brenda S. A. Yeoh (eds), *Theorizing the Southeast Asian City as Text: Urban Landscapes, Cultural Documents, and Interpretative Experiences* (Singapore: World Scientific, 2003), 159–90.

Gupta, Andrea Fraser. 'Singapore Standard English Revisited', in Lisa Lim, Anne Pakir and Lionel Wee (eds), *English in Singapore: Modernity and Management* (Singapore: National University of Singapore Press, 2010), 57–90.

Gwee, Elisabeth. 'Come See the Best of Ramlee', *The Straits Times*, 16 April 1999.

Gwee, Monica. 'National Day to Be a Day of Colour, Movement and Light', *Business Times*, 12 July 1986. Accessed 7 July 2015. http://eresources.nlb.gov.sg/newspapers/Digitised/Article/biztimes19860712-1.2.10.1.

Hack, Karl. 'The Malayan Trajectory in Singapore's History', in Karl Hack and Jean-Louis Margolin with Karin Delaye (eds), *Singapore from Temasek to the 21st Century: Reinventing the Global City* (Singapore: National University of Singapore Press, 2010), 243–91.

Hack, Karl. 'Framing Singapore's History', in Nicholas Tarling (ed.), *Studying Singapore's Past: C. M. Turnbull and the History of Modern Singapore* (Singapore: National University of Singapore Press, 2012), 17–64.

Hartley, L. P. *The Go-Between* (London: Hamish Hamilton, 1953).

Hashim, Rohani and David Hanan. *Malay Comedy in the Colonial and Post-Colonial Context: The Singapore Comedy Films of P. Ramlee, 1957–1964* (Melbourne: Monash University, 2007).

Hayward, Susan. 'Framing National Cinemas', in Mette Hjort and Scott Mackenzie (eds), *Cinema and Nation* (New York: Routledge, 2000), 88–102.

Heide, William van der. *Malaysian Cinema, Asian Film: Border Crossing and National Cultures* (Amsterdam: Amsterdam University Press, 2002).

Heng, Derek. 'Casting Singapore's History in the Longue Durée', in Karl Hack and Jean-Louis Margolin with Karine Delaye (eds), *Singapore from Temasek to the 21st Century: Reinventing the Global City* (Singapore: National University of Singapore Press, 2010), 55–75.

Higson, Andrew. *Waving the Flag: Constructing a National Cinema in Britain* (Oxford: Clarendon Press, 1997).

Higson, Andrew. 'The Limiting Imagination of National Cinema', in Mette Hjort and Scott Mackenzie (eds), *Cinema and Nation* (New York: Routledge, 2000), 63–74.

Hill, Michael and Lian Kwen Fee. *The Politics of Nation Building and Citizenship in Singapore* (New York: Routledge, 1995).

Hjort, Mette. 'On the Plurality of Cinematic Transnationalism', in Nataša Ďurovičová and Kathleen Newman (eds), *World Cinemas, Transnational Perspectives* (New York: Routledge, 2010), 12–33.

Hoe, Irene. 'The Loveliest Night of the Year', *Straits Times*, 10 August 1986. http://eresources.nlb.gov.sg/newspapers/Digitised/Page/straitstimes19860810-1.1.1.

Hong, Lysa and Huang Jianli. *The Scripting of a National History: Singapore and Its Pasts* (Singapore: National University of Singapore Press, 2008). Reprint, paperback. Originally published as Hong Kong: Hong Kong University Press, 2008.

Housing Development Board. 'A Brief Background – Hdb's Beginnings'. Accessed 12 April 2008. http://www.hdb.gov.sg/fi10/fi10296p.nsf/WPDis/About UsA Brief Background - HDB's Beginnings?OpenDocument&SubMenu=A_Brief_Background

Housing Development Board. 'Public Housing in Singapore". Accessed 12 April 2008. http://www.hdb.gov.sg/fi10/fi10320p.nsf/w/AboutUsPublicHousing?OpenDocument.

Housing Development Board. "A Stake in the Nation." *Houseword Commenorative Issue*, 2010.

Housing Development Board. 'About Us: History'. 8 October 2015. Accessed 18 March 2017. http://www.hdb.gov.sg/cs/infoweb/about-us/history.

Housing Development Board. 'About Us'. 16 December 2016. Accessed 18 March 2017. http://www.hdb.gov.sg/cs/infoweb/about-us.

Hsien, Chin Hu. 'The Chinese Concepts of "Face"', *American Anthropologist*, New Series 46, No. 1, Part 1 (Jan–Mar 1944): 45–64. Accessed 23 February 2017. http://www.jstor.org.libproxy1.nus.edu.sg/stable/pdf/662926.pdf.

IMDB. 'Ben Hur: Release Info'. Accessed 2 May 2017. http://www.imdb.com/title/tt2638144/releaseinfo?ref_=tt_dt_dt.

Info-Communications Media Development Authority. 'The Media Development Authority (Mda) Has Classified the Film "To Singapore, with Love" as Not Allowed for All Ratings (Nar)'. 10 September 2014. Accessed 9 January 2015. https://www.imda.gov.sg/about/newsroom/archived/mda/media-releases/2014/mda-has-classified-the-film-to-singapore-with-love-as-not-allowed-for-all-ratings-nar.

Jackson, Peter, Philip Crang and Claire Dwyer. 'Introduction: The Spaces of Transnationality', in Philip Crang Peter Jackson, and Claire Dwyer (eds), *Transnational Spaces* (New York: Routledge, 2004), 1–23.

Jameson, Fredric. 'Third World Literature in the Era of Multinational Capitalism', *Social Text* 15, Autumn (1996): 65–88.

Koh, Edgar. 'Bogdanovich Says It Again . . .', *New Nation*, 9 December 1978.

Koh, Tai Ann. '"It's Like Rice on the Table It's Our Common Dish": The English Language and Identity in Singapore', in Terence Chong (ed.), *Management of Success: Singapore Revisited* (Singapore: Institute of South East Asian Studies Publishing, 2010), 536–60.

Kong, Lily. 'Music and Cultural Politics: Ideology and Resistance in Singapore', *Transactions of the Institute of British Geographers* 20, No. 4 (1995): 447–59. http://www.jstor.org/stable/622975.

Kong, Lily and Brenda S. A. Yeoh. 'The Construction of National Identity through the Production of Ritual and Spectacle: Analysis of National Day Parades in Singapore', *Political Geography* 16, No. 3 (1997): 213–39.

Kuo, Eddie Chen-Yu. 'Languages in the Singapore Social Context', in Teodoro A. LIamzon (ed.), *Papers on Southeast Asian Languages: An Introduction to the Languages of Indonesia, Malaysia, the Philippines, Singapore and Thailand* (Singapore: Singapore University Press, 1979), 159–60.

Kutty, N. G. 'Flexible Policy in Long-Hair Clamps', *The Straits Times*, 11 January 1972. Accessed 23 June 2016. http://eresources.nlb.gov.sg/newspapers/Digitised/Article/straitstimes19720111-1.2.9.aspx.

Kutty, N. G. 'Asean Bid to Revive Our Film Industry', *The Straits Times*, 6 November 1978. http://er esources.nlb.gov.sg/newspapers/digitised/article/straitstimes19771106-1.2.60.aspx.

Kwa, Chong Guan, Tai Yong Tan and Derek Heng. *A 700 Year History from Early Emporium to World City* (Singapore: National Archives of Singapore, 2009).

Lee, Boon-Hiok. 'Reconciling the Survival Ideology with the Achievement Concept', *Southeast Asian Affairs* (1978): 229–44.

Lee, Hsien Loong. 'National Day Rally Speech, 21 August 2016'. Prime Minister's Office, Singapore. 25 August 2016. Accessed 25 August 2016. http://www.pmo.gov.sg/national-day-rally-2016.

Lee, Hsien Loong. 'Uphold Meritocracy but Guard against Elitism: Esm Goh', 28 July 2013. Accessed 20 July 2016. https://www.facebook.com/notes/lee-hsien-loong/uphold-meritocracy-but-guard-against-elitism-esm-goh/553208454741865/.

Lee, Kuan Yew. 'Excerpts of Broadcast of an Address by the Prime Minister, Mr. Lee Kuan Yew, on "Changing Values in a Shrinking World" at the Political Study Centre, July 13, 1966'. 18 July 1966. Accessed 11 July 2016. http://www.nas.gov.sg/archivesonline/speeches/record-details/73d5f696-115d-11e3-83d5-0050568939ad.

Lee, Kuan Yew. 'Transcript of the Interview Given by the Prime Minister of Singapore, Mr Lee Kuan Yew, at the "Meet the Press" – NBC's TV Press Conference of the Air – Held in New York, Recorded April 11 and Telecast on April 15'. Meet the Press. Dennis (Observer Bloodworth, London), John (The Age Bennetts, Melbourne, and Canberra Times) and Peter (ABC and VISNEWS) Hollinshead. 1967.

Lee, Kuan Yew. *From Third World to First: The Singapore Story* (Singapore: Times, 2000).
Lee, Kuan Yew. *The Singapore Story: Memoirs of Lee Kuan Yew* (Singapore: Times, 1998).
Lee, Siew Hua. 'Less Ado About Men with Long Hair', *The Straits Times*, 9 March 1986. Accessed 23 June 2016. http://eresources.nlb.gov.sg/newspapers/Digitised/Article/straitstimes19860309-1.2.21.9.aspx.
Lim, Edna. 'Coming up for Air: Film and the Other Singaporean', *Kinema* No. 28 (Fall 2007). Accessed 15 March 2017. http://www.kinema.uwaterloo.ca/article.php?id=384&feature.
Lim, Edna. 'Countrperformance: The Heartland and Other Spaces in *Eating Air* and *15*', in Lilian Chee and Edna Lim (eds), *Asian Cinema and the Use of Space: Interdisciplinary Perspectives* (New York: Routledge, 2015), 187–203.
Lim, Edna. 'Singapore Cinema: Connecting the Golden Age and the Revival', in Khai Khiun Liew and Stephen Teo (eds), *Singapore Cinema: New Perspectives* (New York: Routledge, 2017), 20–36.
Lim, Edna and Lilian Chee. 'Asian Cinemas and the Potential of Cinematic Space', in Lilian Chee and Edna Lim (eds), *Asian Cinema and the Use of Space: Interdisciplinary Perspectives* (New York: Routledge, 2015), 1–18.
Lim, Kay Tong. *Cathay: 55 Years of Cinema* (Singapore: Landmark Books Pte Ltd, 1991).
Lim, Lisa, Anne Pakir and Lionel Wee. 'English in Singapore: Prospects and Policies', in Lisa Lim, Anne Pakir and Lionel Wee (eds), *English in Singapore: Modernity and Management* (Singapore: National University of Singapore Press, 2010), 1–18.
Lim, Lydia (ed.). *Vintage Lee: Landmark Speeches since 1955* (Singapore: Straits Times Press Pte Ltd, 2016).
Lim, Song Hwee. '15: The Singapore Failure Story, "Slanged Up"', in Chris Berry (ed.), *Chinese Films in Focus II* (London: BFI, 2008), 9–16.
Low, Donald. 'Good Democracy, Bad Democracy', in Donald Low and Thomas Sudhir Vadaketh (eds), *Hard Choices: Challenging the Singapore Concensus* (Singapore: National University of Singapore Press, 2014), 48–58.
Lowenthal, David. *The Past Is a Foreign Country* (Cambridge: Cambridge University Press, 1985).
Loxley, James. *Performativity* (London: Routledge, 2007).
Lu, Sheldon Hsiao-Peng. 'Historical Introduction Chinese Cinemas (1896–1996) and Transnational Film Studies', in Sheldon Hsiao-Peng Lu (ed.), *Transnational Chinese Cinemas: Identity, Nationhood, Gender* (Honolulu: University of Hawaii Press, 1997), 1–31.
Lui, John. 'Singapore Film *Ilo Ilo* on Track to Break Even Thanks to International Acclaim', 4 December 2013. Accessed 5 January 2015. http://www.straitstimes.com/singapore/singapore-film-ilo-ilo-on-track-to-break-even-thanks-to-international-acclaim.
Lui, John. 'Tough Luck for Arthouse Cinemas in Singapore', 19 August 2015. Accessed 5 December 2016. http://www.straitstimes.com/lifestyle/tough-luck-for-arthouse-cinemas-in-singapore.
Mahbubani, Kishore. 'Why Singapore Is the World's Most Successful Society', TheHuffingtonPost.com Inc., 4 August 2015. Accessed 12 July 2016. http://www.huffingtonpost.com/kishore-mahbubani/singapore-world-successful-society_b_7934988.html.
Margolin, Jean-Louis. 'The People's Action Party Blueprint for Singapore, 1959–1965', in Karl Hack and Jean-Louis Margolin with Karin Delaye (eds), *Singapore from*

Temasek to the 21st Century: Reinventing the Global City (Singapore: National University of Singapore Press, 2010), 292–322.
Margolin, Karl Hack and Jean-Louis. 'Singapore: Reinventing the Global City', in Karl Hack and Jean-Louis Margolin with Karin Delaye (eds), *Singapore from Temasek to the 21st Century: Reinventing the Global City* (Singapore: National University of Singapore Press, 2010).
Maugham, W. Somerset. *The Letter: A Play in Three Acts* (New York: George H. Doran Company, 1925).
Millet, Raphael. *Singapore Cinema* (Singapore: Didier Millet, 2006).
Ministry of Information and The Arts, Media Division. *Prime Minister's National Day Rally Speech, 1999: First-World Economy, World-Class Home*. www.nas.gov.sg. National Archives of Singapore, 1999.
Muhammad, Amir. *120 Malay Movies* (Malaysia: Matahari Books, 2010).
National Heritage Board. 'National Anthem'. 2016. Accessed 20 July 2016. http://www.nhb.gov.sg/resources/national-symbols/national-anthem.
National Heritage Board. 'National Pledge'. 2016. Accessed 20 July 2016. http://www.nhb.gov.sg/resources/national-symbols/national-pledge.
Ong, Teng Cheong. *Report on Moral Education 1979* (Singapore, 1979).
Ooi, Giok Ling. 'Singapore's Changing International Orientations, 1960–1990', in Karl Hack and Jean-Louis Margolin with Karin Delaye (eds), *Singapore from Temasek to the 21st Century: Reinventing the Global City* (Singapore: National University of Singapore Press, 2010), 323–44.
Parliament, Singapore. *White Paper on Shared Values (Cmd 1 of 1991)* (Singapore, 1991).
Prakash, Pravin. 'Understanding Meritocracy', *Today*, 25 June 2014. Accessed 26 July 2016. http://www.todayonline.com/singapore/understanding-meritocracy?singlepage=true.
Reid, Anthony. 'Singapore between Cosmopolis and Nation', in Karl Hack and Jean-Louis Margolin with Karin Delaye (eds), *Singapore from Temasek to the 21st Century: Reinventing the Global City* (Singapore: National University of Singapore Press, 2010), 37–54.
Salleh, Nur Asyiqin Mohamad. 'Exiles in "To Singapore, with Love" Shouldn't Get Chance to Air 'Self-Serving' Accounts: Pm', 3 October 2014. Accessed 9 January 2015. http://www.straitstimes.com/singapore/exiles-in-to-singapore-with-love-shouldnt-get-chance-to-air-self-serving-accounts-pm.
Salleh, Nur Asyiqin Mohamad. 'Parliament: "To Singapore with Love" Has "Distorted and Untruthful" Accounts of Past History: Yaacob', 7 October 2014. Accessed 9 January 2015. http://www.straitstimes.com/singapore/parliament-to-singapore-with-love-has-distorted-and-untruthful-accounts-of-past-history.
Samsuddin, Mohd Effindi and Rahmah Bujang. '"Bangsawan": Creative Patterns in Production', *Asian Theatre Journal* 30, No. 1 (Spring 2013): 122–44. http://search.proquest.com/docview/1370866746?accountid=13876.
Seah, Janice. 'The Light Fantastic', *The Straits Times*, 10 August 1986.
Siddique, Sharon. 'Singaporean Identity', in Kerniah Singh Sadhu and Paul Wheatley (eds), *Management of Success: The Moulding of Modern Singapore* (Singapore: Institute of Southeast Asian Studies, 1989), 563–77.
Sim, Gerald. 'Historicizing Singapore Cinema: Questions of Colonial Influence and Spatiality', *Inter-Asia Cultural Studies* 12, No. 3 (2011): 358–70. http://dx.doi.org/10.1080/14649373.2011.578792.
SINdie. '@Sgiff2015: Production Talk with Eric Khoo on "In the Room"'. 2015. Accessed 7 April 2017. http://www.sindie.sg/2015/11/sgiff2015-production-talk-with-eric.html.

Singapore Department of Statistics. *Census of Population 2010 Statistical Release 1: Demographic Characteristics, Education, Language and Religion.* singstat.gov.sg: Ministry of Trade and Industry, Republic of Singapore, 2010.

Singer, Irving. *Reality Transformed: Film as Meaning and Technique* (Cambridge, MA: MIT Press, 1998).

Slater, Ben. *Kinda Hot: The Making of Saint Jack in Singapore* (Singapore: Marshall Cavendish Editions, 2006).

Slater, Ben. *Saint Jack and the Singapore(Ean) Cinema.* TS2238/SSA2218 Singapore Film: Performance of Identity lecture: National University of Singapore, 2009.

Slater, Ben. 'Coming of Age: "Hollywood" in Singapore: Pt. 1'. *'Clearly you've never been. . .'*, 2013. Accessed 3 August 2015. http://sporeana.blogspot.sg/2013/05/coming-of-age-hollywood-arrives-in.html.

Sontag, Susan. 'Film and Theatre', in Gerald Mast, Marshal Cohen and Leo Braudy (eds), *Film Theory and Criticism: Introductory Readings* (Oxford: Oxford University Press, 1992, 4th edn).

Sorlin, Pierre. 'That Most Irritating Question: Images and Reality', *Historical Journal of Film, Radio and Television* 16, No. 2 (1996): 263–5. http://dx.doi.org/10.1080/01439689600260261.

Sorlin, Pierre. 'Endgame', *Screening the Past*, No. 6 (1999). Accessed 10 March 2010. http://tlweb.latrobe.edu.au/humanities/screeningthepast/firstrelease/fr0499/psfr6a.htm.

Stam, Robert. *Film Theory: An Introduction* (Malden, MA: Blackwell Publishers, 2000).

Sung, Bailyne. 'First S'pore-Made Film Good Effort', *The Straits Times*, 16 March 1975. http://eresources.nlb.gov.sg/newspapers/Digitised/Article/straitstimes19750316-1.2.33.3.aspx.

Sunshine, Linda. *Crouching Tiger, Hidden Dragon: A Portrait of the Ang Lee Film* (New York: Newmarket Press, 2000).

Tan, Dylan. 'Basking in *Ilo Ilo*'s Afterglow', *The Business Times*, 29 November 2013. http://www.businesstimes.com.sg/lifestyle/basking-in-ilo-ilos-afterglow.

Tan, Hwee Hwee. 'A War of Words over Singlish', *TIME*, 22 July 2002. http://hweehweetan.yolasite.com/articles.php.

Tan, Pin Pin. 'To Singapore with Love (2013)'. Accessed 9 January 2015. http://www.tanpinpin.com/wordpress/tswl/.

Tan, Pin Pin. 'Statement by Tan Pin Pin'. 10 September 2014. Accessed 9 January 2015. https://www.facebook.com/tosingaporewithlove/posts/585957814848416.

Tan, Suat Lian. 'Let Singapore Sing', *The Straits Times*, 9 August 1980. Accessed 24 September 2016. http://eresources.nlb.gov.sg/newspapers/Digitised/Article/straitstimes19800809-1.2.118.2.aspx.

tanpinpin.com. '*Singapore Gaga*: A Documentary by Tan Pin Pin'. Accessed 16 March 2016. http://www.tanpinpin.com/sgg/story.html.

Thum, P. J. 'Constance Mary Turnbull 1927–2008: An Appreciation', in Nicholas Tarling (ed.) *Studying Singapore's Past: C. M. Turnbull and the History of Modern Singapore* (Singapore: National University Press, 2012), 1–17.

Toh, Hun Ping. 'Bujang Lapok/*The Mouldy Bachelors* (1957)'. Accessed 17 March 2017. https://sgfilmlocations.com/2014/12/05/bujang-lapok-the-mouldy-bachelors-1957/.

Tong, Lim Kay. *Cathay: 55 Years of Cinema* (Singapore: Landmark Books, 1991).

Turnbull, C. M. *A History of Modern Singapore* (Singapore: Oxford University Press, 2009).

Uhde, Jan and Yvonne Ng Uhde. *Latent Images: Film in Singapore* (Singapore: Oxford University Press Pte Ltd, 2000, 1st edn).

Uhde, Jan Uhde and Yvonne Ng Uhde. *Latent Images: Film in Singapore* (Singapore: National University of Singapore Press, 2010, 2nd edn).
Uhde, Jan and Yvonne Ng Uhde. 'The Substation and the Emergence of an Alternative Cinema Culture', in May Adadol Ingawanji and Benjamin McKay (eds), *Glimpses of Freedom: Independent Cinema in Southeast Asia* (New York: Southeast Asian Program Publications, 2012), 209–22.
Urban Redevelopment Authority of Singapore. 'Our History'. Accessed 10 March 2012. http://www.ura.gov.sg/about/ura-history.htm.
Velayutham, Selvaraj. *Responding to Globalization: Nation, Culture and Identity in Singapore* (Singapore: ISEAS Publishing, 2007).
White, Timothy. 'Exactly the Same but Completely Different: Product Differentiation in the Singaporean Films of Shaw Brothers' Malay Film Productions and Cathay-Keris', *Screen Histories and Historiography*. Accessed 23 July 2015. http://courses.nus.edu.sg/course/elltrw/Film/history.html.
White, Timothy. 'P. Ramlee's Cinema of the Kampong'. Accessed 10 March 2012. http://courses.nus.edu.sg/course/elltrw/Film/history.html.
White, Timothy. 'Historical Poetics, Malaysian Cinema, and the Japanese Occupation', *Kinema* (Fall 1996): 5–23. Accessed 18 June 2015. http://www.kinema.uwaterloo.ca/article.php?id=292&feature.
White, Timothy. 'When Singapore Was South East Asia's Hollywood', *The Arts*, 1997.
White, Timothy R. 'The Cinema of Southeast Asia: Malaysia and Singapore, Pt 1'. Accessed 16 May 2016. https://courses.nus.edu.sg/course/elltrw/history/malaysia&singapore.doc.
Willmott, W. E. 'The Emergence of Nationalism', in Kerniah Singh Sadhu and Paul Wheatley (eds), *Management of Success: The Moulding of Modern Singapore* (Singapore: Institute of Southeast Asian Studies, 1989), 578–600.
Winchester, Hilary, Lily Kong and Kevin Dunn. 'Insights into Human Geography', in Paul Knox and Susan Smith (eds), *Landscapes: Ways of Imagining the World* (New York: Routledge, 2013. Originally published in 2003 by Pearson Education Limited).
Wu, Wang Gung. 'South China Perspectives on Overseas Chinese', *The Australian Journal of Chinese Affairs*, No. 13 (January 1985): 69–84.
Yeh, Ray. 'Reworked "In the Room" More Spunky: Eric Khoo'. 2016. Accessed 7 April 2017. http://www.channelnewsasia.com/news/singapore/reworked-in-the-room-more/2545004.html.
Zhiming, Bao and Khin Khin Aye. 'Bazaar Malay Topics', *Journal of Pidgin and Creole Languages* Vol. 25, No. 1 (2010): 155–71. http://dx.doi.org/http://dx.doi.org.libproxy1.nus.edu.sg/10.1075/jpcl.25.1.06bao.

INDEX

7 Letters, 18, 173
12 Lotus, 62
12 Storeys, 140–2, 145, 148–9, 165–7
15, 149, 166
881, 62, 182

accent, 49, 56, 85, 87, 96–7, 108, 139, 160
Across to Singapore, 14, 92–3
Ah Boys to Men 2, 182
Ahmad, Noordin, 32
Aloha, 33
America, 75, 79, 96, 104, 141, 157; see also US
Anak Pontianak, 50
Anaku Sazali, 51, 55
Anderson, Benedict, 10–11
Andrew, Dudley, 13–14
ASAS 50, 32
authentic, 32–3, 101, 104–6, 108, 116, 148
Avellana, Lamberto, 30

bangsawan, 16, 21–2, 34, 43–6, 48–51, 55–6, 80
Barnard, Timothy, 19, 31–2, 57
BAS Films International, 83, 89, 105, 117

Batu Belah Batu Bertangkup, 32–3
Bazaar Malay, 55–6, 63
Berry, Chris, 10, 12–13
Bhabha, Homi, 9–10
bilingual, 64, 78, 119, 128, 141, 146–8
Bionic Boy, 83–7, 89
Blood Valley, 36
Board of Film Censors, 103
Boat Quay, 78, 102, 112
Bogdanovich, Peter, 8, 17, 102, 104–5, 115
Bollywood, 46, 52, 55, 100
Bond, James, 7, 83, 98
Bride from Another Town, 36
Britain, 25, 71; see also UK
British, 1, 3–5, 16, 24–6, 30–1, 44, 49, 71–2, 74–5, 87, 101, 104, 114, 121–2, 125, 173, 176
Bugis Street, 99, 101, 103, 105, 108–12, 115
Bugis Street – The Movie, 139
Bujang Lapok, 33, 43, 52, 55, 57–9, 61–2, 153–4
Buloh Perindu, 28–9
Butler, Judith, 10, 127, 163

campaign, 31, 77, 82, 105, 122, 131–2, 146

INDEX

Cantonese, 36, 82, 96, 118, 139
Carlson, Marvin, 15, 159
Cathay, 19, 23, 27–9, 35–7, 56, 65, 178, 180–1
Cathay-Keris, 6–7, 28–30, 32, 35, 37, 39, 56, 80, 89
censorship, 81–82, 103
Chen, Anthony, 17, 165
China, 3–4, 11–12, 16, 22, 24, 27, 35–6, 70–1, 81, 87, 122, 143, 161, 168–9, 178, 180
China Wife, 36
Chinatown, 85, 94, 96, 99, 105, 115–16, 141, 149
Chinese, 2, 5–6, 8–9, 11–12, 16, 22–30, 35–9, 41–2, 44–6, 55, 57, 70–1, 80–1, 84–5, 87–8, 92–3, 95–100, 102, 105, 108–9, 111, 118, 120–2, 125, 127, 139, 141, 146–7, 152–3, 160, 166, 168–9, 173, 180–1, 188, 190, 192
Chinese Garden, 85
Chong Gay, 87–8
Cinta, 29
City Hall, 31, 57, 85, 99
Collyer Quay, 99
colonial, 3–5, 7, 41, 45, 55, 62, 70, 71–2, 76, 81, 93–4, 96, 99–100, 103, 108, 112, 114, 121–3, 135, 176
Commonwealth, 30, 74
Connaught Drive, 57
cosmopolitan, 1, 4–5, 45, 57, 59, 62, 93
cosmopolitans, 141
Crime Does Not Pay, 88
Crown Colony, 3, 16, 25

Dang Anom, 33
Daud, Ahmad, 29
Devdas, 46
dialect, 55–6, 139, 146–8, 154–5, 160–1, 163
Ďurovičová, Nataša, 15, 66, 68
Dynamite Johnson, 87, 89

Eating Air, 149
Economic Development Board (EDB), 74, 76, 124
Elgin Bridge, 99
Emergency, 31, 41
Empress Place, 57
Eng Wah, 36, 178

English, 7, 9, 25–6, 49, 64, 71, 78, 80, 83, 85, 87, 94, 98–9, 103, 108, 120, 127–8, 139, 141, 146–8, 152, 154–5, 158–60, 165–6
Enter the Dragon, 82–3
Estella, Ramon, 30, 33, 50
Eurasian, 44, 87, 122, 147
Euro-spy, 98, 108

Federation, 3, 25–7, 30–1, 34, 38, 41–2, 57
Filipino, 30, 33, 83, 87, 166–8
Five Ashore in Singapore, 98
Five Cs, 136, 149, 152–3, 183
foreign, 5, 9, 14, 16–17, 31, 36, 64–7, 73–5, 89, 93, 98, 101, 104–5, 116–17, 127, 131, 147, 166, 168–70, 177–8, 183

garden city, 77, 112–13
General Post Office, 112
Ghani, Salleh, 32
global city, 5, 122
Goh Chok Tong, 120, 126, 130, 140–1, 147
golden age, 2, 6–7, 9, 13, 16–17, 22–4, 26–7, 29–30, 32, 34–5, 37, 39–40, 43, 45, 62, 64–7, 80, 82–3, 87, 89, 139, 173, 182
Golden Lotus, 35
Goodwood Park Hotel, 99, 108

Hack, Karl, 2, 5, 25–6, 31, 38, 57
Hai Seng Company, 22
Hang Jebat, 32, 52–3, 56, 62, 64–5
Hang Tuah, 33–4, 64
Haniff, Hussein, 32–3, 39
Haw Par Villa, 98–9
Hawaii Five-O, 105
heartland, 140–1, 143, 145, 148–52, 154, 165–6, 168, 173
heartlander, 140–1, 145, 149–51, 154, 165–8
Higson, Andrew, 11
Hikayat Hang Tuah, 32–3, 64
Hindi, 46–7, 49
Ho Ah Loke, 28–9, 37
Hokkien, 36, 55, 106, 108, 139, 146, 148, 150–1, 154
Hollywood, 8, 11, 14, 16–17, 22, 27, 30, 43, 46–9, 51–2, 55, 62, 80–1, 83, 85, 88–9, 94, 96, 101, 108, 178, 180–2

Hong Kong, 6, 8, 11–12, 16, 22–3, 28, 35–7, 39, 74–5, 80, 82–3, 85, 87–9, 101, 118, 125, 180–1
Honour and Sin, 27
Housing Development Board (HDB), 76, 90, 99, 128, 139–41, 150, 152, 157, 163, 167
Hujan Panas, 34
hybrid, 16, 55, 62, 118
hybridity, 13, 16, 40, 43
Hypocrite, 88

I Not Stupid, 169, 181–2
Ibu Mertua Ku, 43, 51–2
identity, 2, 7, 9–11, 17, 25–6, 32–3, 39–40, 48–9, 54, 71, 78, 101, 119–21, 125, 127, 129, 135–6, 148–9, 183–4
Ilo Ilo, 17, 165–6, 168, 182
Iman, 33
In the Room, 176
independence, 4, 7, 16, 24, 27, 30–1, 39, 41, 69–71, 73–4, 78–9, 120–1, 125, 129, 135, 173
India, 3–4, 21, 70, 155, 160
Indian, 3–4, 10, 16, 22, 25, 27–30, 32–4, 41, 43, 46–7, 49, 51, 55, 57, 80, 93, 99–100, 105–6, 108, 121–2, 125, 128, 160, 173
Indonesia, 6, 23, 34, 70–2, 83, 186
Infante, Eddy, 30
international, 3, 5, 11–13, 23, 28, 39, 55–7, 59, 73, 75–6, 78–81, 83, 84–7, 89, 101, 105, 124, 132, 140–1, 165, 178–9
Israel, 71–2

Jack of Hearts, 105
Japan, 75, 125
Japanese, 3, 6, 11, 23–5, 41, 43, 49, 55, 84, 96, 99, 177
Japanese Occupation, 24–5, 27, 35, 41, 71
Johor, 3, 4, 171, 175
Jurong Town Corporation (JTC), 74, 76

Kallang Basin 77–8
kampong, 7, 57, 59, 60–2, 80, 139, 154, 173
Khoo, Eric, 18, 139, 165, 173, 176–7, 180

Kommissar X, 98
Kong Ngee, 36
Krishnan, L., 29, 56

Labu dan Labi, 49, 57, 59–60
Laila Majnun, 6, 21–2, 45
language, 6–7, 9–10, 16–17, 25, 27–9, 31, 33, 44, 55–6, 63–5, 67, 78–80, 83, 118–19, 120, 125–8, 139, 145–8, 154, 158, 160, 173, 180–1
Lee, Bruce, 7, 81–3, 85, 87
Lee, Kuan Yew, 2–3, 17, 24, 31, 69–70, 72, 77–8, 120–1, 125, 133
Leila Majnu, 22
Lim, Sunny, 83
Loke Wan Tho, 23, 28, 39
Lost Souls Abroad, 27

Madu Tiga, 56
Mahabharata, 32, 44
Mahadi, Haji, 30
Majnun lover, 46
Majulah Singapura, 9, 127
Majumdar, Pani, 33
Malay, 2, 5–6, 7, 9, 16, 22–3, 25–9, 30–5, 37–40, 43–7, 49–52, 55–7, 59, 62–5, 67, 71, 78, 80, 87–8, 93–4, 98–9, 118, 122, 125, 127–8, 139, 146–7, 173
Malay Film Productions (MFP), 6–7, 27–30, 39, 57, 80
Malaya, 3, 6, 22–8, 30–2, 34, 36–9, 42, 44–5, 51, 118
Malayan, 21–2, 25–8, 30–1, 34, 38–9, 50, 57, 70, 128, 170–1
Malayan Communist Party, 30–1, 41, 170
Malayan Union, 25–6
Malaysia, 3, 6–7, 16, 25, 38, 57, 69, 71–2, 75, 81, 119, 122, 128, 130, 152, 154, 170–1, 174–5
Mambo Girl, 35
Mandarin, 7, 27, 64, 78, 81, 88, 127, 139, 146, 148, 154, 160
Margolin, Jean-Louis, 5, 18–19, 67, 73, 90, 137
Media Development Authority (MDA), 170, 184, 191
MediaCorp, 180
Mee Pok Man, 139
Meet Me in St Louis, 51
Meeting the Giant, 17, 168–9

Melaka, 2–5
merdeka, 7, 29, 31, 32, 36
Merdeka Bridge, The, 36
merger, 3, 31, 37–9, 57, 69, 177
meritocracy, 70, 78, 125–6, 128
Millet, Raphael, 22–3, 27–8, 30, 34, 36–8, 43, 81, 83, 85, 87–90, 104
Ministry of Education, 1, 123, 161
Ministry of Home Affairs, 81–2
Ministry of the Interior and Defence (MINDEF), 71
Miskin, 34, 47
Mizuguchi, Kenji, 43
Money No Enough, 140–1, 145–6, 148–9, 154, 167
Money No Enough 2, 181–2
Mother Tongue, 78, 119, 147
Motion Picture & General Investment Co. Ltd (MP&GI), 35–7
Muhammad, Amir, 32–4, 47
multicultural, 2, 35, 123, 125–8, 159
multilingual, 70, 78, 108, 125, 139
multiracial, 9, 21, 35, 70, 76, 125–6, 173
musical, 11, 16, 44, 49–55, 62, 127, 157

Nan Hua Film Company, 22
nansensu-mono, 49
Nanyang, 22, 27, 36
Nanyang Film Company, 22, 35–6
Nanyang Trilogy, 36
Nasib, 33
Nasib Si Labu Labi, 33
nation, 2, 8, 9–18, 38, 70, 77–9, 89, 101, 119–24, 126, 129, 131–6, 139, 141, 151, 153, 163–4, 168, 170–1, 176, 183–4
nation-building, 7, 17, 25, 70, 89, 105, 120, 122
national, 1–2, 7–14, 16–18, 31, 70–4, 76, 78–80, 84, 89, 116, 119–22, 126–7, 129, 131–2, 136, 149, 155, 163, 168–71, 183, 184; see also nationalism
national anthem, 9, 79, 127, 129, 134
national cinema, 8–14, 16–18, 80, 89, 101, 116, 163, 184
National Day, 17, 125–6, 128–9, 132–3, 135–6, 140, 147, 161–2
National Day Parade, 17, 126, 129–32, 134–6, 138, 161, 163
National Day Rally, 128, 140, 147
National Heritage Board, 126

national identity, 10, 17, 71, 78, 119, 121, 129, 136, 149, 183
national language, 9, 31, 63, 127
national pledge, 79, 120, 126–30, 134
nationalism, 10–11, 26, 31, 33, 71, 134, 163
Neo, Jack, 173, 180–2
Noor, S. Roomai, 30, 33
Noor Islam, 33
Nusantara Film, 27–8, 41

Oily Maniac, 37
Omar, Latifah, 29, 45
Orchard Road, 57, 105, 115, 149
Orient, 86, 96, 99
Oriental, 84–5, 93–4, 96
other Singaporean, 18, 183
Ozu, Yasugiro, 43

Padang, 99, 135, 138
Panji Semerang, 57
Parsi Theatre, 44, 67
Pelangi, 28
Penarik Beca, 34, 47
People's Action Party (PAP), 1, 31, 37–8, 70, 73, 120–1, 128
Peranakan, 36, 108
performance, 2, 10–11, 13, 15–18, 33, 44–6, 51–52, 55–6, 62, 66–7, 69, 89, 96, 100–1, 106, 109, 111, 117, 124, 126–7, 129, 131–2, 134–6, 139–41, 148–9, 154–9, 161–3, 168, 177, 183–4
performative, 10, 17, 127, 134, 140, 145–6, 154, 158, 183
performativity, 10, 121, 127, 135–6, 163, 183
Philippines, 71, 83, 85, 87, 124, 166
pontianak, 29–30, 33, 50, 64, 173–4
post-studio, 2, 7, 16–17, 24, 64, 80, 83, 89, 101, 104, 117, 182
postcolonial, 2, 7
Pretty Polly, 99–100, 106, 109–10
Prime Minister, 3, 31, 69–70, 120, 126, 128, 130, 134–5, 140, 147, 154

Raden Mas, 45, 52, 56, 62, 64
Raffles, Stamford, 1, 3, 57, 121–2
Raffles Hotel, 96, 99, 102, 114
Raintree Pictures, 8, 180, 181
Raja Bersiong, 33
Raja Laksamana Bintan, 32
Rajaratnam, S., 79, 82, 126

Ramayana, 32, 44
revival   2, 6–8, 16–17, 27, 64, 89, 105, 136, 139–41, 149, 163, 165, 168, 172, 178, 180, 183
Rimau Film Productions, 28, 41
Ring Around The World, 98
Ring of Fury, 80–2, 88–9
Rojik, Omar, 32

Saint Jack, 8, 17, 101–3, 105–6, 109, 111–12, 114–17
Saloma, 29, 50, 55
Samarang, 6, 21–2
Sanskrit Natyasastra, 46
Sarimah, 57–8
Satar, Aziz, 57
Second Home, 27
second language, 78, 119, 146–7; see also Mother Tongue
Sejarah Melayu, 32, 64
Seniman Bujang Lapok, 33, 57–8
Seniyati, 28
Sentosa, 85
Sentul, Mat, 32
separation, 3, 25–6, 31, 34, 37–9, 69–70, 130, 133, 160, 176
Serangan Orang Minyak, 56
Sergeant Hassan, 43
Seruan Merdeka, 27, 29
Sesal Tak Sudah, 28
Shall We Dance?, 51
Shamsudin, Jins, 29
Shanghai, 12, 22
Shared Values, 120
Shaw Brothers, 6–7, 22, 27–30, 35–7, 39, 56, 65, 178
shomin-geki, 49
Singapore (1947), 14, 96–8
Singapore dream, 136, 148, 152–4
Singapore Dreaming, 149, 151–4, 167
Singapore Film Commission, 39, 178
Singapore Gaga, 149, 154–5, 159, 162
Singapore Malay Journalist Association, 32
Singapore River, 77, 115, 149
Singapore Story, 1–2, 17, 64, 79, 120–2, 128–9, 135–6, 177–8
Singapore Tourism Board, 123, 129, 137
Singapore Woman, 14, 96
Singapura, The, 176–8
Singlish, 139–40, 146–8, 154, 158
Six Million Dollar Man, 7, 83

Slater Ben, 19, 92, 98, 100, 105, 108, 112, 114, 115–16
Song of Singapore, 27
sook ching, 24
South Korea, 74, 178, 180, 182
Southeast Asia, 4, 22, 24, 35–7, 55, 69, 74
Standard English, 139, 146–8, 154
Straits Settlements, 3, 16, 25
Straits Times, 80, 82, 108, 130, 135
Suarez, Bobby, 83, 87
success, 2, 4, 17, 23, 27, 29, 37–8, 69, 70, 77, 79, 119–25, 127–30, 133–6, 139–41, 143, 145–54, 165, 177, 181, 183
Sulong, Jamil, 30, 32
Sumpah Orang Minyak, 56, 62
survival, 2–4, 69–70, 89, 119, 122, 128, 130, 133–4

Taiwan, 11, 35, 74–5, 82–3, 87
Tan Pin Pin, 149, 170, 174
Tarantino, Quentin, 87, 104
Tay Ping Hui, 17, 168, 181
Teochew, 55
Thailand, 6, 22, 27–8, 71, 83, 170
The Blonde from Singapore, 96
The Blood and Tears of the Overseas Chinese, 27
The Broadway Melody, 51
The Letter (1929), 93–4
The Letter (1940), 94
The Light of Malaya, 27
The Two Nuts, 82, 88
The Whispering Palms, 36
They Call Her . . . Cleopatra Wong, 85–7, 89, 101
Tian Yi Film Co., 22, 40
To Singapore with Love, 17, 170, 172
Tong, Kelvin, 149, 175
transnational, 2, 5, 11–13, 16, 21, 23–4, 26, 29, 33–5, 37, 40, 43, 55–6, 89, 184
transnational space, 5, 13, 16, 23, 35, 40
transnationalism, 12–13
Turnbull, C. M., 1, 6, 24, 40–1, 74, 78–9
Two Sides of the Bridge, 87–8

Uhde, Jan and Yvonne, 6, 21–3, 34, 38, 65, 80–1, 88, 91

UK, 28, 31, 116, 170–1
Unbearable Days, 27
United Malays National Organisation (UMNO), 25, 31, 37–8, 128
Urban Redevelopment Authority (URA), 62, 68, 76
urbanisation, 62, 69, 75, 79, 119, 123
US, 11, 103, 107

van der Heide, William, 34, 42–4, 46–7

wayang kulit, 34, 43–45
When Durians Bloom, 36
White, Timothy, 23, 43, 49–51, 60–1, 79–80, 87–8
Winsemius, Albert, 72, 74
Winyo, Jaafar, 30

Yeow, Tony, 80, 82, 105

Zaiton, 29, 61

EU representative:
Easy Access System Europe
Mustamäe tee 50, 10621 Tallinn, Estonia
Gpsr.requests@easproject.com

www.ingramcontent.com/pod-product-compliance
Lightning Source LLC
Chambersburg PA
CBHW051058230426
43667CB00013B/2354